The Worst School in England

Tim Dowley

Also by Tim Dowley

Defying the Holocaust
I'm Talking About Jerusalem
Taking Off: An Anthology of Pasrodies, Send-ups & Imitations
Atlas of World Religions
Nowell!: A Christmas Miscellany
Johann Sebastian Bach
Christian Music: A Global History

The Worst School in England

The rise and fall of Hackney Downs –
the 'Jewish Eton'

Tim Dowley

The Clove Club

THE WORST SCHOOL IN ENGLAND
The rise and fall of Hackney Downs – the 'Jewish Eton'

First published in Great Britain in 2025
Copyright © Tim Dowley 2025

All rights reserved. Except for brief quotations in critical publications or reviews, no part of this book may be reproduced or transmitted in any form or by any means, electronic or mechanical, including photocopying, recording, or by any information storage and retrieval sysatem, without prior permission in writing from the publisher.

Gorringe Press
Tim Dowley Associates Ltd
44 Carson Road
London SE21 8HU

timdowleyassociates.com

British Library Cataloguing in Publication Data

ISBN 978-8369-12571-1

Printed in Great Britain by Lighning Source

Contents

Abbreviations 6
Foreword 9
Prologue 12
1. An Experiment in Education 17
2. Silence in the Ranks! 37
3. Progressive Conservatism 54
4. Weathering the War 81
5. Steady as she goes . . . 113
6. Fire! Fire! 126
7. Hopes and Fears 147
8. Endgame 166
Afterwords: Writers at Grocers' 198
Afterthoughts 207
Some former pupils 210
Index 217

Abbreviations

Admission	Hackney Archives: Admission Register R/DOW/4/1
Adonis	Andrew Adonis: *Education, Education, Education: Reforming England's Schools*. London: Biteback, 2012.
Alderman	Geoffrey Alderman: *Hackney Downs 1876-1995*. Whittlebury: The Clove Club, 2011.
Black	Gerry Black: 'The Jews of Hackney Downs School,' *Jewish Year Book 2001*. London: Vallentine Mitchell, 2001, p. 5.
Bryant	Margaret E. Bryant: *The London Experience of Secondary Education*. London: Athlone Press, 1986.
Elks	Laurie Elks ed.: *Hackney: portrait of a community 1967–2017*. London: The Hackney Society, 2017.
Hadden	R. H. Hadden: *Reminiscences of William Rogers, Rector of St. Botolph Bishopsgate*. London: Kegan Paul, Trench, 1888.
Hardcastle	John Hardcastle: 'Something More than Straws and Sticks and Bits of Coloured Paper: English at Hackney Downs (formerly The Grocers' Company's School), 1876–1881', *Changing English*, Vol. 18, 2011, Issue 1.
Harrison	*Paul Harrison: Inside the Inner City: Life under the cutting edge*. London: Penguin, 1983.
Kemp	John Kemp: *The Last Thirty Years*. Whittlebury: The Clove Club, 1996.
Letter book	Hackney Downs Grammar School: Clerk's Letter Books 1873–86. London Metropolitan Archives: Guildhall Library MS 11821.
LMA	London Metropolitan Archives.
Maclure	Stuart Maclure: *A History of Education in London 1870–1990*. London: Allen Lane, 1990.
Magee	Frances Magee: 'Working with boys at Hackney Downs School 1980–4', in Kate Myers ed.: *Whatever happened to equal opportunities in schools?: gender equality initiatives in education*. Buckingham: Open University Press, 2000.
Medcalf	J. E. Medcalf: *Hackney Downs School 1876–1926*. London: Parkins, 1926.

Minutes	Governors of Grocers' Company's Schools, Minute Book 1. London Metropolitan Archives: Guildhall Library MS11633/001–4.
NA	National Archives.
Neurath	Susanna Reisz Neurath, 'The Murder of Hackney Downs', Hamish Canham Prize Essay of the Tavistock Society, 2011.
O'Connor	Maureen O'Connor, Elizabeth Hales, Jeff Davies and Sally Tomlinson: *Hackney Downs: The School that Dared to Fight.* London: Cassell, 1999.
ODNB	*Oxford Dictionary of National Biography.*
Race	Richard Race, 'Analysing the Historical Evolution of Ethnic Education Policy-Making in England, 1965–2005'. *Historical Social Research*, 2005, Vol. 30, 4.
Reports	Reports to Company, London Metropolitan Archives; Guildhall Library MS 11633A/1, 2.
Review	*The Review*, termly magazine of Hackney Downs School, London.
Spector	Cyril Spector: *Volla Volla Jew Boy*. London: Centerprise, 1988.
TCL	*The Clove's Lines.* Magazine of the Clove Club, former pupils of Hackney Downs School.
Tomlinson	Sally Tomlinson: 'Sociological Perspectives on Failing Schools'. *International Studies in Sociology of Education*, Vol. 7 No. 1, 1997, p. 92.
Wartime	Ogilvie, D. B. and G. L. Watkins ed.: *Hackney Downs Boys in Wartime 1939–1945: An anthology of the Grocers' School's experience*. Whittlebury: The Clove Club, 2005.

The reforming of Education . . . one of the greatest
and noblest designs that can be thought on,
and for want thereof this Nation perishes.
John Milton, *Of Education*, 1644[1]

What a wise parent would wish for their children,
so the State must wish for all its children.[2]
R. H. Tawney

---

5. I owe this quotation to former pupil Charles Heller.
2. R. H. Tawney, *Education: The socialist policy*. London: Independent Labour Party, 1924. Quoted by James Callaghan at a foundation stone laying at Ruskin College, Oxford, 18 October 1976. Jarvis, Peter and Colin Griffin ed.: *Adult and Continuing Education: Major Themes in Education*, Vol I. London: Routledge, 2003, p. 145.

Foreword

Over its 125-year history Hackney Downs School, often known popularly as 'Grocers", exemplified many significant phases in the development of boys' secondary education in England during the same period. Founded in 1876 as a charitable endeavour by the Grocers' Company, a leading City of London livery, the school was intended originally to provide education for the lower-middle classes, with a novel emphasis on the teaching of English. To satisfy aspiring parents, it soon changed course and attempted to emulate the public school model, exemplified by such London institutions as St. Paul's School and Dulwich College, with a new emphasis on Latin instruction. Early in the twentieth century, when the Grocers' Company decided they no longer wished to subsidize the school, the livery gifted Hackney Downs to the London County Council, which took over responsibility for the city's education from the London School Board[3] – the 'LSB' – in 1903.

Until this date, all Hackney Downs pupils paid for their schooling. The London County Council now introduced a number of scholarships, opening entry to less well-off families, including Jewish refugees from Eastern Europe, thus broadening the class make-up of the school. However, Hackney Downs continued to attempt to emulate other leading London public schools. The headmaster during this period met the difficult years of World War I and the ensuing economic crisis with a policy of educational conservatism and considerable austerity.

During the 1930s, increasing numbers of Jewish boys joined the school, many from families that had fled the late-nineteenth and early-twentieth century pogroms of Eastern Europe. Just before World War II, a change of headmaster introduced much-needed reform, a more liberal regime and a humane response to the particular problems of wartime evacuation, when the school relocated to King's Lynn, Norfolk. The decade following R. A. Butler's 1944 Education Act saw outstanding academic achievement; pupils of this period later flourished in science, politics and the arts. Alumni of these years include Harold Pinter, Steven Berkoff, Michael Caine, Leon Kossoff, Lord Clinton-Davis, Professor Barry Supple, the entrepreneur John Bloom, Lord Maurice Peston and the former Head of Mossad, Efraim Halevy – helping Hackney Downs earn the sobriquet 'the Jewish Eton'.

In the 1970s the school converted early and optimistically from grammar school to comprehensive – and continued to thrive. However

---

3. The popular name for the School Board for London, set up under the Elementary Education Act, 1870.

during the late 1980s, for political, financial and demographic reasons, the school declined rapidly, ultimately dubbed the 'worst school in the country' by the tabloid press.[4] In 1995, following months of disruption, inspections, reports, protests and persistent uncertainty, Hackney Downs School was summarily closed by Conservative education minister Gillian Shephard. A decade later, in 2004, Mossbourne Community Academy opened on the same site – a pioneer city academy, with new buildings designed by Sir Norman Foster.

Between 1875 and 1995 Hackney experienced massive demographic changes. When the school first opened, Hackney had barely evolved from a series of closely-linked villages on the fringes of the City to a lower-middle class suburb, with battalions of clerks boarding the frequent commuter trains to Liverpool Street. From the first years of the twentieth century, aspiring first-generation Jewish immigrants moved into Hackney from the traditional East End – Whitechapel and Spitalfields. World War II brought major social disruption to the area, with schoolchildren evacuated to the country for safety and younger men away on active service. By the 1960s, the Windrush generation was starting to move into Hackney, followed by refugees and immigrants from Vietnam, Hong Kong, Turkey, Syria, India, Pakistan and elsewhere, creating a diverse, impoverished demographic profile within the borough and the school. During this period Hackney also began to develop into a favoured location for aspiring artists seeking low-rent properties, a trend that helped initiate a process of gentrification in parts of the borough.

Here, the school's story is retold chronologically, each chapter covering a different headship, a structure supported by the educationist Gerald Grace:

> Historically, headteachers in English schools have
> been powerful definers of the culture, organisation
> and ethos of schooling . . . Once appointed, they had,
> in comparative terms, a large degree of professional
> autonomy . . . English headteachers have historically
> constituted a leadership class in schooling . . .
> Headteachers in England are the inheritors of a school
> leadership culture which for over a hundred years gave
> priority to spiritual, moral and pedagogical leadership in
> education.[5]

---

4. For example, 'Is this the worst school in Britain?' *Mail on Sunday*, 20 March 1994.
5. Gerald Grace, 'Research and the Challenges of Contemporary School Leadership: The Contribution of Critical Scholarship', *British Journal of Educational Studies*, Vol. 48, No. 3, September 2000, pp. 232, 238, 241.

In writing this history I have been fortunate in being able to draw on a broad range of sources. The copious records of the Grocers' Company, now housed at the London Metropolitan Archives, offer rich and extensive evidence covering the school's first thirty years. For the years following, quinquennial HM Inspectors' Reports provide comprehensive evidence of the school's profile and performance. I have also been able to draw on the contents of the school magazine, *The Review*, which appeared three times a year, and covered the period of World War II in particular in fascinating detail. During its life as a grammar school, former pupils ran a thriving 'old boys'' association – the 'Clove Club'[6] – which published its own journal, *The Clove's Lines*, which included many valuable reminiscences and records of school life. The Chairman of the Clove Club, Glyndwr 'Willie' Watson, not only re-energised the club's activities after the school's closure but also built up a wide-ranging archive of school records, photographs and memorabilia to which he generously allowed me access. Finally, the school's last tumultuous years threw up their own accumulation of source material, both published and archival.

Particular thanks are also due to a number of other former pupils, especially the late Dr. Melvin Brooks, who rescued much of the school archive from the rubble of the school fire in 1963, Professor Barry Supple, Professor Henry Grinberg and Alan Ruston, and former Hackney Downs teacher, Dr. John Hardcastle, for information, memories, advice and encouragement in undertaking this project.

Tim Dowley

---

4. Named after the spice depicted on the badge of the Grocers' Company.

Prologue

Grocers' Schools

London's Guild of Pepperers, with records dating to 1180, were traders, or 'engrossers', in spices, gold and other luxury goods and controlled the weighing of goods imported into the city. In 1348, the guild changed its name to the 'Company of Grossers'; whilst the first known reference to the 'Company of Grocers of London' dates to 1376. In 1428, the Grocers' Company was granted a royal charter, and in 1512 recognized as second in precedence – after the Mercers – of the Great Twelve livery companies of the City of London.

The Grocers were originally an active and efficient trade organization. Members were required to be trading as grocers and to subscribe to a common fund. If in need, members could expect relief from the company and burial at the fraternity's expense. Among the company's tasks was ensuring that food standards were upheld throughout the city. In 1456, for instance, the Grocers' Company ruled 'John Ayshfelde shall make a fine of 6s 8d for offens don in makynge of untrewe powder gingere and cynamon'.

Over the centuries, regulation of trading standards slipped and the company became increasingly distanced from the day-to-day business of importation and distribution. By 1875, a London grocer could add sand to his sugar, or mix his powdered ginger with powdered bones, yet fear no investigation by what had evolved into a wealthy corporation. Members' responsibilities had dwindled to overseeing a handful of charities and enjoying numerous splendid dinners.

Hackney Downs School was founded by the Worshipful Company of Grocers in 1876, at a time when public elementary education was still a novelty and secondary education the privilege of the wealthy. Members of the company had previously founded several schools. In 1614 Humphrey Walwyn (c. 1558–c. 1612), a member of the Grocers' Company, founded the Free School, Colwall, Herefordshire;[7] while in 1660 Henry Box (1585–1662)[8] founded Witney Grammar School, Ox-

---

7. Now The Elms co-educational boarding school.
8. Box was elected Master of the Grocers' Company in 1640, but turned the post down due to 'many infirmities' – possibly to avoid public office during the turbulence of the English Civil War.

fordshire,[9] with four wardens of the company as governors. In 1873 the Grocers' Company declared this school '...to a very high degree unsatisfactory', and two years later the Charity Commission condemned it as 'absolutely useless'. Oundle 'Free Grammar School' Northamptonshire, was founded in 1556 by Sir William Laxton (c. 1500–1556) – Lord Mayor of London and eight times Master of the Grocers' Company – and taken over by the company in 1573 with money endowed by Laxton. Although all these schools benefited from the generosity of the Grocers' Company, none had been founded by the company, a distinction enjoyed by Hackney Downs alone.

We must educate our masters

Around the time of the founding of Hackney Downs School, three events triggered a national debate about education. The British army had failed dismally during the Crimean War of 1853–56, prompting calls for improvement in education and technical training. Secondly, the passing of the Reform Act 1867[10] almost doubled the number of males in England and Wales who could vote – an increase from 1.4 million to 2.5 million – shifting power from the landed classes towards the industrial and commercial bourgeoisie and skilled working-class, a revolution that prompted the much-repeated response of Lord Sherbrooke (1811–92), often paraphrased as 'We must educate our masters'.[11] Thirdly, the creation of a united Germany in 1871 challenged the military and economic hegemony of the British Empire, raising concern in Britain about the breadth and effectiveness of educational training and skills.

In 1864 Lord Palmerston's reforming government set up a Royal Commission under Lord Taunton to investigate the hundreds of endowed grammar schools and privately-owned 'proprietary' schools, many of which were operating archaically. To implement the resulting Taunton Report's recommendations of 1867 – most significantly the proposal to establish a national system of secondary schools providing a modern education – Gladstone's government passed the Endowed Schools Act 1869 and appointed a commission to draw up new schemes of governance for these endowed schools.[12] The resulting report rated and ranked schools by how many years pupils spent there and by their father's occupation. 'First-Grade' or 'First Class' schools – richer, en-

9. Now The Henry Box School.
10. Also known as the Second Reform Act.
11. His actual words were: 'I believe it will be absolutely necessary that you should prevail on our future masters to learn their letters,' House of Commons, 15 July 1867.
12. In 1874 the Commission's extensive powers were transferred to the Charity Commissioners.

dowed institutions, many of them boarding schools – turned themselves into what we now recognise as 'public schools', concentrating largely on Latin and Greek – emulating reforms introduced by Dr Thomas Arnold at Rugby between 1828 and 1841. By contrast, 'Middle Class' schools taught only basic Latin – if any – and offered instead a curriculum that included commercial subjects appropriate to their pupils' perceived needs: the majority were expected to leave school aged fourteen or fifteen to take up a middle-class occupation.

To fund the new 'Middle Class' schools, it was proposed that obsolete endowments, originally set up for non-educational purposes be appropriated. The Merchant Taylors', Mercers' and Stationers' Companies already maintained London schools; the Grocers' Company was now spurred into action by the Endowed Schools Act. The company administered a number of obsolete bequests; with these assets, together with revenue from gifts and rents, it reckoned it could raise around £30,000.[13] In December 1870, the Grocers requested the Charity Commissioner's permission to utilise this money to set up a new 'Middle Class school' in North London. Their proposed scheme was advertised in *The Times* on 10 May 1872, and received royal assent on 24 March 1873, following which the company instructed its solicitor to arrange the purchase of their favoured site, immediately south of Hackney Downs, in north-east London.[14]

Hackney: a peaceful haven

A stranger visiting the parish of Hackney in 1600 would have discovered an area of green fields and woods, with clusters of linked settlements. The village of Hackney centred around the parish church of St. Augustine, built above the confluence of the Hackney and Pigwell brooks, yet was situated only two miles from Bishopsgate, on the edge of the City of London, with access via Ermine Street, the Roman road from Lincoln – today's busy A10 Kingsland Road – and from Cambridge, along today's Mare Street. There were also tracks leading eastwards to the River Lea, and roads and tracks connecting Hackney with the neighbouring, but as yet still separate, hamlets of Clapton, Dalston, Shacklewell, Stamford Hill, Homerton and Hackney Wick.

The seventeenth-century diarist Samuel Pepys was charmed by both Hackney's rural attractions and its women,[15] and described a summer

13. Roughly equivalent to £3.25M in 2025.
14. NA ED 27/13054 and 3055. To set up the school, the Charity Commissioners empowered the Grocers' Company to sell rent charges and hereditaments (18 June 1873), together with houses in Old Jewry and Walbrook for £8400 and £5000 respectively (23 July 1873). Minutes 1, ff. 1–2.
15. He confessed in 1667 'we went chiefly to see . . . the young ladies of the schools.'

trip from his city home in 1664, when he '...played a shuffle-board, ate cream and good cherries', contrasting the tranquil village with the chaos of the teeming city. Eighteenth-century Hackney remained both prosperous and peaceful, the village essentially a single street; however proximity to London constituted much of its appeal – it was part of London, but not yet London. Georgian Hackney became a playground of the middle classes, housing aspirational citizens who had risen through trade and finance. Dr. Johnson reckoned 'The greatest ambition of the London shopkeeper is to retire to Stratford or Hackney.' Yet over centuries Hackney had also absorbed outsiders and immigrants, offering a haven for Huguenots, Jews, religious dissenters and political controversialists.

Eighteenth-century Hackney boasted several private schools for the upper classes. Most celebrated was Newcome's Academy, or Hackney School, which attracted such Whig patrons as the Cavendish and Fitzroy families, the Duke of Devonshire and the Earl of Hardwicke. The school was noted for its plays, their prologues and epilogues performed by contemporary leading actors, including David Garrick. The diarist Thomas Creevey (1768–1838), a former pupil, recalled bullying at the school and younger boys despatched to pilfer turnips on icy evenings. Judging by a 1722 newspaper report, Hackney schools could be hazardous:

> A few days ago two Lads had some Words at Mr W's Boarding School in Hackney: the one being stronger than the other ty'd him up by his hands to a beam in his room, and after having stripped and beat him, he drew his sword and stabbed him in several places under the arm; which not content with the cruel youth exercised his penknife on him too. He then took him down and finding he was not despatched, hung him up again by the neck and so left him . . .

The Madras House School, founded in Hackney's Mare Street in 1817, took on national significance, its name deriving from the Madras teaching system, by which monitors taught the younger boys. Pupils included a future Bishop of Zanzibar and Charles Reed (1819–81), subsequently Hackney's first MP and Chairman of the London School Board. In 1830, Hackney Proprietary Grammar School opened, the first boys' grammar school in the locality, admitting the sons of city shopkeepers but excluding those of local tradesmen. Later the same year, a rival Church of England Grammar School, with links to King's College, London, opened in Hackney's Clarence Road. By 1861 there were at least 61 private schools in Hackney, among them St. John's Foundation

School for the sons of poor clergymen, with pupils who included Antony Hope,[16] author of *The Prisoner of Zenda* (1894).

There are no firm population figures for Hackney earlier than 1801, but it is estimated the parish numbered around 1,940 persons in 1640; 5,900 in 1756; and 7,270 in 1779, while the 1801 census recorded 12,730 inhabitants. At the turn of the nineteenth century, two-thirds of the parish of Hackney remained farmland, while Clapton, Dalston, Shacklewell, Stoke Newington and Homerton continued to be rural communities, beyond the urban sprawl of London, described in 1822 as a 'great festering sore' by the journalist William Cobbett.

Over the next seventy years, the parish of Hackney metamorphosed rapidly from a series of linear hamlets and villages separated by fields into an inner London suburb. In 1867 it was awarded parliamentary representation, and by 1899 was sufficiently populous to become an autonomous borough, with its own elected council. In 1850, the village of Hackney started to take on a modern, urban appearance, with the opening of the East and West India Docks and Birmingham Junction Railway[17] and construction of a railway bridge across Mare Street, which remains Hackney's main thoroughfare. The railways, with their affordable fares, followed by horse-drawn trams in the 1870s, offered the legions of clerks who soon swelled the population rapid access to the city. In 1866, an additional railway line into the city's Broad Street terminus opened, while the Great Eastern Railway inaugurated a branch through Hackney in 1872, with stations at London Fields and Hackney Downs, and at Rectory Road and Stamford Hill on its Enfield branch.[18] Between these two lines, the Grocers' Company proposed to build their new school.

---

16. Sir Anthony Hope Hawkins (1863–1933).
17. Renamed the North London Railway Company in 1853.
18. Local pressure ensured the Chingford branch tunnelled beneath Hackney Downs.

Chapter 1
An Experiment in Education
Herbert Courthope Bowen, Headmaster 1876–81

> *There is no better passport to a City bank or counting house than an education at the Middle Class Schools.*[19]

Armed with both the requisite funds and the necessary government consent, the Grocers' Company proceeded to draft a scheme specifying the Middle Class day-school for boys they planned to open in Hackney. With little or no experience of running an educational establishment, the company asked the advice of Revd. Prebendary William Rogers (1819–1896), a bachelor of radical views and wide educational experience who had served on the Royal Commission on education set up by Lord Derby's government in 1858. A product of Eton and Balliol College, Oxford – he rowed in the fourth University Boat Race – Rogers was dedicated to educating London's poor. In 1845 he became the incumbent of St. Thomas, Charterhouse, Islington: 'Costermongery was the industry of the place: the district was Costermongria'.[20] Within months, Rogers had set up an elementary school for ninety boys in a blacksmith's shed, followed by several larger and more conventional schools for both boys and girls. In the process, Rogers gained valuable knowledge about London's educational needs, together with vital expertise in extracting funding from charities and upper-class philanthropists: 'I tried in turn every society, corporation, livery company, charity, and fund in London, and I dunned my private friends till I was ashamed to look them in the face.'[21] In 1863 Rogers, a 'Liberal Churchman of the strenuous sort'[22] became Rector of St. Botolph-without-Bishopsgate, where his parishioners initially regarded him with suspicion as a 'Radical'.[23] He compared his new parish with Jerusalem for its variety: more than one-third was Catholic and Jews proliferated – although he

---

19. Bryant p. 244.
20. Hadden, p. 51.
21. Hadden pp. 62–63.
22. Obituary in *Daily Chronicle*, 20 January 1896.
23. He was known popularly as 'Hang theology Rogers'.

affirmed 'I am dead against "converting" Jews' When he arranged a special service for Jews ejected from Russia, the church was packed with Jewish parishioners.

Rogers now turned his sights on secondary education. He 'dreamed a dream. It took the shape of an organized scheme of middle class education, and, for the money, [his] longing eyes were fixed upon the parochial charities of the City.' With his habitual energy and ingenuity, By 1866, Rogers had set up Bath Street School, in a former French Protestant Hospital just off City Road, Shoreditch.[24] The school soon moved to purpose-built premises in nearby Cowper Street and was renamed Finsbury Middle-Class Boys School, and later, more famously, Central Foundation School.[25]

Middle Class secondary education acquired sudden importance nationally following Prussia's shock defeat of France in 1870 and German unification the following year. The educational system of Prussia, Britain's new continental rival, was regarded as one of the engines of that country's economic and military success: there was a popular maxim that the Franco-Prussian War was 'won by Prussian schoolmasters'.[26] As early as the 1830s, the Prussian system featured progressive characteristics not generally seen elsewhere, including free primary education, teacher training, funding for building schools, oversight to ensure high standards, a curriculum inculcating national identity and specialist instruction in science and technology. The new Middle Class school was seen as an institution that might help Britain catch up with Germany, by providing secondary education for the sons of skilled workers, tradesmen and the professional middle classes.

At the Cowper Street School's foundation ceremony the Lord Mayor of London complained 'for years past our middle class education had been inferior to that of France and Germany'. The new school's most distinctive feature was the omission from its curriculum of Latin and Greek; an early university examiner of the school judged: 'the absence of classics is more than compensated for by the sciences and the proficiency evinced in English and French'.[27] As a model Middle Class school, Finsbury attracted official visits by the Prince of Wales in 1870, the King of the Belgians in 1872 and the future King George V in 1874.

William Rogers was a leading proponent of Middle Class schools for the children of tradespeople and clerks, precisely the pupils the Gro-

---

24. Hadden pp. 114, 157–167.
25. Today a voluntary-aided comprehensive school, at the same address.
26. A variant on the Duke of Wellington's apocryphal claim: 'The battle of Waterloo was won on the playing fields of Eton.'
27. Bryant p. 244–245

cers' Company envisaged would fill their new school.[28] He was generous in the information he offered the company, including the number of pupils at the Finsbury School, the salary of its head, Dr Richard Wormell (1838–1914)[29] and even its accounts. The Grocers decided that the Company's Court in toto would be recognized as their new school's governing body, with no distinction between the Court and the Governors, while an executive committee of eight members of the Court – the Hackney, or School, Committee – would 'superintend' the school.[30] It seemed not to occur to them that some knowledge or experience of education on the part of the governors might prove useful in effectively administering their school. Following Rogers' example and advice, it was decided the new school should be 'Third-Grade', as defined in the Taunton Report, with minimal time devoted to Latin. The syllabus would favour English as well as commercial subjects regarded suitable for middle-class occupations, to assist meeting national requirements amid the anxiety about Prussian militarism and industrialization.

The new school was to accommodate 500 boys, giving 'a practical education suitable for the children of that class who desire to educate their children up to the age of fourteen years or thereabouts' and would be open to 'all boys who are of good character, and of sufficient bodily health'. The entrance fee for pupils was set at not more than one pound, and annual fees at between three and six pounds.[31] The Grocers' Company would decide the curriculum, length of terms and number of assistant masters, while the headmaster – who was to be paid £200 per annum plus a capitation fee of £1 per pupil – would specify textbooks, school hours and teaching methods. The Head had the power to appoint and dismiss staff, but could himself be suspended, and dismissed upon six months' notice, with no reason given.[32]

The Endowed Schools Commission required that the new school should be sited within three miles of the City of London, since its funding derived from charities originally set up to support London citizens. The company purchased for £8,250 from the Amherst family[33]

28. As Chairman of Governors of Dulwich College, South London, Rogers waged a long and bitter struggle with its headmaster, Revd. Alfred Carver (1826–1909), who by contrast wanted his college to become and remain 'a first grade school'. Sheila Hodges, *God's Gift: A Living History of Dulwich College*. London: Heinemann, 1981, pp. 38–39.
29. '£600 or thereabouts' – around £90,000 in 2025. Wormell was a pioneer in the teaching of science: see *ODNB*.
30. Minutes f. 5, 7 January 1874.
31. At this time a skilled artisan typically took home around £1 – 12s per week, a teacher £2.
32. The headmaster's salary was very generous, comparable to that of a contemporary senior civil servant.
33. William Tyssen-Amherst, first Baron Amherst of Hackney (1835–1909), whose father inherited property in Hackney.

a triangular site of roughly three acres immediately south of Hackney Downs, bounded by Downs Park Road and two forking branches of the Great Eastern Railway. In January 1874, the company tasked the School Committee with overseeing the design and construction of the new school, specifying:

> [The] Middle Class School for 500 boys – no boarders – should comprise a Hall, Theatre, or large room capable of accommodating on Speech-day eight hundred people.[34] That there should be from twelve to sixteen classrooms, a kitchen to provide dinner for about 250 boys and for the Masters (about twenty in number) daily, a Clerk's office, Accommodation for the Head Master and Assistant Masters, Rooms for hats and coats, Lavatories etc. and a Porter's Lodge separate from the main building.

The Headmaster was not expected to live on site:

> not only will non residence induce a better class of man to apply for the appointment, but . . . a nonresident [sic] Master comes fresher to his work.[35]

Building estimates were agreed in spring 1874 and an architectural competition announced, attracting 47 design submissions by the closing date of 1 June 1874. Of the plans presented, 43 were disqualified out of hand for exceeding the specified funding – which suggests the company seriously underestimated the realistic price. Successfully meeting the condition that construction had to cost less than £13,200,[36] the winning design was that of the celebrated architect Theophilus Allen (1846–1929),[37] an exponent of the 'Domestic Gothic' style.[38] His plans were featured in a contemporary issue of *Building News*.[39] The building contract was awarded to Holland & Hannen, of Duke Street, Bloomsbury – who, the company was informed, 'hold a high position in the building trade'[40] – and construction completed by summer 1876. The company insisted on cutting costs, for instance saving £150 by

---

34. The completed theatre could not accommodate this number.
35. Minutes ff. 12–13, 11 March 1874..
36. Minutes f. 15–16, 22 July 1874. By comparison, initial estimates for building St Dunstan's College, Catford, in 1887 were as high as £58,000. (L. F. Morris: *A History of St. Dunstan's College*. London: St Dunstan's College, 1970. pp. 35–36.
37. Best known today for his Grade II* listed Dome Cinema, Worthing, West Sussex.
38. The design was not dissimilar to that of several contemporary schools, such as Alleyn's, Dulwich, and St Dunstan's, Catford, apart from its distinctive amphitheatre.
39. 7 May 1875.
40. Minutes ff. 17–18, 16 December 1874.

using yellow bricks instead of the stone specified by the architect.[41] Constructed of red brick with Bath stone dressings, the new building consisted of fifteen classrooms fitted in the 'Prussian system' – that is, state-of-the-art educational design – with a large, semi-circular amphitheatre for school assemblies and even a tuck-shop – but neither science rooms nor gymnasium.[42]

The next crucial step was the appointment of a suitable headmaster. In June 1876 160 applications were received for this post.[43] The clerk of the company was singularly unforthcoming when approached by potential applicants for information about the school, though he did reply to one candidate: 'All I can say about the neighbourhood round the school is that it is a rapidly growing and rather thickly populated suburb within easy reach of the City.'[44] From the large number of candidates, a short list of six was drawn up, all Cambridge graduates under the age of forty. Revd. Rogers' influence is surely evident in the choice of the successful candidate, Herbert Courthope Bowen, Second Master at Finsbury School,[45] appointed first Headmaster of the Grocers' Company's Middle Class School on 5 July 1876.[46] On 27 September 1876, Stephen Goodhart, Master of the Grocers' Company, drove to Hackney with the Wardens and Court of Assistants, officially to open the new school, which initially enrolled 210 pupils, taught by just four assistant masters.[47]

Born in Trinidad,[48] Herbert Courthope Bowen (1847–1909) attended the island's prestigious Queen's Royal College, or 'QRC',[49] graduat-

41. Minutes f. 21, 19 May 1875.
42. There followed a series of problems with the building, particularly with its heating system, although it is unclear whether this was due to cost economies, flawed specifications or poor workmanship. For instance, in November 1882 it was reported that insufficient iron tyes and straps had been used to attach the roof of the theatre (Reports, 1.11.1882).
43. Minutes f. 38, 21 June 1876.
44. Letter Book 1, f. 179, 30 May 1876.
45. There was a final run-off ballot between Bowen and Revd. Edward Stafford Carlos, a maths master at Christ's Hospital, Horsham, Sussex. Minutes f. 40, 5 July 1876.
46. Letter Book 1, f. 270, 5 July 1876.
47. Three masters were on a salary of £120 per annum, one on £75. Minutes f. 48, 27 September 1876.
48. Pupils recalled his reading aloud to them Charles Kingsley's travel book, *At Last: A Christmas in the West Indies* (1871). Herbert's father, Jerome Jeremiah Townshend Bowen (1808– 86), was a planter, and his mother Jessie née Courthope, daughter of a Rotherhithe shipbuilder. (*The Clove Review*, Spring 1953, pp. 6–7.) Jerome Bowen received £558 18s 6d compensation for 19 enslaved people on his cocoa estate at El Socorro, Trinidad, under the agreed settlement scheme for the emancipation of slaves. (Centre for the Study of the Legacies of British Slavery database, UCL.)
49. Distinguished alumni include the historian C. L. R. James (1901–89), novelist Sir Vidia Naipaul (1932–2018) and Eric Williams, TC CH (1911–81), first Prime Minister of Trinidad and Tobago.

ing in 1864. He recalled a childhood 'spent amidst the woods and hills of a West Indian Island' and collecting local facts.[50] Although Bowen had entered Cambridge University in 1866 to study Classics and mathematics at Corpus Christi, his first love was English prose and poetry, but at this date there was no Honours School of English.[51] After graduating in 1870, he was appointed an assistant master at Dulwich College, where his cousin Revd. Robert Jardiner was a master,[52] before moving to a similar position at Highstead School, Torquay, in 1871. In 1872 Bowen was awarded Cambridge's LeBas prize for his essay 'The present condition and influence of Mahommedanism [sic] in India' and in 1873 the Maitland Prize for 'The Principles of Buddhism and Christianity compared with Special Reference to the History of their Comparative Success'.[53] Between 1873 and 1876, Bowen taught at the Finsbury School.[54]

Contemporaries describe Bowen, who never married, as tallish, thin, with fair hair, a light flowing beard and blue piercing eyes. He was an English specialist – rare when there was no final Oxbridge exam in the subject – and during his career developed a strong interest in progressive pedagogy and the psychology of learning. An early follower of the German educationist Friedrich Froebel, Bowen pointed out that, in contrast with most other educational reformers, Froebel 'starts from psychology and endeavours to make his practice an orderly application of its methods'.[55] Froebel described the process by which children express their inner thoughts and needs as a kind of 'unfolding'. Following Froebel, Bowen shifted his focus from the content of school subjects and methods of instruction to the nature of learning and the role of 'self-activity' in children's early development. In 1876, the year he was appointed to Hackney Downs, Bowen published *Studies in English*, a textbook for secondary schools, where he laid out some of his thinking:

> It is a matter of deep importance in education... that method of style of thought and expression should be closely attended to. The mere accumulation of facts may

---

50. As Dr Hardcastle points out, it is ironic that Bowen's Trinidadian connection had been forgotten when, in the 1970s, almost 60 percent of pupils at Hackney Downs came from a Caribbean background. (Hardcastle, p. 12.)
51. The Oxford University English Faculty was not founded until 1894, while Cambridge did not introduce an English tripos until 1917.
52. Jardiner subsequently became Senior Master at St Paul's School.
53. *The Clove Review*, Spring 1953, No. 4, p. 6. His family was disappointed he failed to achieve a First, complaining he 'wasted his time writing poetry'.
54. *Alumni Cantabrigienses*; Minutes f. 39, 21 June 1876.
55. H. C. Bowen, 'Hints to Froebel students', a paper read to the Froebel Society, 24 November 1886, (London: Hodgson, 1886).

The architect's visualisation of his design for the Grocers' Company's School, Hackney.

    come at any time… [T]he mere piling together of facts is as the piling together of loose stones without mortar and without design…[56]

English language and literature took pride of place in Bowen's preferred curriculum:

    It is clear… what must be gained by bringing those whose minds are fresh and open to all noblest impulses, whose ears have not yet forgotten the sounds, nor their eyes the sights of heaven – which still they hear and see, and smile at in their sleep – into closest contact with true greatness, earnest longings, noble purity and strength, passionate or tender love of beauty.[57]

He believed that if pupils were exposed to their

    native literature… rules of grammar will come to them

---

56. H. C. Bowen, *Studies in English*. London: 1876, p. vi. In the same year Bowen wrote to Monckton Milnes, Lord Houghton, requesting access to the John Keats manuscripts, as he was thinking of publishing a complete edition. (Rollins: *The Keats Circle* Vol. II pp. 349–50). Bowen was a member of the New Shakespeare Society.

57. Medcalf, p. 15. Bowen seems to be referencing Wordsworth: 'But trailing clouds of glory do we come / From God, who is our home: / Heaven lies about us in our infancy! / Shades of the prison-house begin to close / Upon the growing Boy…' ('Ode on Intimations of Immortality from Recollections of Early Childhood').

sure enough, but unconsciously... there is no necessity for these rules to be known in a codified form.[58]

Bowen had the following, slightly amended, words by the Christian Socialist author Charles Kingsley (1819–1875) inscribed around the walls of the school theatre:[59]

> Be good, sweet child, and let who can be clever,
> Do noble things, not dream them, all day long,
> And so make life and death and that for ever
> One Grand Sweet Song.[60]

In January 1877, Bowen set out his new school's course of study: English language, literature and composition, History, Commercial and Physical Geography, Arithmetic, Mathematics, Surveying, Writing and Book-keeping, Drawing, French, Vocal Music and the elements of Science – a curriculum specifically designed for boys to leave school equipped for employment in the commercial world of late nineteenth-century London. For an additional fee, and after school hours, boys could also take classes in Latin, German, Shorthand and Water-colours.[61] In the earliest years, there was no provision for organized sports. Parents had to buy all textbooks, and were charged two shillings per term for pens, ink, paper, slates, slate-pencils and reading books. Pupils had to wear a school cap (or straw boater in summer) – on its peak a yellow camel laden with cloves, part of the insignia of the Grocers' Company.

Boys could be admitted to the school between the age of seven and twelve, having passed a simple entrance exam. Those under the age of ten had to be able 'to read words of three syllables, to write text hand, to know the multiplication tables, and to be able to work easy sums in simple addition and subtraction.' Those aged over ten had to demonstrate 'a knowledge of vulgar fractions and the outlines of commercial geography and English history.'[62] For the school's first two decades the local community from which most of the boys were drawn 'was almost exclusively Christian, and most fathers of boys at the school were bank

---

58. H. Courthope Bowen, 'The Teaching of English Grammar: A New Method', paper read to the College of Praeceptors, 17 June 1885.
59. The distinctive amphitheatre: at assembly, the boys sat on its steps. The Speech Room of Harrow School is of similar design.
60. Medcalf, p. 29. Adapted from Charles Kingsley's 'A Farewell', which reads: 'Be good, sweet maid, and let who will be clever; / Do noble things, not dream them, all day long: / And so make life, death, and that vast for-ever / One grand, sweet song.'
61. Minutes f. 60, 10 January 1877.
62. Minutes f. 61, 10 January 1877.

officials, civil servants and professional or businessmen.'[63] The school's admission register recorded fathers' occupation and the family's address. Of the first twenty pupils recorded in October 1876, fathers occupations were: solicitor's managing clerk, boot manufacturer, commercial clerk, corn merchant, master mariner, wine merchant, merchant, butcher, lithographer, Australian agent, coal merchant, HM Customs clerk, brewer's manager, timber merchant, brass founder, merchant's clerk, stationer, commercial traveller, Civil Service clerk, surveyor and oilman. All lived in Hackney or the adjoining districts of Clapton, Stoke Newington, Dalston, Victoria Park and Kingsland.[64]

The school's front playground, knee-high in grass in summer, was 'Lammas' land, much used as a fairground. By custom, between 12 August and 6 April each year this area had been utilised by Hackney parishioners for pasturing cattle.[65] Hackney Downs had recently been acquired by the Metropolitan Board of Works, and to mark the school's boundary with the Downs the Grocers' Company enclosed their estate with a low white fence, which aggravated some local residents. In November 1876, John de Morgan, founder and president of the Commons Protection League, wrote to the company demanding the fence be removed.[66] On Easter bank holiday 1877, a crowd tore down the fence-posts. In May, 'anticipating a recurrence of the nuisance caused on the previous Easter Monday by the assemblage of disorderly persons on the ground in front of the School' the Headmaster wrote to warn the Company and was instructed to contact the police. Despite an injunction against the ringleader,[67] further damage was caused, and in July the Company resolved to build a 760-foot-long wall to protect the school's land.[68] Despite this obstacle, people bound for Hackney Downs Station continued to use the playground as a short-cut, presuming it to be a right-of-way.

63. Black, p. 54.
64. Admission, October 1876.
65. Medcalf, p. 14.
66. In the 1870s several popular movements were protesting about the enclosure of public land. One such dispute concerned Hackney Downs, hitherto common grazing land. Matters came to a head on 11 December 1875, when a crowd of up to 50,000 gathered on Hackney Downs. The outnumbered police withdrew and fences were pulled up and burnt. *Punch* published mock-medieval verses about the destruction, entitled 'A Fytte of Hackney Downs'. The **Metropolitan Board of Works** eventually bought out Lord Tyssen to ensure the Downs remained open. (Layers of London website; Silvester St Clair, *Sketch of the Life and Labours of Jno. De Morgan, Orator, Elocutionist, and the Tribune of the People*. Leeds, 1880, pp. 8–10.
67. Granted by the Master of the Rolls, 29 June 1877 (Minutes f. 69, 14 July 1877).
68. Minutes f. 71, 18 July 1877. The Lammas land dispute rumbled on for the next two decades. In 1888, Hackney Downs was transferred from the Metropolitan Board of Works to the London County Council.

Headmaster Bowen came down hard on pupil absence. The Governors 'entirely approved' his excluding two boys for attending the Lord Mayor's Show during school time.[69] Nor was pupil behaviour always gentlemanly: in 1877 the Great Eastern Railway complained to the school that boys had thrown stones at signals and broken the windows in a signal-box. On another occasion the governors – presumably anticipating disorder – instructed the headmaster to ensure sufficient police were on hand for speech day.[70] Frequent fights took place between the 'printers' boys' – apprentices at Eyre & Spottiswoode's Bible printing works in nearby Shacklewell – and Grocers' pupils, summoned by the battle-cry 'The camels are coming!'[71]

Until 1881, independent inspectors reported positively every year. In December 1877, Revd. Reginald Broughton (1836–1912), of Balliol College, Oxford, described the strict discipline he observed at Hackney Downs:

> The boys are never allowed to run up and down stairs or along the passages, nor is any shouting or talking allowed in the precincts of the School during school hours… Whenever in the course of the day changes from one class-room to another are necessary the same vigorous system of military discipline is observed…

Broughton's report continued:

> For enforcing the discipline of the School the Head Master has recourse to various methods of punishment, such as fines, detention and occasionally corporal punishment...

Broughton confirmed that 'English is the main stuff of learning in the school,' while French was taught 'not so much grammatically as with a view to giving the boys a French vocabulary and teaching them to express themselves both in speaking and writing'. Although this sounds unexceptionable, 'the Court [i.e. the Governors] did not consider [this] quite satisfactory'.[72] However, overall the Governors were so pleased with Broughton's assessment that they suggested the Headmaster have it printed in local newspapers.[73]

---

69. Minutes f. 54, 10 November 1876. Another parent appealed in vain to Shoreditch County Court after Bowen excluded his son for unauthorised absence. (Minutes f. 57, 27 November 1876). When the *Hackney Express* reported the case, the Governors instructed Bowen to stop advertising the school in that newspaper. (Letter Book 1, f. 392, 27 February 1877; f. 396, 16 March 1877.)
70. Medcalf, p. 10.
71. Medcalf, p. 26. Another reference to the Grocers' insignia.
72. Minutes f. 81, 83, 86, 10 January 1878.
73. Letter Book 1, f. 601, 25 July 1878.

As to religious education, Bowen seems to have sympathized with Revd. Rogers' rather agnostic views, and minimized such activity:

> The whole School once a week on Friday afternoon after 4 o'clock meets together in the Theatre and all unite together in offering up praise to God by singing one of the Psalms of the Old Testament to the accompaniment of an organ. This is the only strictly religious part of the School discipline, but it is one in which all the members of the various religious denominations[74] to which the boys belong can join and in it they join most heartily.

Anxious to correct the impression that this was the only religious exercise, Bowen reported he had also introduced an hour on Wednesday mornings 'devoted to an Old Testament Scripture Lesson,' to which only one boy objected. He also noted that, lacking a laboratory, the school could offer no tuition in chemistry, despite contemporary awareness that chemistry was a vital component in German industrialization; in its place Bowen proposed Mechanics and Botany.[75] From 1876, the Hackney Choral Society, led by the eminent musician Ebenezer Prout (1835–1909),[76] was permitted to use the school theatre for rehearsals, provided school pupils could also attend.[77] From 1877, university extension lectures were also held in the theatre, on a similar basis.

In 1878, Joshua Girling Fitch (1824–1903), a leading educationalist and one of Her Majesty's Inspectors of Schools, undertook the second annual inspection. Having heard pupils read, he criticized their Cockney accent:

> The reading throughout the school is intelligent though not always accurate, and not wholly free from those special faults of intonation and pronunciation which are apt to prevail among London-bred boys…

But overall his impression was very positive. He singled out Bowen's approach to the teaching of history, 'fastening the thoughts of scholars upon a few of the greatest events, the turning points in our National history…' supplementing the lesson 'by reference to text books' Fitch singled out language teaching for his highest praise, noting that Latin was not regarded as 'an essential ingredient' for boys 'the great majority of

---

74. It is unclear whether this included Jewish pupils, though observant Jews would presumably have left before sundown in winter months.
75. Minutes f. 83, 84, 90, 30 January 1878.
76. Many of Prout's Novello editions of Handel oratorios are still in print.
77. The Governors reckoned 'the society was likely to be a great use to the school, and had amongst its members many relatives of the scholars.' Minutes f. 45, 1 November 1876.

whom will enter probably on some business or profession at the age of 15'. He assessed 'the mode in which English is taught in this School as exceptionally skilful and successful' and concluded:

> On the whole I may honestly congratulate the Company upon the great success and high promise of the important Educational Experiment they have made... I cannot doubt that under its present management it will soon take the highest rank among the Public Schools of the Metropolis.

It is important to note his description of the school's programme as an 'educational experiment': Cowper Street, and in turn Hackney Downs, seem to have pioneered an educational path preparing the middle classes for commercial and business life. Yet, ominously, by this same date the Governors were anticipating a financial deficit, to be met by the Grocers' Company.[78]

In 1879, the school was inspected by J. M. D. Meiklejohn (1836–1902), first Professor of Education at St. Andrew's University and – like Bowen – a follower of German philosophy. By this date the school's pupils numbered 376, still far short of the budgeted 500. Meiklejohn summarized the school's aims:

> The chief purpose of the School appears to be to give its pupils a commercial education of the best and most solid kind, and to combine with that a liberal education in the literature of our own country, along with such a knowledge of French as may be useful to a man of business.'

The inspector focused on the exceptional teaching of English:

> A special feature in the School is the teaching of English Literature. It is on the one hand difficult to over estimate [sic] the value of this as a means of education; while on the other hand it seems to be the duty that lies nearest to us, to train our children to know and to be fond of the best literature of their own country. This object appears to me to be carried out with great success, with greater success indeed than in any School I know, or know of in Great Britain....
>
> English Grammar is more sensibly and efficiently taught in this School than in any other I have had to examine. The boys are made to think, to observe, to

78. Minutes f. 101–104, 107, 29 January 1879.

draw conclusions for themselves and to give reasons for whatever they say… [T]he methods and plans on which the school is worked thoroughly fulfil the aim and purpose of the Founders; and… the teaching of English Literature is a gain, not only in itself but for the other subjects of the School. It seems to me to make the boys more open minded, more alert, more quick in perception more pervious to learning and to good teaching than if they were kept constantly upon the lines of mere drill and dull lesson work…

The organisation of the School and the administrative arrangement are excellent, and the Head Master has a perfect check upon the work and conduct of each individual boy in the school…. The foundation of this School cannot but be of the greatest benefit to the neighbourhood, and I am satisfied that the working of it is in complete accord with the generous spirit and intention of the Founders.[79]

High praise indeed; and – in view of later developments – it is important to note Meiklejohn's belief that the Headmaster was thoroughly fulfilling the stated aims and goals of the company. In 1879 the Governors discussed the provision of university exhibitions for pupils, but deferred any decision until there were more boys of an age intending to progress to tertiary education. An exception was the first school captain, an able scholar named Harry James Thompson, who was granted 25 guineas to support him at King's College, London.[80]

Despite these glowing reports, the Grocers' Company was increasingly concerned about the school. From the outset, there had been anxiety about the financial burden the school laid upon the company. In May 1876, before the school opened, the company had anticipated a £660 deficit in annual running costs. To reduce outgoings, they cut the projected salary for the Headmaster by half, from £200 to £100, and his proposed capitation fee from one pound to ten shillings for every boy over the number of 400. Nevertheless running costs soon rose rapidly: when the school opened there were four assistant masters; three years later there were eighteen, more than quadrupling the cost of staff salaries. In 1880, the

---

79. Minutes ff. 123, 126–128, 11 July 1879.
80. In his final report to the Governors, presumably to bolster his own reputation, Bowen quoted from the *City Press*: at his university graduation, Thompson had 'probably the strongest list of honours ever gained by a student of the Engineering Department' (Reports to Company, 16 July 1881).

Governors recorded a deficit of £1201 – 9s – 1d for the previous year.[81]

The Company's scheme for the school included religious instruction, but permitted parents to exempt their sons from prayers, religious worship and instruction.[82] Outside of religious instruction classes, school staff were prohibited from teaching 'systematically and persistently any particular religious doctrine'. When the Governors proposed the introduction of morning prayers, Bowen responded this 'would take up too much time and necessitate the omission of a subject.'[83] A year later, under continuing pressure from the governors, the Headmaster reported:

> I have introduced Prayers at the opening of School every Monday mornings [sic]… and have had no objection from any parent – even some of the Jews attend.[84] I read part of the Gospel for the day and then we say the Lord's Prayer… On Wednesdays (as before) we begin with 3/4 of an hour's study of the Old Testament.[85]

Still not satisfied, the company's clerk wrote peremptorily to Bowen in April 1881: '…let me have a written report as to the Religious information given in the school under clause 37 of the Scheme.'[86] Bowen responded that every class now studied part of the Old Testament each term, and the sixth form 'sometimes' worked on a New Testament book. The school week commenced with a 'ceremony' where the Head read part of the Gospel for the day,[87] and everyone joined in the Lord's Prayer, after which the Head 'asking for a blessing on our work'. Wednesday mornings began with a 45-minute Bible lesson and reading,

81. The Governors also interested themselves in such insignificant matters as the installation of fountains in the playground, coat-hooks beneath the theatre, and the purchase of a looking-glass for the school secretary's wife, an inkstand for the office and a box for dumbbells. (Letter Book 1, f. 632, 16 November 1878.)
82. William Rogers, Bowen's mentor and patron, though an ordained priest, had strong reservations about religious education: 'I take the position that what is generally regarded as religious instruction conduces neither to religion nor instruction . . . On the first London School Board I advocated a strictly secular education . . . ' (Hadden pp. 205–206).
83. Medcalf p. 21. Bowen did not subscribe to conservative Christian beliefs: in his Maitland Prize essay, 'The Principle of Buddhism and of Christianity compared . . .' (1874), he wrote: 'The theory that Christ's death was a propitiatory sacrifice, made to appease the wrath of God, is untenable…' and 'The picture of a never-ending damnation of the majority of the human race… can never be reconciled with the conscience and reason of mankind' (pp. 56, 59).
84. There was already a Jewish presence in the locality before the major immigration of Jews to the UK in the following decades. In his examination of the earliest registers of the school (1876), Gerry Black identified 'a sprinkling of Jewish names' (Black, p. 55).
85. Minutes f. 136, January 1880.
86. Letter Book 2, f. 89, 7 April 1881.
87. i.e. the set passage from the Anglican *Book of Common Prayer*.

and the week concluded with 'a short address, singing a psalm, and a short prayer'. Bowen reckoned that at this date the school numbered roughly 120 [Protestant] Dissenters and 230 Anglicans.[88]

It appears Bowen did not always act diplomatically, which caused further friction with the Company. In June 1879 he requested the Grocers' Company to provide a covered area in the playground, since the space beneath the theatre was providing inadequate shelter in bad weather. It transpired that Bowen had already asked an architect to prepare plans for the proposed structure, costed at £1000. Ambushed by their employee, the company turned down his request.

The Oxford and Cambridge Examinations Board report of 1880 was more critical than previous school inspections, concluding:

> The results at present attained are excellent in the department of English History and Literature; but where thought is required they [the pupils] are hardly equal to what might have been hoped; still it must not be forgotten that the boys leave school at such an early age that their reasoning powers, however carefully cultivated, have not had time to mature.[89]

On the Headmaster's recommendation, the Governors agreed to set up a carpenter's shop.[90] They also agreed to Bowen's proposal that the sixth form be entered for the Oxford and Cambridge Local Examinations, 'established by the Universities with a special view to the needs of Middle Class Schools' and accepted as a preliminary qualification for pupil teachers.[91] In addition, the Governors agreed to spend £40 on apparatus for teaching 'mechanics, hydrostatics and heat'.[92]

In April 1881, the Governors had further cause for concern, when Bowen dismissed an assistant master named W. E. Burford for having struck a boy. Burford demanded an inquiry, but was informed the Company had no jurisdiction in the matter, upon which he launched a protest campaign, circulating leaflets and picketing Grocers' Hall[93] – an embarrassment for which the Governors blamed Bowen.[94] On top of this, the

---

88. Reports to Company, 27 April 1881.
89. Reports to Company, 19 July 1880.
90. Reports to Company, 26 January 1881.
91. Maclure, p. 52.
92. The Governors now agreed to the use of the school theatre by an external 'Debating Society', whose members included such 'influential Gentlemen' as Lord George Hamilton (1845–1927), later First Lord of the Admiralty, Mr Coope – possibly Octavius Coope (1814–86), MP for Middlesex from 1874 – and Mr Fawcett – presumably Henry Fawcett (1833–84), MP for Hackney 1874–84. (Reports to Company, 26 January 1881.)
93. Letter Book 2, f. 94, 28 April 1881.
94. The Governors absolved themselves of any responsibility: 'the Head Master has the sole

Governors voiced concern that Bowen was preparing few, if any, pupils for the Cambridge Local Examinations, which could have opened up entry to one of the major public schools – something the company had explicitly ruled out at its foundation.

Above all, the Governors were worried that the school roll – and thus income from fees – was dwindling. 210 boys had been enrolled at the school's opening; that number increased to 389 by 1878, which was still 111 short of the planned capacity of 500. However, by January 1880 numbers had fallen back to 354. Roughly two-thirds of the pupils came from the immediate neighbourhood, so the Governors adopted Bowen's suggestion of publicizing the school more widely, with advertisements in twenty local newspapers. Despite this campaign, by March 1881 pupil numbers had dropped to 333.[95]

The falling roll can in part be explained by the impact of W. E. Forster's Elementary Education Act of 1870, which provided for universal free elementary education for the lower classes, the sons and daughters of working men.[96] Paradoxically, this educational revolution led to lower middle-class and 'respectable' working-class parents, keen to distinguish their children at fee-charging private schools from those attending free Board Schools, demanding their sons be taught Latin. The classics, and Latin in particular, became a desired social marker among the parents – skilled workers, tradesmen and professional middle-classes – whose children the Governors were striving to attract. The classical languages took on symbolic significance for these aspiring parents.

In a letter to the Governors dated 7 March 1881, Bowen argued that the school faced fierce competition from the growing number of free Board Schools,[97] and was seriously undercharging tuition fees – currently £6 per head per annum. The Headmaster proposed raising fees by 50 percent to £9 per head, which he reckoned would bring in an extra £1000 per annum, equalling the regular annual deficit. Bowen also proposed that – to meet the new competition – Hackney Downs should become 'higher than a Middle Class School, or one in which something higher than ordinary Middle Class Education can be procured'. He suggested recruiting another Oxbridge-educated teacher – at this date

power of appointing and dismissing all Assistant Masters' (Letter Book 2, f. 120, 4 August 1881.)
95. The financial loss for the year ending December 1880 amounted to £1017 – 17s – 8d: Reports to Company, 26 January 1881.
96. The London School Board, the new education authority for London, was first elected on 29 November 1870 (Maclure, p. 15–16).
97. Bowen appended a list of 43 schools within 25 minutes' walking distance of Hackney Downs, all offering Elementary and/or Middle Class Education, and catering for around 4,500 pupils.

of thirteen masters, only two (including the part-time music teacher) possessed a university degree.[98] Bowen also noted that, compared with other City Company schools, such as Merchant Taylors' and St Paul's, which offered more than 100 scholarships, the Grocers' Company provided just three, adding force to the contemporary epithet 'the Graceless Grocers'.[99] He added: 'the smallness of my salary naturally leads me to look out for promotion elsewhere' – the earliest direct evidence of his unhappiness at the school.[100]

In July 1881, the Governors heard that Bowen intended to hand in his notice at Christmas.[101] He had clearly lost the confidence of the Governors, though whether mainly as a result of the falling roll and failing finances or because of his reforming, English-centred curriculum and liberal regime is unclear. His resignation letter leaves no doubt he felt he had been forced out:

> It being impossible for me any longer to avoid noticing that you do not appreciate my past or present work at Hackney Downs, and feeling that, without your active sympathy it would be impossible for me to effect anything worthy of the Grocers' Company or the Schools,[102] or satisfactory to myself, I beg hereby to place in your hands my resignation of the post of Head Master... [103]

Two years later G. S. D. Murray, an Assistant Commissioner of the Charity Commission, interviewed the new headmaster, Charles Gull,[104] who blamed his predecessor:

> The former decline of the School is attributed to the system pursued by the late Headmaster. The Scheme of work was badly arranged, Latin being made an extra subject & taught out of the regular School hours, and undue attention being given to English Literature, which was taught from textbooks edited by the Headmaster himself.[105] There were no School games, nor any

98. Reports to Company, July 16 1881.
99. Livery Companies' Commission, I, p. 287.
100. Reports to Company, 27 April 1881.
101. Minutes 6 July 1881.
102. i.e. the junior and senior sections of the school.
103. Minutes f. 159, 16 July, 1881.
104. See below for the context of the interview.
105. This was, and remained, a common and accepted practice. Bowen published a number of textbooks including: *Studies in English for the Use of Modern Schools* (London: Henry S. King, 1876); *Simple English Poems* (London: Kegan Paul, 1879); and *English Grammar for Beginners* (London: Kegan Paul, London, 1879).

religious instruction. The School was consequently
in bad odour, and it was found advisable that the
Headmaster should retire.[106]

Gull's criticism is incorrect and self-serving, ignoring the fact that the scheme set up by the Grocers' Company specifically excluded Latin and had never included sports. His gratuitous swipe at Bowen for teaching from his own textbooks is tendentious; the term 'bad odour' might more fairly be applied to the behaviour of the company towards their first Headmaster.

After leaving Hackney Downs, Bowen applied for the headship of a grammar school, but the Grocers' Company refused to give him a testimonial, on the specious grounds of 'never having done so' previously.[107] In 1882, Bowen was appointed Principal of the Finsbury Training College (FTC) for Secondary Schoolmasters, the first English institution for training secondary teachers, set up by a number of headmasters of 'First Grade Schools', and for which Canon Rogers provided rooms and teaching practice at the Cowper Street School. However Bowen encountered major obstacles, both financial and professional, in attempting to sustain the college.[108] He enlisted the support of Oscar Browning (1837–1923), another early advocate of professional teacher training, appointed to a lectureship at King's College Cambridge in 1880.[109] In December Bowen wrote to Browning, who had apparently suggested Bowen apply for the post of Headmaster of the Perse School, Cambridge, a step he was reluctant to take as he believed the FTC would collapse if he resigned.[110] By this date, the FTC was in dire straits financially: Bowen asked Browning for £5 to help support it[111] and implored

106. NA, Records of the Ministry of Education: ED 27/3058.
107. Minutes f. 174, 5 July, 1882; Letter Book 2, f. 251, 6 July 1882.
108. '…headmasters of [this] date had no belief in training, and the most advanced of them offered only lip service.' *The Clove Review* Spring 1953, No. 4, p. 6.
109. Browning was a colourful Cambridge personality – 'Falstaffian, shameless, affectionate, egoistic, generous, snobbish, democratic, witty, lazy, dull, worldly, academic' (G. Lowes Dickinson), dismissed as a master at Eton ostensibly for disregarding rules but apparently also for inappropriate relationships with pupils. See Ian Anstruther: *Oscar Browning: A Biography*, London: John Murray, 1983. On teacher training at Cambridge see: Mark McBeth, 'The Pleasure of Learning and the Tightrope of Desire,' in ed. Joyce Goodman and Jane Martin, *Gender, Colonialism and Education: The Politics of Experience*. London: Woburn Press, 2002 pp. 61–64.
110. 12 December. Bowen listed his qualifications: 'I am unmarried, aged 36. MA, 4th Senior Optime 1870, Le Bas Prizeman and Maitland Prizeman. Headmaster of the Grocers' Company's schools Hackney Downs 1876–1881. I am not in orders.' (Cambridge University: King's College Archive Centre OB/1/191/A.)
111. Bowen seems to have spent the early part of January, and possibly Christmas, in Italy (20 January 1884, Bowen/Browning Letters). His nephew, H. T. Bowen, reported he often holidayed with his brother Horace in southern France or Italy. (*Clove Review*, spring 1953, p. 7.)

him to encourage men from King's to apply for admission, explaining he was unable to supply candidates to all the schools who were requesting teachers.[112] In November 1884, Bowen reported that the college had just four students: 'poverty culled the rest'. The writing was on the wall, and in September 1886 Bowen told Browning 'You will soon get formal notice the Finsbury Training College is to be closed... It has had no funds for a year past and has no encouragement to struggle any more ... . I am literally on my beam ends.'[113] Desperate for employment, Bowen reported to Browning that he was considering applying for the Chair of Modern Literature at the University of Sydney, Australia.[114] In the event he remained in England, reviewing, lecturing and writing on education and the professional training of teachers.[115]

As a follower of Froebel, Bowen now devoted his energies to teaching at Cambridge and to the work of educational societies. He joined the Council of the College of Pr[a]eceptors, became Chairman of the National Froebel Union and was one of the founders of the Teachers' Guild. In 1885 he published a collection of poems and sonnets, *Blossom from an Orchard*,[116] while *Froebel and Education by Self-Activity* appeared in 1893.[117] Bowen also published a number of papers on key topics in education,[118] explaining

112. 12 May 1884, Bowen/Browning Letters.
113. 14 September 1886, Bowen/Browning Letters.
114. 15 October 1886, Bowen/Browning Letters.
115. Ten years later Bowen accepted an invitation from Browning to give a series of lectures at Cambridge on the History of Education for a fee of £50, an arrangement it is implied he had also made in previous years (28 May 1896, Bowen/Browning Letters). Bowen was now living in rooms at 3 York Street, Portman Square 'surrounded by his beloved books... never other than a poor man'. He was a member of the Savile Club, whose members included 'one of his closest friends', Sir E. Ray Lankester (1847–1929) a leading biologist, who never married; Sir Owen Seaman (1861–1936), another friend who never married, editor of *Punch* from 1906. See H. T. Bowen: 'Herbert Courthope Bowen,' *The Clove Review*, Spring 1953, pp. 6–8. Bowen's brothers were W. H. Bowen, Paymaster-in-Chief of the Navy, and Horace George Bowen, Chief Cashier of the Bank of England from 1893.
116. London: David Stott. Several poems are noted as written in Italy. 'After Failure' includes the lines:
    Youth, disappointment, and that fatalist
    Debauching idleness abide with me:
    These three are plotting how my soul to twist
    And bend it in a dread deformity.
It is tempting to read them as confessional.
117. Published by William Heinemann, London, and since reprinted at least 54 times.
118. 'The Teaching of English Literature in Middle-Class Schools', College of Praeceptors, March 16, London: C. F. Hodgson, 1881; 'Is Knowledge Power?', Education Society, June 16, London: Hodgson, 1884; 'The Training of Schoolmasters for Middle and Higher Schools', College of Praeceptors, March 19, London: Hodgson 1884; 'The Teaching of English Grammar – A New Method', College of Praeceptors, June 17, London: Hodgson, 1885; 'The Training of the Constructive Imagination', Education Society April 20, London:

> My attention was first called to [Froebel's] system when, as headmaster of a large London school [Grocers'] many years ago I had occasion to notice the extra brightness and teachableness of some little boys who had been, at least partly, trained on Froebel's plan.[119]

Bowen believed English teaching should be centrally concerned with the development of mind.

Herbert Courthope Bowen died in London on 9 April 1909, aged 61.[120] Some accounts have criticised him for his shy, withdrawn nature; one pupil found him 'reserved... with no sympathy for boys as boys'[121] However the tribute published in the *Review* was warm and well-informed:

> He was a man of marked individuality, caring little for ordinary assessments of success, and he gave to a certain number of boys a conception of their life-work which has been a stimulating influence . . . [E]verybody who had had anything to do with him would testify that he was just. To boys not clever, but willing to work, he was kind and fair, and many a boy of this sort must look back with gratitude to helpful words and deeds . . . Mr. Bowen will be recalled most vividly, perhaps, as he read to the boys in the theatre during some luncheon hour when the weather was too bad for play. Passages from Kingsley's *Westward Ho!* would be chosen, or an extract from some other stirring story. A real sympathy could then be discovered . . . beneath his austere manner...
> In the attention which he paid to the study of English he anticipated by many years the present movement.[122]

Hodgson 1885; 'Hints to Froebel students', Froebel Society. November 24, London: Hodgson 1886; 'Connectedness in Teaching or, The School Curriculum as One Organic Whole', College of Praeceptors, May 14, London: Hodgson, 1890; '"Creativeness" or Self Activity as a means of Education', College of Praeceptors, April 13, London: Hodgson 1892. For a discussion of Bowen's educational thinking see Hardcastle pp. 7, 9.

119. While teaching art at Hackney Downs during Bowen's headmastership the art educationist Francis Henry Newbery (1855–1946), Director of the Glasgow School of Art between 1885 and 1918, encountered and embraced Froebel's ideas. (TCL , January 1953, p. 7; see also ODNB.)

120. His address, 14 Castletown Road, West Kensington. An obituary in the *Journal of Education* (May 1909), described him as 'impulsive, generous, warm-hearted, he had many friends and, in spite of quarrels, no lasting enemies'. He left £3815 – worth roughly £500,000 in 2025.

121. Hackney Archives R/DOW 0/7.

122. Review 67, Summer term 1909, p. 56.

Chapter 2
Silence in the Ranks!
Charles Gull, Headmaster 1882–1905

> ...*my best efforts shall be given to maintain the School at a high standard of discipline and efficiency.*
> Charles Gull

57 candidates applied for the post of second Headmaster of Hackney Downs School; by 25 October 1881 these had been whittled down to a shortlist of six, three of whom were ordained clergymen.[123] Finally, Charles George Gull was selected 'by a large majority'.[124] Born in 1851, Gull entered St. Alban Hall, Oxford,[125] in 1869 and graduated B.A. from Hertford College[126] in 1875. Before coming to Hackney he had taught for two years at Colwall Grammar School, Malvern, a Grocers' Company foundation; for one year at Farnborough School, Hampshire; and from 1877 until 1881 at Dulwich College,[127] where he was praised by the Headmaster for having founded the College Rifle Corps. By 1880, Gull's corps numbered 100 members. At a parade of 55,000 volunteers before Queen Victoria in Windsor Great Park in 1881, the Manchester Guardian singled out Gull's Dulwich company for praise.[128] While in Dulwich, he took deacon's orders in the Church of England, serving as curate at St Peter's, Lordship Lane.

It is difficult to understand what attracted the Governors of Hackney Downs to Gull. He was more junior, had less teaching experience and was less academically qualified than any of the other shortlisted

---

123. Letter Book 2, f. 193, 25 October 1881. Reports to Company, 2 November 1881.
124. Letter Book 2, f. 205, 16 November 1881. Gull was then living at Cedar Villa, Underhill Road, Dulwich.
125. Now part of Merton College.
126. However, Crockfords records he was an open scholar at Magdalen.
127. There is scant record of Gull in the extensive archives of Dulwich College, where he had been a pupil between January 1861 and June 1869. His father, Joseph Winney Gull, a Camberwell ship- and insurance-broker, was a governor of Dulwich College from 1868 until 1872 or 1875.
128. Sheila Hodges, *God's Gift: A Living History of Dulwich College*. London: Heinemann, 1981, p. 243.

candidates. He was unmarried, and – apart from his work with the corps – seems to have left little impression at Dulwich College. In his covering letter to the Governors listing his referees, Gull set out his agenda: 'Should you think well to elect me, my best efforts shall be given to maintain the School at a high standard of discipline and efficiency.' There is no reference to educational methods or standards, or to his views on the curriculum or examination system. Gull's referees described him as 'a man who can create enthusiasm', and focused on his 'attention to physical education' and 'acquaintance with financial matters'; the 'support he has given in the gymnasium and play-ground, and to everything that is manly in the sports and amusements of the boys'; his 'power as a disciplinarian'.[129] Sporting a patriarchal beard, and habitually riding to school on a horse, Gull was clearly a commanding presence, a contrast to 'shy, withdrawn' Herbert Bowen.

On Gull's first morning at Hackney Downs, the boys assembled, chatting companionably, before marching into school. The new Headmaster stood at the top of the steps, imperious in cap and gown. 'Silence in the ranks!' he yelled in a stentorian voice – with immediate impact. He announced that in future, upon the first bell, pupils would walk 'like gentlemen' to their classrooms, before proceeding silently to the theatre for morning prayer, making it clear there had been a major shift in the school's dispensation. Former pupil Frank Thompson described the change in literary terms, referencing Bunyan and Mallory:

> 'Mr. Faithful' had given place to 'Mr. Greatheart', or to change the simile, . . .the lonely Sir Galahad with his passionate quest for high ideals had retired to make room for King Arthur with his Round Table.[130]

From the outset, Gull determined to create a new ethos, as summarised by another former pupil:

> Mr. Gull altered the regime to more of a public school type, with emphasis on Latin. He also introduced mortarboards and gowns for the form masters, whereas under Mr. Bowen they wore a rounded hat.[131]

Immediately, Gull presented the Governors with his 'ideas on the management, the scope and the needs' of the school. A classics graduate, recently ordained, he immediately added Latin and Religious Knowledge to the examination curriculum, specifying that 'Latin should be taught as the best vehicle of instruction in Grammar', overturning Bowen's

---

129. Reports to Company, 2 November 1881.
130. Medcalf, p. 28.
131. A. L. Solomon, *Review* 165, Summer term 1948.

policy and satisfying reported pressure from parents. Gull also asserted: 'French should be taught as a living language; sufficient time should be given to this subject to make boys able to speak and write the language fluently' – despite Bowen having fostered a similar approach. Gull proposed a similar method for German teaching. Evidently keen to define the school as Christian – and indeed Anglican – the new Head informed the Governors he intended to introduce a 'short Divine Service' at the beginning and end of the school day.[132] Gull persuaded the Governors to buy a second-hand pipe organ for use during the now daily services, and introduced two Scripture lessons weekly throughout the school, a practice that contrasted markedly with the minimal religious observance during Bowen's headmastership.

In his first Annual Report, on 18 July 1882, Gull expanded on his reforms. He took this opportunity to attack Bowen's approach, claiming his predecessor's 'system of instruction was so very unusual that we have been compelled to begin *de novo* in almost every subject' – an evaluation contradicted by the generally very positive annual reports by inspectors and examiners between 1876 and 1881.[133] The school roll remained low, numbering only 309 pupils.

According to Dr. Alderman, Gull's military-style discipline resulted in a virtual strike by the sixth form.[134] The Headmaster caned almost the entire set – a feat he recalled with 'no little pleasure and pride'. Gull's recipe was: 'Keep them hard at it and have no nonsense while they are at it, but don't forget to give them an "easy" now and then…'. Boys were permitted to move freely and noisily between classrooms, as Gull believed it to be good policy to allow them to let off steam.[135] Gull was a committed believer in corporal punishment for both laziness and insubordination: a favourite axiom: 'If a boy doesn't work he must be whipped.' For major offences, the cane was supplanted by the birch, newly-prepared by the school porter from shrubs in the front playground and administered upon the bare skin. In 1898, Gull was sued for assault by a father whose child had been caned for visiting the London zoo during schooltime.[136] Revd. Gull attempted to follow

132. Reports. In his first Annual Report, 18 July 1882, Gull allowed that 'Boys of the Jewish faith' could absent themselves 'under the conscience clause'. Although Gull was ordained deacon in the Church of England in 1881, he was not priested until 1899. (Freddie Witts, Dulwich College.)
133. Gull requested the Governors to supply a new bell: 'confusion is sometimes caused by the Railway Bell at Hackney Downs Station being mistaken for the School Bell... The Porter, whose lot it is to ring the hand bell, has been rendered inconveniently deaf in the execution of his duty.' Minutes 2: 12 July 1884, f. 6.
134. Alderman, p. 26.
135. Medcalf, p. 31; Review 153, Summer 1940 p. 33.
136. The father won the case, but was awarded only nominal damages. Such was Gull's

playwright W. S. Gilbert's nostrum in *The Mikado,* of making the punishment fit the crime: when he caught two boys smoking, he forced them to smoke two of his foulest pipes, taking sadistic pleasure in their suffering; 'They are getting greener and greener every minute,' he commented. 'It's lovely!'[137]

During his first term as Headmaster, Gull appointed a drill sergeant,[138] just as he had at Dulwich College, and soon established a non-uniformed school battalion[139] comprising almost every boy. In due course, Gull installed two miniature rifle ranges at the school, one in the gymnasium, the other outdoors, where boys aged fourteen and over were instructed in musketry. Parades were conducted on Hackney Downs, accompanied by a school drum and fife band, the boys armed with 'flat pieces of wood fashioned like rifles'.[140]

The Grocers' Company was concerned, as ever, at the continuing expense of maintaining the school, which required a subsidy of around £1,200 every year to balance the books. In 1882, the Company proposed raising the school fees by fifty percent, from £6 to £9 per annum, a strategy vigorously opposed by Gull, who threatened to resign in protest. Such an increase would have required the assent of the Charity Commissioners, whose Assistant Commissioner, G. S. D. Murray, interviewed Gull in an attempt to understand the situation before giving judgment.[141] Murray recorded that, after leaving school, most boys 'take to their Father's business, or become Clerks'. He reported 347 boys currently on the school roll, although it could accommodate 550; and that between 150 and 200 pupils lived within fifteen minutes' walk of the school.[142] He noted that few boys came from (free) public elementary schools – it would be necessary to offer scholarships to attract them – and that some of those transferring from private schools were 'very ignorant'.

During his interview with Murray, Gull claimed that raising the fees above £6 would 'inflict a serious blow on the rising [educational] prosperity of the School' and 'drive more children to the Board Schools'. Murray was swayed by the Head's arguments, pointing out that other local endowed schools charged a maximum of £6 per annum, so raising

---

popularity with a large number of parents that a fund-raising campaign was launched to compensate him for his supposed ordeal. He used the money to construct new fives courts.
137. Medcalf, p. 33.
138. Minutes 1, f. 162, 11 January, 1882.
139. Boys were not required to wear a uniform as it was thought some families would have been unable to afford it.
140. Review 166, Easter term 1949, p. 25.
141. Reports, 16 April, 5 May 1882.
142. 46 came by train 'chiefly from the Eastern Suburbs'.

Charles George Gull, second Headmaster of Hackney Downs School.

the fees would leave Grocers' at a competitive disadvantage. Fees were not raised and financial concern continued; two years later, the Company was still pressing to reduce its grant to the school by raising pupils' fees. Gull argued that the school's high educational standards would be jeopardised by any cost-cutting, and repeated his argument that raising the fees by the proposed fifty percent would result in the short-term loss of pupils, and hence lower income, still leaving the Company with an annual deficit of around £1,000.[143]

The Company remained concerned. In 1887 the Grocers wrote to the Charity Commission, arguing they had never intended to support the school financially once established; rather, they had planned 'to

143. Reports, 11 May 1882.

found an Institution which should be self supporting [sic].'[144] They argued 'the class now benefitted [sic] by the School is to a great extent not that for which the Institution was originally designed . . .' and objected to 'so large an annual expenditure of the Company's funds . . . giving an education so much below cost price to those who have no claim upon them'. The Grocers rejected the Commissioners' proposed solution – that the company provide an endowment in the form of 'investment of capital in trust for the School' – which might have given the school long-term financial stability similar to that enjoyed by Dulwich College and Alleyn's School, both sustained by Edward Alleyn's historic endowment. Eventually, numbers began to increase. In July 1887, pupils totalled 455; in December 1889, 485. Finally, in June 1888, school fees were raised to £8 per annum for boys under eleven, and £10 for those eleven and over, with current pupils exempted.[145] It was reckoned receipts would increase by £1,500 as a result of this rise in income, greatly reducing the annual deficit.

Under Gull's regime, physical education provision improved considerably. In 1883, the Company agreed to build a fives court in the back playground,[146] while five years later the Head persuaded the Governors to acquire a playing-field in Lower Edmonton, together with neighbouring Hydeside House, which became Gull's residence. Having finally agreed to increase fees, the Grocers' Company now also yielded to Gull's request to fund, at a cost of £4,000, a combined swimming pool and gymnasium – possibly to economise on expense: a gym with flooring that could be removed in summer to access a pool.[147] The 80-foot swimming pool was opened in June 1889.[148]

Further emulating the practice of public schools, Gull proposed the formation of an Old Boys' Club, for which he hoped the Grocers' Company might provide 'a suitable Shed'. The inaugural meeting of the Clove Club (named after the cloves featured on the Grocers' Company's coat-of-arms) was held on 27 September 1884, its activities soon ranging from rugby, cricket, swimming and water-polo to an orchestra, debates and drama. Again following the example of public schools, and despite the fact that Hackney Downs was not a boarding school, in 1902 Gull introduced a house system, rather unimaginatively naming the four 'divisions' by the points of the compass, and populating them with the pupils living in each respective direction.[149]

144. Minutes 2, f. 111, 24 November 1887.
145. Minutes 2, 20 June 1888.
146. Minutes 1, f. 189, 21 November 1883.
147. Minutes 2, f. 93, 4 May 1887.
148. Minutes 2 f. 206, 6 December 1889.
149. Since most boys lived east or north of the school, this system was inherently impractical.

Upon the outbreak of the Boer War in 1899, his military enthusiasm to the fore, Gull founded an Old Boys' Rifle Corps attached to the London Rifle Brigade, the 4th London Volunteer Regiment .[150] 'Here is a chance for us of the middle classes, the backbone of the country, to do our part,' he trumpeted. When the war ended, Corps numbers fell; those remaining were absorbed into what became the 5th (City of London) Battalion, London Rifles, who were among the first Territorials dispatched to France in September 1914, on SS *Chybassa* with the British Expeditionary Force, following the outbreak of World War I.[151]

In 1896 Gull finally overcame his prejudice against science and persuaded the company to build laboratories[152] and appoint a chemistry teacher; a large art room was also added 'for instruction in drawing'. Gull's predecessor had started a school library in 1880, after the Grocers' Company made a grant of £10 for a bookcase and £20 for books.[153] The school magazine, *The Review*, offers a glimpse of pupils' choice of reading at the turn of the century. Sixth-formers preferred S. R. Crockett, a prolific Scots writer of historical adventure romances; Robert Louis Stevenson; Rider Haggard; and (Francis) Marion Crawford, an American novelist noted for his weird, fantastical stories. Lower forms were reading almost exclusively the historical and patriotic derring-do of G. A. Henty, George Manville Fenn, W. H. G. Kingston, Jules Verne and R. M. Ballantyne – best-known today for *The Coral Island*.[154]

During Gull's headship, music came to occupy a significant role in school activities. In the 1880s, the tradition of an annual Christmas concert was established, whilst an oratorio or sacred cantata was performed each year during the Easter term. The school's music master, choirmaster and organist, Ernest Newton (1856–1929), a noted composer of light music, directed annual productions of Gilbert and Sullivan operettas, with boys playing roles of both sexes. Hackney Downs was apparently the first school to be permitted to perform the Savoy operas.[155] Beginning in 1890, for fifteen years *H.M.S. Pinafore*, *The Pirates of Penzance*, *Iolanthe*, *The Mikado* and *The Gondoliers* were staged in rotation, in productions that achieved London-wide renown. In 1896 *The Musical Times* reported:

> . . . we have rarely heard chorus-singing from boys that pleased us so much. The tone was full, round, perfectly

---

150. Minutes 3, f. 224, 29 January 1900.
151. Watkins, G. L. and S. J. Bench: *Roll of Honour and Service*. Twig Books: Dinton, 2014, p. 218.
152. Minutes 3, f. 122, 13 April 1896; f. 166–67, 12 July 1897.
153. Alderman, *Hackney Downs*, p. 22.
154. Review 126, p. 18.
155. Review 153, Summer term 1940, p. 18.

in tune, and produced with ease . . . It says volumes for the boys and the all-round ability of the headmaster, the Rev J. [sic] Gull, who coached all the performers, that in view of their age their acting was remarkably good.[156]

The Easter concerts featured such works as Sir Arthur Sullivan's *The Prodigal Son*, *The Martyr of Antioch* – 'an exceptionally good performance' according to *The Musical Herald*[157] – and *The Golden Legend*; Spohr's *The Last Judgement*; Mendelssohn's *Lobgesang* and *Elijah* and – inevitably – Handel's *Messiah*. *The Musical Times* noted in 1898, 'no more intelligent or persevering body of youthful amateurs is to be found in the metropolis and its suburbs than the boys of the Grocers' Company's School'.[158]

In the first years of the twentieth century, debates staged by upper-school pupils reflected current political and social issues: the wide range of topics discussed included such contentious issues as Anarchism, conscription, the Boer War, railway nationalization, state education – one speaker condescendingly considered 'the education given in Board Schools was far too advanced for the people for whom it was intended' – and women's suffrage.

By the mid-1890s, Hackney could be described as 'a district thickly populated by the better class of Jewish working man'.[159] Regardless of the fact that there were Jewish pupils at the school, during a 1904 debate on the motion 'Alien [i.e. Jewish] immigration is a check upon the amelioration of the Housing of the Poor' (unanimously carried) one boy argued 'something would have to be done with the present Jews who occupied the East End of London in large numbers'. Another speaker took a callously jocular approach, claiming you 'might tell whether a labourer lived in the Enfield direction or in the Poplar district by the amount of the dust on the man's coat'.[160] Such remarks convey a certain middle-class complacency among some pupils. The following year the Aliens Act was passed, the first restriction on immigration to the United Kingdom in modern times.[161]

Annual school inspections continued to result in positive feedback. In 1892, G. Brandon Grundy, of Brasenose College, Oxford, summarized his findings:

156. *The Musical Times*, 1 February 1896, p. 99.
157. *The Musical Herald*, May 1 1896, p. 144.
158. *The Musical Times*, 1 May 1898, p. 318.
159. *Jewish Chronicle*, 12 April 1895.
160. *Review*, March 1904, p. 9.
161. Alderman, p. 33. In 1905 the *Manchester Evening News* suggested 'the dirty, destitute, diseased, verminous and criminal foreigner who dumps himself on our soil and rates simultaneously, shall be forbidden to land'.

School chemistry laboratory, c. 1900.

> I consider the results of the Examination to be eminently creditable to the School as a whole . . . I have been much struck by the excellence of the work in some departments . . .

The following remarks must have been especially gratifying to Revd. Gull:

> There is one institution in the School to which I was introduced with which I was peculiarly struck. I refer to the Boys' Drill. I do not suppose there is another School in England where this special and valuable form of Physical Education is carried on to such perfection...[162]

By this date, Hackney Downs teaching staff included a higher proportion of university graduates: in July 1893, of fifteen teachers, eight had been to Oxford or Cambridge and one to Trinity College, Dublin.[163]

During this period, most boys left the school at the age of fifteen. The highest examination they could take was the Junior Cambridge Local Examination; candidates were not allowed to sit the London [University] Matriculation Examination until they reached the age of sixteen. Many pupils spent only two or three years at Hackney Downs,

---

162. Minutes 3 f. 32, 3 August 1892. At this date the Headmaster reported heavy absences due to an influenza epidemic, with up to 25 percent of boys out of school.
163. Minutes 3 f. 52, 25 July 1893.

limiting their educational progress. Gull constantly urged parents to keep their sons at school, perhaps for financial as much as academic reasons. When the Master of the Company sang the praises of German education at a prizegiving, Gull immediately responded indignantly:

> The reasons why German boys are better educated than English boys are that they stay at school much longer and the German Headmaster will brook no interference from parents, governors or anyone else.[164]

The idea that German education might have been superior in content or methodology was anathema to him.[165] However, over time, more boys remained at school longer and matriculated, with some sixth-formers being prepared for the Second Class Civil Service Examinations and a minority gaining university scholarships. Gull was concerned the school offered few scholarships for entry to the school or for admission to university. In 1896 he complained to the Governors:

> The school is losing ground both in numbers and in distinction . . . [because] the Scholarships given by the [London] County Council and others from the Elementary Schools are not tenable at Hackney [Downs School], and . . . promising boys are attracted elsewhere by the chance of getting leaving Exhibitions to assist them to go to the Universities.

He pleaded with the Grocers' Company to offer leaving exhibitions so the school could compete 'on fair terms with the higher grade secondary Schools, such as the City of London School, Merchant Taylors', St Paul's, &c.'[166] Yet the company remained opposed to encouraging university entrance, and reminded Gull that Hackney Downs was purposed for preparing the sons of the middle classes for commerce and manufacturing rather than university:

> the policy . . . from the first has been against the development of Hackney into a School in touch with the Universities . . . [the Governors] have aimed at providing an education calculated to train the children of middle class parents to earn their living by commercial and industrial pursuits, and not to rouse an ambition for a more advanced course of study, resulting too often in an addition to the already excessive number of Schoolmasters and Curates.[167]

164. Review 151, Summer term 1939, p. 24.
165. Medcalf, p. 38.
166. Reports 2, 20 January 1896.
167. Minutes 3 f. 119, 20 January 1896.

In other words, remember your station in life; do not try to break through the class ceiling.

Despite the continuing anxiety over finances and pupil numbers, the 1898 Inspector's report was once again outstanding:

> I was well satisfied with the work as a whole. The methods of instruction appeared to me excellent, the teaching efficient and painstaking, and the organisation admirable, while the tone and discipline of the boys and their demeanour . . . left nothing to be desired.[168]

From 1898, in addition to offering pupils in the Upper Fourth form and above English, Mathematics, French and Latin, boys intending to proceed to university could now also take Greek classes; those preparing for office work could learn shorthand and book-keeping; those aiming for 'higher commercial work' could take German; and those aiming for a career in science or mechanical work could opt for physical science.[169]

Exam results remained excellent; at the turn of the century, Grocers' and Dame Alice Owen's School, Islington, topped the list for the entire country. And, despite the Company's misgivings, the trend towards pupils achieving university entrance persisted. The first boy to gain a scholarship direct from the school was D. L. Bryce, to Emmanuel College, Cambridge, in 1898, whilst the greatest academic success of the Gull era was Arthur George Heath (1887–1915), who in 1904 won a classical scholarship to New College, Oxford, where he was awarded the Craven Prize.[170] Other notable pupils of Gull's era included R. W. Chambers (1874–1942), later Quain Professor of English Language and Literature at University College, London (1922–41), and Sir John Jarvis (1876–1950), Conservative M.P. for Guildford, who campaigned on behalf of depressed areas of the country.

As Headmaster, Charles Gull exhibited a bewildering mixture of sternness and ruthlessness bordering on cruelty combined with acts of spontaneous generosity, and was described as 'an autocrat of the "just beast" tradition and a born leader'. He broke down while announcing

168. Minutes 3 f. 209, 8 February 1899.
169. Review, February 1898, p. 9.
170. Heath's family background reveals something of the class make-up of the school in this period: his father was Assistant Principal Clerk in the Inland Revenue, and both sides of his family inherited significant wealth. Heath was killed in action during World War I. His wartime letters were published by the Classical scholar Gilbert Murray in *Letters of Arthur George Heath* (Blackwell, Oxford, 1917). Murray wrote: 'all of us prophesied for him a name famous in Europe, for never had we known an intellect so clear, so subtle, so profound' (J. E. Medcalf, 'The Grocers' School', in *The London Teacher* 1000, 25 February 1938). See also Review 86, Christmas term 1915, pp. 11–14.

the death of a pupil, donated £30 when a master's wife needed an operation, pressed the Grocers' Company to offer scholarships for masters' sons and persuaded the Headmasters' Association to establish a pension scheme for assistant teachers.[171] To mark the school's twenty-first anniversary in 1897, Gull chartered a steamboat, and the entire school sailed down the Thames aboard the Clacton Belle to Chatham, where they toured the dockyard and observed warships under construction.[172] The school magazine noted the 'journey by train to Woolwich was not so pleasant as it might have been, since the route lay mainly through the East End of London', contrasting the lower middle-class profile of Hackney with working-class East London, and revealing the middle-class condescension of the writer.

Gull's teaching methods could be crude and cruel. When a boy made a series of mistakes in translating Latin, the Head made him stand on a form and administered a cut of the cane for every error.[173] This unabashed disciplinarian was responsible for preparing boys for Anglican confirmation; until 1904, the school participated in regular corporate services of holy communion at the end of term.[174] Despite his paternalistic and despotic methods, Gull seems generally to have been popular with boys, parents and staff, with some pupils regarding him as legendary. Harry Cape, pupil between 1891 and 1895, offered a vivid impression of the second Headmaster:

> Staff and boys alike – rumour added the Governing Body also – were dominated by the Headmaster. Mr Gull was a great man, of commanding physique and wonderful voice, a great disciplinarian and a born administrator. He was respected, but hardly loved... He was not, in the strict sense of the term, a great scholar, but he had originality and fertility of ideas and he was devoted to his school. He was an active member of a group of very able men whose work has never received the recognition which it deserves... Gull, of the Grocers' School, Scott,[175] of Parmiter's,[176] Easterbrook,[177] of Owen's, Islington... pioneers of what in common parlance is now called the Secondary School as contrasted with the great Public School... [178]

171. Medcalf, pp. 36, 41.
172. Review, 3 August 1897, p. 6.
173. Medcalf, p. 42.
174. For instance at St. Mark's, Dalston. Review 137, Christmas term 1934, p. 17.
175. Dr. Robert Pickett Scott, Headmaster 1887–1904.
176. Parmiter's School, Bethnal Green, now at Garston, Hertfordshire.
177. James Easterbrook, Headmaster 1881–1909.
178. Cape later taught at the school. Review 153, Summer term 1940, pp. 14–15.

Teaching staff c. 1890.

As we have seen, almost from the outset the Grocers' Company had been concerned about the ongoing cost of maintaining Hackney Downs, with staff salaries a particular worry. The number of pupils at the school rose to a peak of 495 in July 1890, but soon began to fall rapidly again. Gull attributed this to changes in the profile of the local population and the spread of tenement buildings, although some parents were still comparatively prosperous – several arrived at the twentieth Annual Sports day in Edmonton in 1901 in 'horseless carriages . . . to the admiration of all and sundry'.[179] The sudden fall in numbers was also due to the abolition of fees at state elementary schools in 1891.[180] School attendance to the age of ten had been made compulsory nationally in 1880, raised to eleven in 1893 and twelve in 1899.

Parents' occupations were similar to those listed at the school's opening twenty-five years earlier. A sample of 20 between April and July 1900 shows parents still largely drawn from the lower middle class: grocer, wholesale milliner, retired army officer, Bank of England clerk, wine merchant, merchant, gentleman, piano-maker, estate agent, commercial travellers, solicitors, Barnardo's Homes governor, civil engineer, shipping agent, Methodist minister, outfitter and dentist. While most lived in the Hackney area, some now lived further away, in the City of London, Chingford, Walthamstow, Wood Green and Tottenham – all accessible by train.[181] At least five pupils were of German origin.[182]

179. Review July 1901, p. 11.
180. David Cannadine: *Victorious Century: The United Kingdom 1800–1906*. London: Allen Lane, 2017, pp. 412, 502.
181. Hackney Archives: R/DOW/4/.1, April–July 1900.
182. The Wettern brothers, whose father came from Hamburg in the 1860s. Three served in

By April 1903 the school had as few as 355 pupils – only fifty more than when Gull had become Head – and the company, which by 1903 was subsidizing the school to the tune of £4,066, could see no end to deficit financing.[183] As with other secondary schools in the capital, the London County Council offered a grant to the Grocers' Company in 1894, on condition they offered free places to 'Junior County Scholars' – pupils successful in the L.C.C. scholarship exams. Any such scheme was anathema to the autocratic Gull, who claimed: 'The London County Council are attempting to dominate Secondary Education in London . . . to compel Governing Bodies to receive representatives of the Council on their Boards.' The company rejected the scheme, which put Hackney Downs at a disadvantage financially and educationally vis a vis schools that accepted the L.C.C. grant and its scholarship boys.[184]

When it was suggested the school might be placed under the L.C.C.'s Technical Education Board,[185] Gull wrote to the Grocers' Company objecting forcibly, claiming the board's secretary, Dr. William Garnett,[186] was 'an enthusiast for the teaching of Science and Art' – both subjects abhorrent to Gull. The Head also objected to the alleged 'interference and alteration of the Board's Inspectors' in the internal organisation of schools they supported. But Gull was rowing against the tide: eleven reputable London schools joined the L.C.C. scheme, including Alleyn's, Dulwich; Coopers' Company, Bow; Parmiter's, Bethnal Green; Dame Alice Owen's, Islington and Central Foundation.[187]

The Education Acts of 1902 and 1903 abolished the School Boards set up in 1870. London's entire educational system – Board schools, church schools, special schools, evening schools, art schools, technical institutes and polytechnics – were now brought together under the L.C.C. Henceforth, both elementary and secondary education became the responsibility of elected local government bodies and was funded through the rates. The London County Council inherited a number of 'higher grade' schools that aspired to secondary status. Sir Robert Morant, Permanent Secretary to the Education Board, specified that a secondary school should provide a 'general' course – that is, neither specialized nor pre-vocational – leading to a prescribed standard at six-

the British army in World War I. TCL February 2006, p. 4.
183. Minutes 4 f. 70.
184. Minutes 3 f. 65–67, 5 June 1894.
185. The L.C.C. set up the Technical Education Board in 1891; a major part of its work consisted of providing scholarships and exhibitions from elementary to secondary schools. Maclure p. 26.
186. Dr William Garnett (1850–1932), scientist and educational adviser to the London County Council.
187. Minutes 3, f. 219–21, 2 June 1899.

teen plus. His proposed curriculum was closely aligned with that of the traditional grammar school, and new 'county grammar schools' were based on this model. The L.C.C. began to increase the number of secondary school places available, converting a number of existing schools to this new status.[188] In the light of this development, and following discussions with the L.C.C., on 28 June 1904 the Grocers' Company minuted:

> We recommend that the site and buildings at Hackney be handed over to the London County Council as a free gift, subject to such provisions in the interest of the present scholars as may be agreed upon.[189]

On 8 July they wrote to Sir William Collins, Chairman of the London Education Committee of the L.C.C., offering to hand over Hackney Downs, subject to

> an assurance that certain existing interests which have been allowed to grow up in connection with the school will not suffer under the changed conditions of government.

The L.C.C. accepted the offer, but asked the company to continue running the school for the time being, with the council meeting all costs. The council planned to maintain the school 'as a public Secondary School for boys as day scholars'.[190] They would appoint the majority of the Governors, who would prescribe:

> the general subjects of instruction, the relative prominence and value to be assigned to each group of subjects, the arrangements respecting the school terms, vacations and holidays, and the payments of day scholars.

while the Headmaster would prescribe:

> the choice of books, the method of teaching, the arrangement of classes and School hours, and generally the whole internal organisation, management, and discipline of the School, including the power of expelling boys from the school with the sanction of the governors.

Boys were to be aged eight or over, and could not remain at school

---

188. Maclure, pp. 78, 88–91.
189. Minutes 4, f. 53, 28 June 1904. The playing field at Edmonton and Hydeside, the Headmaster's residence, were to be let to the L.C.C. for five years.
190. The new scheme received government approval on 22 October 1906 (LMA: ILEA/S/SB/23/02/10).

beyond the age of eighteen without special permission. The school was based on selective entry: candidates had to prove they were 'fit for admission in an examination'. It had been proposed to call the re-constituted institution 'Hackney Downs Grammar School', but the Clove Club argued for the retention of the existing name, so a wordy compromise was agreed: 'Hackney Downs School, formerly the Grocers' Company's School'.[191] At a meeting on 20 December 1904, Sir William Collins guaranteed:

> parents who sent, or intended to send, their boys to the
> School need have no apprehension as to what might
> happen in the immediate future, since the same, or, at
> any rate, a similar education would certainly be given.[192]

It is unclear why the company decided to stop maintaining Hackney Downs, which it had founded, but continued to support Oundle, which it had not.[193] The parents of potential pupils in Hackney may not have been as well-off as those sending their sons to Oundle, but giving the latter school to Northamptonshire County Council could have released company funds to Hackney Downs. Immediately after the transfer of Hackney Downs and Witney schools to their respective county councils, the company poured funds into Oundle, funding its new Great Hall (1907). Gull was in competition with Oundle's ambitious Frederick William Sanderson (1857–1922), one of the leading headmasters of the period, who lobbied hard and successfully for the resources to transform it into one of the major public schools. The Grocers' Company chose to fund Sanderson's vision of an elite school for gentlemen and abandon the school for the sons of the lower middle classes in Hackney, which was rapidly transmuting into a largely working-class district.[194]

Charles Gull now opted to retire leaving the school at the end of summer term 1905.[195] To Gull, the concept of serving a public body such as the L.C.C. was intolerable. The school set up a Gull Memorial fund, which paid for a 'grim crayon drawing'[196] of the Headmaster, and

---

191. NA, Records of the Ministry of Education, ED 35/1671 (B).
192. Review, March 1905, p. 8.
193. In contrast with the parsimonious policy of the Grocers' Company towards Hackney Downs, in 1884 the relatively modest Parmiter's Foundation supported Parmiter's School, Bethnal Green, with two-thirds of its net income of £3,112, and from 1888 with its entire income. Andrew Lewis and Brian Coulshed: *A History of Parmiter's Estate Charity*, Watford: Parmiter's Foundation, 1999, p. 7.
194. MS 11588/31: Orders from the Court of Assistants, p. 217, 20 March 1905.
195. Gull married in December 1900, aged 49. (Review 126, Spring 1931, p. 17.) The Grocers' Company offered him a pension of £500. (Minutes 4: ff. 52–53, 28 June 1904.)
196. Review 147, Spring term 1938, p. 10.

The battalion on parade in front of the school during the Gull era.

a casket trophy as annual prize for the 'Best Boy'.[197] For two years Gull ministered as army chaplain at St Paul's, Valetta, Malta, then as parish priest successively at Hounslow, Hendford, Yeovil and St. Michael the Archangel, Litlington, East Sussex.[198] He stayed nowhere long, as he had the unfortunate ability of provoking antipathy. Revd. Gull died of throat cancer in 1918.[199]

197. Review 62, Christmas term 1907, pp. 7–10. The portrait was destroyed in the 1963 fire.
198. LMA EO/PS/4/34 26 Feb 1918, f. 20.
199. An obituary notice appeared in Review, XXI 93, Summer term 1918.

Chapter 3
Progressive Conservatism
William Jenkyn Thomas, Headmaster 1906–1935

I always thought he imagined himself as the head of Greyfriars. He used to ... wear a mortarboard and walked about swishing his gown.
Alexander Baron

As next headmaster of Hackney Downs School the L.C.C. Education Committee selected William Jenkyn Thomas (1870–1959),[200] who came with a first in Classics from Trinity College, Cambridge. Born in North Wales, in 1896 Thomas became the first head of the Aberdare Intermediate School, which he built up to become the largest secondary school in the Principality. Just nine years later, aged only thirty-five, Thomas was appointed the third Headmaster of Hackney Downs. He had a distinctive appearance, his silvery-white hair and blue eyes often remarked upon. One former pupil remembered:

> complete in top hat and morning coat [he] cycled, on a very high frame bicycle... being remarkable in that he proceeded by a method of one half revolution of the crank, followed by a period of free wheel.[201]

Under the new L.C.C. regime, and following the autocratic Gull, there were fears the school's distinctive character might be threatened. An editorial in the school magazine raised the question:

> What will the School be like next term? was the enquiry heard on all sides at the end of last term. Will the school be altered or will it remain the same ... We are now in a position to assure these same small boys ... that there is no need for them to fear either for their school or for their privileges. There certainly have been changes, but

---

200. According to W. W. Grantham, Chairman of the Governors, it was an 'open secret' that they received 'numerous applications' for the post (Medcalf, p. 12). Thomas had apparently considered moving into journalism, having written frequently for the *Manchester Guardian*.
201. Letter from Roy A. Waters to Howard Freeman, 26 July 1976, HDS Archive.

they will not affect the School adversely . . . [202]

At the 1906 prize-giving, Dr. Baxter Foreman, deputy chairman of the L.C.C., claimed there was 'no foundation for the rumour that the status of the school was to be lowered'. The status of Grocers' School at this date is revealed in a letter from Dr. Garnett, Educational Advisor to the L.C.C., to Sir William Collins, suggesting there should be a first-grade school in each division of London: City of London School in the centre; St Paul's in west London; King's College School, Wimbledon, in south-west London; Dulwich College in the south-east; and 'the Grocers' School . . . for the north-east'[203] – placing Hackney Downs on a level with those leading public schools.

On 22 October 1906, the L.C.C. approved the new scheme drawn up for the school.[204] The Governors, a sub-committee of the council, were authorized to set 'the general subjects of instruction, the relative prominence and value to be assigned to each group of subjects,' while the Headmaster was responsible for 'the choice of books, the method of teaching, the arrangement of classes . . . and generally the whole internal organisation, management, and discipline of the School'. The Council held the school site 'in trust,'[205] and was required to administer the school in conformity with the scheme's provisions. Contemporary sensitivity over the religious question is evident in a lengthy section:

> The parent or guardian of . . . any scholar attending the School as a day scholar may claim by notice in writing addressed to the Head Master the exemption of such scholar from attending prayer or religious worship, or from any lesson or series of lessons on a religious subject...
>
> If any teacher, in the course of other lessons at which any such scholar is in accordance with the ordinary rules of the School present, shall teach systematically and persistently any particular religious doctrine from the teaching of which any exemption has been claimed . . . the Governors shall, on complaint made in writing to them . . . inquire into the circumstances, and if the complaint is judged to be reasonable, make all proper provisions for remedying the matter complained of.[206]

---

202. Review 51, November 1905, p. 1.
203. Bryant, p. 436.
204. LMA ILEA/S/SB/23/02/10.
205. Clause 15.
206. 'Approval of the Scheme for Grocers' Company's Schools', LMA EO/PS/3/179. The wording is similar to that in the religious clauses [4(1) and 4(2)] in Balfour's 1902 Education Act.

Legal transfer of the school's ownership to the L.C.C. on 1 January 1907 heralded a 60-year period during which the school became a leading publicly-funded selective boys' secondary school, a 'first grade Public Secondary School', according to the L.C.C. Prospectus. This marked a turning-point in the school's constitution: fee-paying pupils now sat alongside L.C.C. scholarship holders, with the council's Junior Scholarship scheme enabling a large number of boys from poorer homes and from public elementary schools to enter the school. Boys could enter from the age of eight and stay on until their nineteenth birthday. For fee-payers, the cost in 1911 was three guineas per term for boys aged under eleven at entrance, and four pounds for boys above that age.[207] In 1908, 38 percent of the school's pupils were wholly or partially exempt from fees, a proportion which rose to 49 percent by 1932.[208] The number of boys coming from public elementary schools began to exceed the number exempt from fees, showing that some parents on lower incomes were willing and able to pay to educate their sons at Hackney Downs.[209] As Stuart Maclure has pointed out:

> Secondary education remained a normal progression for the middle-class children . . . but for the elementary school classes secondary education represented a distinct and positive social movement – a transition only to be made by those able to prove by some early achievement that they were specially marked out from their fellows by 'a capacity to benefit from secondary education'.[210]

Over the school's first thirty years Hackney, had evolved into a bustling, overcrowded London borough. The middle classes were beginning to depart; in their place there arrived poorer families from the East End, many of them Jewish migrants originally from Eastern Europe, occupying a socio-economic space between the manual working-class and lower middle class.[211] Unable to afford private schooling for their children, these families were able to take advantage of the school's new status, using it as a vehicle to elevate their sons into middle-class professional careers.[212] Almost immediately the change in the school's

---

207. *Hackney Downs School Prospectus*, 1911, p. 3.
208. Every school under the L.C.C.'s authority was to have a balance of scholarship-holders and fee-payers 'to help create a social balance'. Maclure p. 90.
209. NA, ED 35/1671(A) and 5252.
210. Maclure p. 53.
211. Between 1881 and 1914, around 150,000 Jews migrated from Eastern Europe to Britain, fleeing pogroms and poverty. Many settled initially in tenement buildings and slum streets in the East End. In 1906, four entrants to Hackney Downs arrived direct from Russia; three from Archangel, one from Vologda. TCL, October 1999, p. 3.
212. At the 1907 local elections the 'Progressives' (in effect the Liberals) lost control of

Hackney Downs School, Downs Park Road, c. 1905.

status was reflected in the occupation of pupils' fathers. While a number of parents still pursued lower-middle class careers, there was a roughly equal number who would be regarded as working-class. The occupations of the fathers of nineteen pupils who entered the school in January 1907 are: stock jobber's clerk, glass merchant, furrier, land proprietor, traveller, decorator, butcher, accountant, stock jobber, chemist, woollen rag merchant, electrical engineer, refreshment caterer, licensed victualler, stock and share dealer, two builders and carpet salesman. Most lived in Hackney and its environs, including Canonbury, Seven Sisters and Green Lanes, one from Chingford, Essex.[213]

Following the L.C.C. take-over in 1905, the school roll increased from 328 to 390, resulting in oversized classes and the need for additional teachers. Because of the overcrowding, science and commercial classes were held in nearby Hackney Technical Institute.[214] The L.C.C. was not slow in modernising the school. At the end of 1908, new science laboratories, handicraft rooms and a photographic darkroom were built; botany, advanced physics and chemistry could for the first time be

the L.C.C. to the 'Municipal Reformers' (the Conservatives). In 1918 the Reformers ruled that, to be eligible for L.C.C. scholarships, children had to be British when applying for the award and be born in, or have fathers who were born in, the United Kingdom or Dominions, thereby discriminating against Jews. A decade later this policy was diluted, but was not rescinded until after World War II. Geoffrey Alderman, *Modern British Jewry*, Oxford: Clarendon Press, 1998, pp. 256–59, 291–92.
213. Hackney Archives. Admissions Register R/DOW/4/1, January 1907.
214. NA, ED 35/1671 (A). The Institute, subsequently Hackney Technical College, was situated in Dalston Lane, next to Hackney Downs Station. By 1926, the school roll had risen to 650, the highest yet recorded (Medcalf, p. 51).

taught at the school. During the construction work, some forms had to walk to the Institute for lessons, which had 'a deplorable effect on the corporate life of the School'.[215] This was not the last time such inconvenience was experienced.

Initially the school was managed jointly with the Hackney School for Girls and the County Secondary School, Dalston, by a new North Eastern Secondary Schools Advisory Committee. However after 1917, the L.C.C. appointed dedicated Hackney Downs School governors, as a sub-committee of the authority's Education Committee, with four ex-officio members – the Chairman and Vice Chairman of the L.C.C. Education Committee, and Chairman and Vice-Chairman of its Higher Education Sub-Committee – with no more than eight others, of whom at least one had to be a member of the Education Committee, and no more than two could be nominated by the University of London.[216] In the school's jubilee year, 1926, the Chairman of Governors, Major W. W. Grantham KC, was both an L.C.C. member and Past Master of the Grocers' Company.[217]

Under the new management, the school's organization and curriculum evolved considerably. The first and second forms – boys under the age of eleven – consisted solely of fee-paying pupils; scholarship boys started in the lower third form, aged eleven. Although in theory every boy had to sit an entrance exam, in practice this was not always the case. Some former pupils recalled they were offered entry simply after an appointment with the Headmaster.[218] The only obligatory item of uniform was the school cap, which had to be destroyed after it was discarded.[219] During this period, forms remained in their classroom, while subject masters changed rooms. Six 'Houses' replaced the previous four 'Divisions', following public school practice. One house was headed by Samuel Richards, a former pupil, awarded a London University MA for a thesis on the surprising subject of 'Feminist Writers of the Seventeenth Century'.[220] William Lucas (c. 1863–1945) another of the new Housemasters, was praised by a distinguished former pupil not only as a fine mathematician but for 'the supreme virtue of provoking the spirit of inquiry among his pupils'.[221] The rest were more often remembered for their respective forms of punishment and bullying.

215. Review 62, Christmas term 1907, p. 4.
216. Review 89, Christmas term 1916, p. 12.
217. Medcalf, p. 47.
218. T. W. Marsden Anderson and Allan Bowler, in the late 1920s. TCL January 2001, p. 2.
219. Prospectus for 1927, p. 5.
220. Later published as *Feminist Writers of the Seventeenth Century*. London: David Nutt, 1914.
221. Obituary by Sir Ben Lockspeiser.

The frequent comparisons with German education voiced during Gull's time grew increasingly jingoistic during the Edwardian period. At Speech Day December 14 1907, Jenkyn Thomas claimed he was
> continually meeting with the statement that Germany was turning out better men than England; to which he could only reply that if boys were withdrawn at 14 years of age they could not be expected to become senior wranglers or expert linguists.[222]

He added xenophobically that English boys 'have other virtues to which the Germans could never pretend' – a remark greeted with applause. Similar sentiments were voiced at Speech Day 1908, when the wife of Lieut.-Col. A. C. E. Welby, Chairman of the L.C.C. Higher Education Sub-Committee, hoped 'boys of the school would always help to maintain England in her position as the greatest nation in the world.'[223] The school magazine, *The Review*, frequently expressed similar rivalry with Germany in the pre-war years.

Yet in these years preceding World War I, the Monitors' Literary and Debating Society evinced considerable political awareness, discussing topics ranging from Irish Home Rule to Socialism. In November 1907, Ben Lockspeiser (1891–1990), later first President of CERN, spoke on the motion 'Will the airship ever become a power in war?', arguing that the aeroplane 'will become the real fighting power, being cheaper, stronger, lighter, and harder to destroy . . . '[224] Even during the war years, surprisingly controversial motions were debated, such as: 'The action of the Northcliffe Press has been detrimental to the nation' and 'There is a Yellow Peril'.[225] In this period the school monitors staged an annual play, usually Shakespeare with all-male casting, a tradition that continued into World War I, with *A Midsummer Night's Dream* in 1915 and *Twelfth Night* in 1916.

In March 1908, the L.C.C. published a brief initial report on its newly-established secondary schools. For 'Hackney Downs Secondary school for boys' (it was not described as a grammar school nor given its desired sobriquet 'formerly the Grocers' Company's School') the report summarised:
> In consequence of the erection of new buildings the school is still in a transition state and the work in some departments has been somewhat dislocated. The

---

222. Review 62, Easter term 1907, p. 54. Gull had previously argued the same point.
223. Review 66, Easter term 1909, p. 45.
224. Review 62, Christmas term 1907, p. 26. At the age of 15, Lockspeiser, the son of Polish immigrants, was awarded a prize as 'the best junior boy in all England'.
225. Review 92, Christmas term 1917, p. 111.

> commercial department is developing satisfactorily and
> is carried on with considerable ability . . .[226]

This was followed by a full HMI[227] Inspection in July 1908. At this date the school numbered 426 pupils, of whom 162 (38 percent) held L.C.C. scholarships, while the rest paid fees. The boys were drawn from several classes: fathers of 70 boys (16 percent) were classed as professional; 72 (17 percent) merchants or manufacturers; 62 (15 percent) retailers; 140 (32 percent) commercial managers and 81 (19 percent) as 'service' – for instance postmen, artisans or domestic servants. 38 percent came from public elementary schools – presumably more or less the same 38 percent who were awarded L.C.C. scholarships. The change in the school's intake following the L.C.C. takeover could not be clearer, in enabling less affluent parents to send their sons to a thriving grammar school. Of school-leavers, it was reported 40 percent started work in the commercial sector, 14 percent became pupil teachers or entered professional training, while the rest moved on to other schools.[228]

The inspectors noted that 'railway lines run on two sides of the site, and the noise of passing trains is at times distracting'[229] and that the corridors were 'cheerless and gloomy'. Under Gull, who had been reluctant to accommodate science, this subject had been offered only as an alternative to his favoured Latin or German; henceforward it was taught throughout the school.[230] The inspectors criticized pointedly the school policy on textbooks, particularly those for English and Latin:

> It is singularly unfortunate that the books used are the
> property of the School and not of the boys themselves . .
> . The result is that they leave School without possessing
> one of the Masterpieces of Literature that they have been
> working at . . . [231]

In 1909 the school replaced the Matriculation and Cambridge Local exams with the School Examination Matriculation Standard and University of London Junior School Examination. Every pupil would now receive a general education to the age of sixteen, leading to the London General School Examination. This curriculum included English language and literature, history, geography, arithmetic, algebra,

226. 27 March 1908. LMA L.C.C./EO/PS/12/MISC/008.
227. His Majesty's Inspectors.
228. 13–17 July 1908. NA ED 109/3729, p. 2.
229. It was impossible to see out of the windows when seated – perhaps a deliberate ploy to avoid distraction, particularly by the frequently passing steam trains.
230. NA ED 109/3729, p. 10.
231. NA ED 109/3729, pp. 12–13

William Jenkyn Thomas, third Headmaster of Hackney Downs School.

trigonometry, elementary calculus, Latin (with German as an alternative), French, botany, physics, chemistry, handicraft and drawing. Report cards were sent home every week for parents to initial, and full reports issued every term. The Science Sixth prepared boys for the Higher School Examination, which could lead to a degree in science or medicine; the Arts Sixth provided for boys wishing to opt for the humanities; while a new Commercial Sixth offered a three-year course preparing boys for the Intermediate BSc (Economics) of the University of London and covered commercial knowledge, economics, banking, trade and finance, British constitution, accountancy, shorthand and typewriting, in addition to regular secondary school subjects.[232] The new commercial classes were introduced in order to:

232. *Hackney Downs School Prospectus*, 1911 p. 3. By 1927, this had been shortened to a two-year course, with the option of a one-year course for early leavers and a less

supply the educational needs of boys entering commercial life, and to prevent the premature removal of boys from School to those establishments where a good general education may be sacrificed to the acquisition of co-called commercial subjects.[233]

Hackney Downs was the first school in the country to present candidates for the London University Inter-Comm exam, and also provided an Employment Bureau, where 'old boys' offered current pupils advice on opportunities and openings.

Many in the Commercial Sixth progressed to the London School of Economics (LSE) or a career in the City. An example is Dr. Cyril James (1903–73), who, from a working-class background, went on to become Principal of McGill University, Montreal. At the age of thirteen, James entered Hackney Downs on an L.C.C. bursary of £15 per year. Although he failed matric, a master named Charles Davenport persuaded James and six friends to return to school. Benefiting from Davenport's coaching, sometimes at his home before school, the entire group passed at the second attempt. Davenport suggested they stay on and prepare for the Intermediate Exam of the London Bachelor of Commerce degree. Having achieved this, James entered the LSE in 1921.[234]

By January 1914, the majority of pupils were from working-class families. The Admissions Register for that year lists twenty fathers' occupations as: wholesale meat salesman, engineer, Professor of Music, medical practitioner, builder, draper, commercial clerk, wood-buyer, exporter, company director, mercantile clerk, retired builder, manager, book-keeper, warehouseman, chair manufacturer, packing-case manufacturer, fancy leather-case manufacturer, chemist-druggist and furrier. Almost all lived in Hackney or immediately surrounding districts.[235]

Another full HMI school assessment took place in March 1915, the second year of World War I. By this date, the number of pupils had risen to 493, the inspectors noting the school 'is quite full, and is likely soon to be in a position of being obliged to refuse pupils fit to attend it'.[236] The class composition of the school was broadly similar to 1908, although the percentage from the professional classes had risen from 16 to 20. The number of grant-aided boys remained similar to 1908, with 209 pupils holding L.C.C. scholarships. The percentage of school-leav-

---

advanced course for others. *Prospectus* 1927.
233. NA ED 109/3729, p. 24.
234. Stanley Brice Frost: *The Man in the Ivory Tower: F. Cyril James of McGill*. Montreal & Kingston: McGill-Queen's University Press, p. xx.
235. Hackney Archives. R/DOW/15/1 January 1914.
236. 23–26 March 1915. NA ED 109/3730, pp. 3, 15.

ers entering commercial life had risen significantly, from 40 percent in 1908 to 65 percent seven years later.

The inspectors expressed concern at the penny-pinching policies of the school, noting that in the 'expenditure on books, stationery and equipment, the limits of justifiable economy appear to have been passed . . . ' and that 'some of the text-books used by the boys are tattered and defaced almost beyond recognition'. As in 1908, the inspectors pressed hard for the school to make some school books the property of pupils:

> To expect boys to learn how to read when they have no books of their own which they can mark is to expect a vain thing. To give them no pride of possession while at school is, moreover, a singular way of encouraging them to use books in after life.

The inspectors were equally critical of the headmaster's practice of allowing some classes to become too large, reminding him 'classes over 30 are contrary to the Board's regulation'. Here again Headmaster Thomas was overdoing his economies. The inspectors concluded: 'The School is a flourishing institution, and is doing good work which may well in some directions be further improved'.[237] In 1917, Russian was introduced to school's curriculum, perhaps in response to the unrest in Russia that led to the November Revolution; it is unclear how long the subject continued to be taught.[238]

World War I impacted the school hugely. *The Review* for Christmas term 1914 included a Roll of Honour listing 144 former pupils and three masters known to be serving in the armed forces. They included a wide variety of postings, including to the Royal Flying Corps, Royal Army Medical Corps, Bahia Light Horse, London Rifle Brigade and Royal Naval Volunteer Reserve, while others were serving as interpreters, rough riders and despatch riders.[239] The following issue of the magazine included a long piece by Lance Corporal W. S. Read describing his experiences with the London Rifle Brigade at Ploeg Striert ('Plug Street') on the Western Front.[240] Subsequent numbers of *The Review* included notices of war casualties as well as further reports from 'old boys' serving at the front. There appears to have been little, if any, censorship of their detailed and easily identifiable frontline accounts.

Former pupils continued to volunteer for active service in large numbers, the school battalion acting as a spur. By Christmas 1916, at least 500 old boys had joined up, and more than 100 had lost their lives. From

237. NA ED 109/3730, pp. 7, 15.
238. Governors' Minute Book, LMA EO/PS/4/34, 26 June 1917, f. 20.
239. Review 83, Christmas term 1914, pp. 3–6.
240. Review 84, Easter term 1915, pp. 53–58.

the trenches around Ypres, former pupil F. J. Roberts (1882–1964),[241] serving with the Sherwood Foresters, published the celebrated *Wipers Times*. Printed initially on a damaged press discovered amid the ruins of the city, the paper was filled with trench humour, coded criticism of the General Staff and adverts for pornography and local brothels. The school also produced pacifists: 'Among the few Old Boys who are "conscientious objectors" is Mr. E. R. Calvert. Whatever we may think of his attitude, there can be no doubt that he is perfectly sincere and that he has held his views for a long time. Essays which he wrote when in the Upper V . . . prove this.'[242]

During the war, the school took in around thirty young Belgian and French refugees as pupils.[243] Speech day for 1915 was postponed 'until a more favourable opportunity [could] be found for its celebration'.[244] In 1917, a boy evacuated with his family to Brighton to escape the Zeppelin raids on London.[245] The worldwide Spanish flu pandemic also seriously impacted the school: in some weeks of autumn term 1918 as many as 20 percent of boys were absent; at the peak, 140 pupils and 6 teachers were absent.[246]

In the war years, with many masters away on active service, women teachers were appointed. Dorothy M. F. Watherstone (?1879–1968) joined the staff in spring 1916, on temporary transfer from the nearby Dalston County girls' school. Barbara Low (1874–1955), whose Jewish parents emigrated to England after the failed Hungarian Revolution of 1848, also taught at Hackney Downs in this period.[247] A Miss Phillips taught science at the school for seven years, until the end of summer term 1922,[248] and the last female teacher did not leave until 1923. Referring to

241. J. Ivelaw-Chapman, *The Riddles of Wipers: An Appreciation of The Wipers Times, A Journal of the Trenches.* Pen & Sword Books, Barnsley, 2010; *The Wipers Times: The complete series.* Little Books, 2008.
242. *Review* 89, Christmas term 1916, p. 8. Roy Calvert (1898–1933) came from a Quaker background. His alternative service was on a fruit and vegetable farm belonging to Chivers, the jam manufacturers. A decade later Calvert became Secretary of the National Council for the Abolition of the Death Penalty. Brian P. Block and John Hostettler, *Hanging in the Balance: A History of the Abolition of Capital Punishment in Britain.* Winchester: Waterside Press, 1997, p. 97.
243. One Belgian refugee, François Dethier, wrote a long piece in French describing his wartime experiences. Review 85, Summer term 1915, pp. 106–10.
244. *Review*, Christmas 1915.
245. TCL April 1997, p. 1.
246. *Review* 94, Christmas term 1918, p. 4.
247. Low was a founder member of the British Psychoanalytical Society and published *Psycho-Analysis: A Brief Account of the Freudian Theory*, London: George Allen and Unwin, 1920. It is still in print.
248. Phillips joined Hackney Downs in 1915 from Moorfields Training College. She subsequently became senior science mistress at Godolphin and Latymer Girls' School,

women teachers at Speech Day 1919, the Headmaster griped ungraciously: 'We cannot profess to have altogether enjoyed the innovation.'[249]

At least 117 former pupils were killed during World War I. On 19 June 1919, a memorial service for former pupils who had fallen was held at St. John at Hackney church. A year later a memorial tablet and roll of honour recording the names of those who had lost their lives was unveiled at the school by the Earl of Denbigh, Colonel in the Honourable Artillery Company.[250] The following year it was decided to build a new pavilion at the school field in Lower Edmonton as a war memorial.[251]

In 1918 inflation reached 22 percent in the United Kingdom; this post-war depression necessitated considerable financial stringency. The Headmaster claimed 1921 was 'the most anxious year in living memory. It was a year of reaction in education, a year of slump in commerce . . .' At the end of 1918, with 544 boys on the school's roll, a waiting list had to be opened. The same year, a further Education Act raised the leaving age to fourteen, helping nudge parents to keep their sons at school for a full five years, to maximize the educational benefit. The school advised parents not to withdraw their sons from school if they had no job to go to.[252] Fees were raised to £18 per year for boys aged under twelve on admission, £21 for boys between twelve and fourteen, and £27 for boys between fourteen and sixteen,[253] while a was fund set up to meet instances of hardship. Some scholarship boys needed an additional council grant to purchase the school uniform.

A further Board of Education Inspection took place in 1922. By this date, the school had grown yet again and numbered 585 pupils,[254] with 41 percent on scholarships, fully exempt from fees.[255] The sixth form

Hammersmith. Review XXIII 101, Summer term 1922, pp. 18–19.
249. Review 95, Summer term 1919.
250. Review 97, Summer term 1920, p. 4. A Roll of Honour and Service for Old Boys and Members of Staff who served and those who were killed 1914–1918 was published by the Clove Club in 2014 (Dinton: Twig Books). It includes detailed accounts of service and photographs, with transcripts of articles by serving soldiers extracted from The Review.
251. Review 98, Spring term 1921, pp. 18–19. The pavilion was destroyed in a fire in 1963.
252. Review 99, Summer term 1921, p. 5.
253. *Prospectus* 1927.
254. In autumn 1923 the school roll reached a peak of 650 pupils – 430 fee-payers and 217 scholarship boys – and additional space had to be made available by re-purposing some rooms. Governors' Minute Book, LMA EO/PS/4/34, 25 October 1922, f. 108.
255. In their response to the report, the Headmaster and the Chair of Governors, Nettie Adler, were keen to claim 'there is no difference in social class between Junior scholars and fee payers, and that a large number of fee payers came from Public Elementary Schools.' (NA, Records of the Ministry of Education: ED27/8001.) Henrietta 'Nettie' Adler (1868–1950), daughter of Chief Rabbi Hermann Adler (1839–1911), was Chairman of Governors between 1910 and 1936. A celebrated social worker and Jewish political activist in Hackney, in 1910 she became one of the first two women elected to the L.C.C. (TCL, November 2008,

had gradually increased in size, from just 17 boys in 1914 to 40 in 1920. By 1923, the school roll reached a new record of 656, the Inspectors noting the local area was 'more and more industrialised'. The class profile of pupils remained similar to 1908 and 1915, apart from an increase in parents engaged in retail trade and a decrease in clerks and commercial agents. Almost all sixteen new parents listed in July 1923 would be classified as pursuing working-class trades or occupations: traveller, fishmonger, butcher, motor driver, mechanical engineer, mantle-maker, schoolmaster, cost accountant, clerk, woodturner, tailor, trimmer, manager, decorator, salesman, police sergeant – and from Hackney, Clapton or Stoke Newington.[256]

Alfred Rayns, who entered the school around this time as a fee-paying pupil aged nine, had only to pass a simple entrance test: 'the headmaster read aloud to us twice a short story about an elephant, which we then had to reproduce on paper from memory'. Rayns also recalled the content of his English lessons:

> We had to learn several poems by heart and recite
> them in front of the class. [Mr Barron] gave us a good
> grounding in paragraphing, sentence construction,
> the usage of capital letters and punctuation, as well as
> regular dictations and the learning of lists of spellings...
> [R]ather surprisingly we had lessons in Phonetics. The
> purpose of this was probably a form of speech training to
> try to correct the cockney accent.

He criticised Barron for telling

> ... stories of life in the trenches which were not really
> suitable for boys of such a tender age. The first world
> war had ended only seven years previously and the poor
> chap could not get it out of his mind.[257]

By now the school was regularly sending students to university, mainly colleges of the University of London, but also to Oxford and Cambridge with scholarships. A large proportion of boys went straight into business in the City, many extending their education at 'night school' or evening classes. The 1922 report singled out the senior French master for praise, noting 'a number of boys visit France under his guidance during the Easter holidays'. Yet again the Headmaster's economising was denounced, the inspectors noting that not a penny had

---

p. 13; see also ODNB.)
256. Hackney Archives. Admissions, 1905–23. R/DOW/15/1 July 1923.
257. Alfred William Rayns: *A Sheep's Head and a Piece of String*, 1998, private publication, pp. 52, 69.

been spent on the school library during the year 1920/21. However, they concluded 'the School generally is in a sound and healthy condition'.[258]

In 1908, pupils' average stay at the school was about three and a half years; this increased to almost five years in 1928, when the average leaving age was sixteen years eight months.[259] By 1931, the school roll stood at 675, meaning additional space was once again urgently required. A new wing was added at the west end of the school, housing an extra classroom, an art room and a library; at the same time the staff common-room was enlarged and the gymnasium equipped with heating. While construction was under way, the first and second forms were accommodated in Hackney Technical Institute, once more utilised as an unofficial annexe. In his report for 1930–31, the Headmaster complained of the impact of the building works.

> The health of the school suffered – there was more illness on the staff than during the great influenza epidemic of 1918… The work of the school also suffered, as the examination results show.[260]

The harsh economic conditions persisted and impacted many pupils. Cyril Spector, a scholarship pupil in the mid-1930s, recalled:

> School uniform presented a problem for my parents. The grant I received was supposed to cover it, but I made do with the school cap and a badge, which was sewn on to my jacket in lieu of a blazer, and a tie…[261]

In 1931 the conservative Municipal Reform Party, which had formed a majority in the L.C.C. since 1907, reduced the education budget, with spending cuts that extended even to school prizes. This policy was attacked in the press as particularly mean and helped Labour gain a majority at the 1934 L.C.C. elections.[262] The prevailing financial hardship is reflected in repeated appeals in the school magazine for books for the school library. Titles of Jewish interest were donated, reflecting the increasing number of Jewish pupils at the school.

The subjects of school debates throw light on issues of concern to older pupils in this period. In 1923 the Commercial Fifth Debating Society voted against military training in schools, claiming it encouraged the love of war. Attempts to revive links between the school and the London Rifle Brigade were defeated: 'After the experience of the Great

---

258. 21–24 March 1921. NA ED 109/3731, pp. 1–5, 8, 11.
259. NA, ED 3 5/1671 (A) and 252; ED 109/3731 and 3733.
260. Hackney Archives. R/DOW/1/32.
261. Spector, p. 44.
262. Graduate unemployment caused by the economic crisis meant that London schools were able to appoint well-qualified teachers (Maclure, p. 113).

War we doubt that any one is overwhelmed with the desire to join the army.'[263] The society also debated such contemporary topics as reparations, nationalizing the land, the power of the trades union, Co-operation and Communism.[264] A similar pattern of debates continued into the following decade, with a wide range of topics discussed during 1931:

> Another war is inevitable, Spending not saving will solve the economic problem to-day, The idea of Progress should be the greatest good for the greatest number, Prohibition in England would lead to National disaster... . Science has done more harm than good, Life is getting too soft, Shakespeare in modern clothes is absurd, War is necessary to Progress.[265]

By the mid-1930s the school could boast:

> Numbers of Old Boys have qualified as Medical practitioners, many Open Science Scholarships have been won at Oxford, Cambridge and elsewhere...[266]

This pattern was sustained. Cyril Domb (1920–2012), who became a distinguished physicist, recalled the impact of a particular maths teacher on his career:

> Swan was a superb teacher and managed to keep his eye on every pupil in the room ... When I moved into the sixth form he gave me complete individual treatment, saying that he wanted to groom me for a Cambridge scholarship...[267]

In 1938 Domb won the first Oxbridge scholarship at the school in six years.[268]

During this period, every boy was scheduled physical instruction in the gym at least twice a week, and an annual gymnastics display with Swedish exercises involved up to fifty pupils.[269] Wednesday afternoons were set aside for sport – cricket in summer and football in winter – while some boys distinguished themselves at athletics. At the 1929 Amateur Athletic Association national championship, A. A. Cooper came second in the two-mile walk; the following year the school sent a team to the Public School Sports for the first time.[270] In 1936 A. A. (later

---

263. Review, 1923.
264. Review 103, Summer term 1923, p. 13.
265. Review 126, Spring Term 1931.
266. Review 133, Summer 1933, p. 5.
267. Cyril Domb, *Reminiscences*, p. 27.
268. In 1954 Domb became Professor of Theoretical Physics at King's College, London.
269. Stanley Quinn, 'My Years at the "Grocers"', 1994; Typescript in HDS Archive, p. 4.
270. In 1935 Cooper broke the word record for the 3,000m and 5,000m walk.

Sir Arthur) Gold (1917–2002) won the high jump at this meeting.[271] Rowing became a school sport, with two clinker fours purchased out of tuck-shop profits raced on nearby River Lea. By 1931 the school possessed its own boathouse. The playing field at Edmont,on was enlarged after the Grocers' Company agreed to the demolition of the headmaster's residence, Hydeside House, and incorporation of its site into the existing open space, with a lease that would expire in 1962.[272]

Physical instruction was under the charge of A. J. Marley, honorary Sergeant-Major of the school battalion and former corporal in The King's Own Yorkshire Light Infantry. Marley was feared for his rigorous control and noted for his malapropisms – he loathed 'them cosmopolitan shoes' – and insisted boys wore 'Thistle' plimsoles purchased from him, though available much cheaper in nearby Chatsworth Road street-market.[273] Before school, Marley trained boys on the rifle range in the back playground; on at least one occasion a stray bullet hit a passing commuter train. One boy, on starting at the school in the 1920s, was surprised to discover in each class-room a rack of dummy rifles, with a tea-tray handle as trigger guard. The school battalion consisted of four companies, one reserved for Jewish boys whose parents objected to military activities on the Sabbath. Marley, who made no attempt to conceal his prejudice, dubbed this fourth company the 'Red Army'.[274] An annual school Field Day was staged at Edmonton, with a high-ranking regular army officer taking the salute.[275] The school battalion survived until 1935, when the L.C.C. terminated all forms of military training for schoolchildren. The Hackney Downs battalion paraded one last time, inspected by no less than the elderly Field-Marshal Viscount Allenby (1861–1936). Former pupils expressed considerable resentment about the closure of the battalion.[276]

Alexander Baron,[277] who entered Hackney Downs in 1929, described the immediate environs of the school around this time:

> Before then, Clapton, which was its immediate
> catchment area, and all those streets on the other side of

---

271. Gold, an outspoken opponent of professionalizing sport and of performance-enhancing drugs, became honorary secretary of the British Amateur Athletics Board (1965–72) and chairman of the British Olympic Association (1988–92).
272. Review 133, Summer term 1933, p. 4.
273. Allan Bowler, pupil 1929–38, HDS Archive.
274. Anonymous letter to Willie Watkins, 20 March 1998.
275. Ralph Willcocks, 'Some Memories of our school in the 1920s', 2 April 1996; HDS Archive.
276. For a brief history of the battalion see S. A. Richards, 'The School Battalion', Review 142, Summer term 1936, pp. 22–27.
277. His pen name: his birth name was Joseph Alexander Bernstein (1917–99).

> the Downs ... seemed to be the quarter of well-to-do, old-fashioned Hackney tradesmen, people who could afford to send their sons because it was mainly a paying school, and they just took a small quota of scholarship boys. In my year, thirty-three scholarship boys applied. My Mum ... took me with fear and trembling for the interview. And I think it was the first year they took all the thirty-three applicants. And I think from more-or-less the time I went onwards – it sounds like I was leading the tribes of Moses into the desert – the proportion of Jews in the school seemed to grow until it was very noticeable.[278]

Baron judiciously distinguishes Hackney from 'the East End':

> Looking back on Hackney in the 1930s up to the war, most of the population were respectable. It's modern journalists who have called Hackney in [sic] the East End ... I would say that the working class was old-fashioned Labour in Hackney, passive, non-political, highly respectable.[279]

In his novel *The In-Between Time*, Baron includes a passage that clearly describes Hackney Downs School as he experienced it:

> The old-fashioned school buildings, in the same ageing red hue as the walls ... [The novel's protagonist] was a complete believer in the school traditions, the school song, the envied sanctuary of the prefects' room which was adorned with such trophies as signboards stolen from railway stations and advertising statuettes taken from shopfronts; he loved the worn front steps that could only be used by prefects and masters; he lived in worship and awe of the white-haired headmaster who flicked at boys with the tail of his gown. Hater of militarism though he was, he enjoyed being a platoon commander in the cadet corps and looked forward to his Saturday mornings on the rifle-range. Tuck-shop, fives-courts, gymnasium, swimming-pool, playing-field, metal-work shop...

---

278. Interview with Ken Worpole in *So We Live: The novels of Alexander Baron*, edd. Susie Thomas, Andrew Whitehead and Ken Worpole. Nottingham: Five Leaves Publications, 2019, pp. 44–45.
279. *So We Live*, p. 52. For a perceptive account of Anglo-Jewry between the wars, challenging the 'myth' of upwards social mobility, see: David Cesarani, 'A Funny Thing Happened on the Way to the Suburbs: Social Change in Anglo-Jewry Between the Wars, 1914–1945' in *Jewish Culture and History*, Vol. 1, 1 (1998), pp. 5–26.

He also sketched the sixth form:
> There were only eight boys in the Arts Sixth and now that the period of examination cramming was over the masters were able to behave more like university tutors, talking to boys individually and treating them (for the first time in their school lives) as young men who were on a more or less equal footing.[280]

For Baron
> School displaced home as a centre of my life. It was the place where I at last fitted in. In time our family home became only an annexe to it, a place where I was little more than a lodger.[281]

Along with some of his fellow sixth-formers, Baron lost interest in his curricular subjects – English, History, French and Latin – exploring instead European films at the Academy Cinema in Oxford Street, ballet at Sadlers Wells, art at the Tate Gallery and left-wing politics, reading *Das Kapital* when he should have been revising for Matric.

In his novel *Failure*, Roland Camberton, who also attended Hackney Downs, describes the social and religious make-up of the school in this period, as he describes its lightly fictionalized counterpart, 'Stenholme College':[282]

> The boys at Stenholme were split twice: into Jews and non-Jews, and into scholarship boys and paying boys. These divisions were not deep enough to be troublesome, but they were noticeably there. One or two members of the staff, for instance, drew attention in class to the difference between 'some of you boys', 'you lot', 'some of you Jewish boys', 'some of you scholarship boys from poorer homes' – or, more brutally, 'Jew-boys' and 'riff-raff' – between these two categories and the true-blue non-scholarship-holding non-Jews.

Cyril Spector, another contemporary, discerned similar distinctions within the school:

> There was a subtle class and social division that soon became apparent. Firstly the division between Jews and

---

280. *The In-Between Time*, London: Macmillan, 1971, p. 23
281. Baron, p. 10. In *The Uses of Literacy* (1957), Richard Hoggart claimed a working-class scholarship boy's attachment to school could act destructively as well as being a liberating influence.
282. Pen name of Henry Cohen (1921–65), who left Hackney Downs in 1938.

non-Jews. Secondly, the division between fee-paying and scholarship boys, and, thirdly, the gap between those who came from the south side – Clapton – and those from the more prosperous north – Stamford Hill . . . Since I was only a Jewish scholarship boy from Clapton, I was at the bottom of the pile.[283]

Allan Bowler, a pupil between 1929 and 1936, recalled that, for prayers, Jewish boys met separately in a form room, while the gentiles assembled in the theatre[284] for 'a shortened form of matins'[285] taken by the headmaster. Roman Catholics were excused.[286] The Jewish Cyril Spector recalled his mother:

refused to allow me to eat at school. Even sandwiches were not allowed, as she feared the food might be contaminated by the school's non-Kosher plates, so I trekked back at lunchtime every day.

As Jewish boys couldn't attend school for detention on Saturdays, they had to stay after school during the week, which was resented by some teachers, who received no additional payment for this work.[287] Jewish boys could find the first two years at school particularly difficult, as most were also attending after-school Hebrew classes to prepare for their Bar Mitzvah.[288]

With – or despite – the increasing numbers of Jewish pupils, there was a marked degree of anti-Semitism in the school. In an anecdote from his book about school leadership, Jenkyn Thomas exhibits the casual anti-Semitism common in this period:

A Jewish boy came for his interview. In the course of it, I asked him,. 'Are you fond of reading?' 'Oh, yeth, Thir, very fond,' he replied enthusiastically. 'What authors do you like best?' 'Thcott, Dickenth, and Thackeray, Thir.' . . .[289]

The English master James Medcalf, later Head of English, was suspected of anti-Semitism for his habitual use of the supposedly humorous

---

283. Spector, p. 46.
284. Allan Bowler, TCL, June 2000, p. 5.
285. i.e. Anglican Morning Prayer. Rayns, p. 67.
286. Stanley Quinn (pupil 1935–39), TCL, October 2000, p. 15.
287. Spector, p. 44.
288. Emanuel Levy, TCL, November 2006, p. 39. He was one of five Levys in his class: Levy, E (1); Levy, E (2); Levy, Sam; Levy, Sid; and Levy, John Sidney.
289. *Letters to a Young Head Master*, p. 141. Dr. Sam Lawson recalled being beaten by Thomas, who cried 'Ichabod' ('the glory of Israel is departed') with each stroke. (Letter to Willie Watkins, 19 April 2013, HDS Archive.)

phrase: 'And a heavy due/Jew fell on each blade of grass . . .'.²⁹⁰ Baron/Bernstein also records that the Catholic Medcalf

> my friendly adviser on reading, remarked in the nicest of ways that the Steins were trying to overturn civilization – Einstein, Epstein and Gertrude, and now they had been joined by Bernstein.²⁹¹

In his novel *Failure*, Camberton describes a character named Sergeant-Major Battersby, 'the gym instructor and factotum of the Cadet Corps' – clearly modelled on A. J. Marley: ²⁹²

> As for the Jews, Battersby usually referred to them as 'Jew-boys', 'Jew-lot' (or, under his breath, 'Jew-bastards') and 'foreigners'; but if in a good mood, he would vary between 'the Yiddisher boys' . . . and his favourite, 'the -vitch's and -sky's'.

As David Cesarani has pointed out, the political situation in Europe in the 1930s meant

> The Jewish schoolboys . . . were not allowed to concentrate single-mindedly on their academic work. The struggle between the Republicans and the followers of Franco in Spain, the plight of German Jews under Nazism and the activity of local Fascists were a constant distraction. They asked themselves: 'could it happen here?'²⁹³

Hackney and Stoke Newington were centres of the longest and strongest support for Mosley's British Union of Fascists.²⁹⁴ Morris Beckman (1921–2015) recalled assaults by Mosley's Blackshirts later in the 1930s, particularly targeting Jews on late-night buses around Dalston Junction.²⁹⁵ Alexander Baron recorded a small group of Fascists in the school,²⁹⁶ and a talk at the school about his tour of Germany in the

---

290. A contemporary pupil rejected this interpretation, claiming 'Medcalf's "heavy Jew" who fell on the grass was one of his pointers towards better English usage, because he was forever correcting the grammar, diction and pronunciation of all his pupils, whether their patois was Cockney, Yiddish, Welsh or Irish.' (Ronnie Hoffman to Willie Watkins, 17 Nov 1999; HDS Archive). The question remains: why choose the 'heavy Jew' as an example? The gentile Allan Bowler, whose father was a Quaker, described Medcalf as 'an anti-Semite and a staunch Catholic' (TCL June 2000, p. 5).
291. Baron, p. 125.
292. In *Failure*.
293. Morris Beckman: *The Hackney Crucible*. London: Vallentine Mitchell, 1995, p. x.
294. John Marriott, *Beyond the Tower: A History of East London*. New Haven and London: Yale, p. 305.
295. Beckman: *Crucible*, pp 105–07.
296. They belonged to a minor organization known as the Imperial Fascist League, who

1930s by former pupil H. A. Jones (1893–1945):[297]

> He described to a crowded audience the renascence of that country in the usual glowing terms. The so-called atrocities were only some excesses committed by over-enthusiastic followers. He had gone to Germany as a guest of the new German government and, having met some of the men at the top, he could assure us that they were pretty decent and responsible fellows who would soon put a stop to this sort of thing.[298]

From the 1930s onwards, a number of Jewish former pupils emigrated to Palestine, particularly following the establishment of the new State of Israel in 1948.[299]

Jenkyn Thomas continued Gull's habit of reacting strongly to pupil absence. When George Macleod, Acting Manager of the Hackney Empire Palace[300] withdrew his son for a day 'to see his King', the headmaster sent the boy home for alleged 'breach of contract'. Macleod challenged Thomas by calling out 'the conduct of your drawing master who continually *hits boys about the head*' [Macleod's emphasis], thereby achieving an honourable ceasefire.[301] Like Gull, Thomas was strongly authoritarian. He operated a system of red and black tickets – signifying commendation or punishment respectively – issued to boys by masters. A black ticket merited at least a severe reprimand or detention, but more serious offences resulted in caning of the hand or backside. Thomas was not slow in employing corporal punishment; almost every account by pupils in *The Clove's Lines* mentions it. In the early 1930s Thomas caned an entire class of thirty boys for classroom disorder;[302] on occasion the beating was carried out in public at morning assembly.[303]

---

denounced Mosley's British Union of Fascists as a tool of the Jews!
297. Jones wrote the official history of the RAF during World War I.
298. Baron, pp. 119–20.
299. Aria Pollak, (HDS 1915–21) emigrated to Palestine in 1930 to farm at Binyamina, near Caesarea; Arthur Citron (HDS 1914–20) arrived in Palestine in 1932, to become chief accountant of the Palestine Potash Company; Meyer Silverstone (1927–33) arrived in Israel after 1948, and served as Director General of the Ministry of the Interior, 1960–70; Bert Ambrose (HDS 1922–28) headed Barclays Bank, Israel; Israel Gal-Edd (Izzy Greenstein, HDS mid-1930s) became Director General of the Israeli Ministry of Development; Dr. Emanuel Levy (HDS 1933–39) became Director of National Accounting. Reflecting the strong tradition of medicine at the school, a number of former HDS pupils became doctors, dentists and academics in Israel. (Handwritten account by the late Dr. Melvyn Brooks (HDS 1957–64), who became a village doctor in Karkur, near Caesarea.
300. Today the Hackney Empire theatre.
301. February 11 1914. TCL, December 2002, p. 15.
302. Henry Welfare, TCL, October 2000, p. 11.
303. Ralph Willcocks, 'Some Memories of our school in the 1920s', p. 5; 2 April 1996; HDS

Jenkyn Thomas officiates at assembly in the school's semi-circular theatre.

In addition to this formal system, duly recorded in a punishment book, former pupils have recounted numerous instances of casual teacher violence and physical control: hitting with rulers, poking in sensitive areas, striking heads, throwing wooden blackboard-dusters and assault with window poles. Particular masters were known for specific cruelties, such as twisting a boy's forelock or grabbing him by the neck. Such arbitrary retribution was the response not only to bad behaviour but could also the reaction to wrong answers or perceived slights. The school was controlled by violence and threats of violence. Baron looked back humorously on all this:

> Well, Hackney Downs was a good school when I was there... I reckon I got quite as good an education as they got at public schools. But the masters – a couple of them were comic characters. The headmaster whom I admired very much – but I always thought he imagined himself as the head of Greyfriars. He used to also wear a mortarboard and walked about swishing his gown. And there were whackings, but they were very rare. On the only occasion when I got whacked – I got four in a form-whacking – it was great fun. I thought: this is just like the *Magnet*...[304]

Archive.
304. *So We Live*, pp. 44–45. *The Magnet* was a weekly boys' story magazine, aimed

According to another former pupil, most boys knew next to nothing about sex:

> I remember no discussion about sex among us boys in the class . . . My ideas about the other sex were derived in large part from the books I read, books by Leslie Charteris (The Saint), P. G. Wodehouse (Jeeves) and others. Girls were a mystery and men were knights in shining armour . . . It was as though babies were ordered from and delivered by a stork to properly married couples.[305]

In his semi-autobiographical novel *The In-Between Time*, Baron reflects a similar picture: 'At school [the protagonist] lived in a self-consciously male world in which sex played a surprisingly small part... One boy at school was supposed to have "done it".'[306] However Roland Camberton intimates a remarkably liberal attitude by one (unnamed) teacher:

> when David asked one of the younger masters what *Lady Chatterley's Lover* was about, he laughed contemptuously and said: 'Oh, *that* book. People make such a fuss, and do you know what it's really about? It's nothing more than – No, but I won't tell you. You read it for yourselves and find out.' And he lent them his Tauchnitz edition of Lawrence.[307]

The school offered boys a wide range of clubs and societies. A radio club was formed in 1923, with lectures by electronics engineers and visits to manufacturers, exhibitions, the BBC and 2LO at Marconi House. By 1927 it had metamorphosed into a Radio and Social Club, and by the 1930s was a solely social club, adding field trips to school-based activities. There were educational visits to a variety of places, including the Old Bailey, Fords of Dagenham, the Carreras tobacco factory, Battersea Power Station, HMV to see an early demonstration of television, Clapton Greyhound Stadium and a 10 p.m. production-run at the *Daily Herald* in Fleet Street, followed by a salutary 1 a.m. visit to homeless people sleeping in the crypt of St. Martin in the Fields.[308] In 1930 a German teacher took a group of pupils to Germany; a former pupil recalled the master denouncing Hitler, not troubling to conceal his Socialist views.[309] School parties also took educational cruises in the

---

primarily at working-class boys, featuring Billy Bunter and Greyfriars School.
305. Stanley Quinn, 'My Years at the "Grocers"' 1994, p. 5; Typescript in HDS Archive.
306. *The In-Between Time*, Macmillan, 1971, pp. 14, 16.
307. This was thirty years before the 1963 'Lady Chatterley trial'.
308. William H. Greaves, TCL, February 2006, p. 12.
309. Sam Feld, open letter to the Clove Club, 13 July 2000, HDS Archive. The master had

Baltic and Mediterranean on the White Star steamer *Doric*.

Throughout Thomas's headship there were annual concerts of solo, chamber or choral music, as well as recitations. In 1934 a school orchestra was formed 'not so much to aim at public performance, but rather to unite in making cheerful and pleasant sounds'.[310] The new ensemble gave its first performance at Speech Day 1936, and was cruelly advised to 'avoid Tchaikovsky until they [had] settled down a little'.[311] There were no more plays or Gilbert and Sullivan operettas, though a plea was made in 1923 that 'theatricals be revived.'[312] It was claimed 'theatricals are notoriously impossible in the School owing to lack of a workable stage'; instead a Sixth Form Union was formed in 1931 to read plays, discuss literary topics and arrange theatre trips.[313] In 1937 pupils saw Shaw's *Pygmalion* at the Old Vic, *The Merchant of Venice* at the People's Palace, Mile End Road and the Habima Players' production of *The Wandering Jew* in Hebrew.[314] Finally, in 1938, English master Stanley Day produced *Twelfth Night* in the school gym, with an all-male cast: 'The LNER [London North Eastern Railway] . . . played its part with monotonous regularity, though its intervention occasionally arrived at an opportune moment.'[315] This was followed in 1939 by Galsworthy's *Escape* and Erich Kästner's *Emil and the Detectives*, performed in German.

In February 1932 there was another HMI inspection, which was much more overtly critical of the Jenkyn Thomas regime. At the beginning of that year the school numbered 675 pupils, with an average class size of 35 – the L.C.C. stipulated 30 or fewer. By this date 47 percent of pupils were wholly exempt from fees. The Inspectors commented that the 'accent of some of the boys might prove a handicap for them in after life' – a recurrent complaint – and recommended speech training. In a typed confidential report attached to the printed public version, the Inspectors were outspoken:

> The English teaching is generally quite uninspired. The H.M. [headmaster] doesn't really care about the subject. Probably nothing can be done while he remains at the School.[316]

They emphasized the continuing problem of excessive class size, pointing

learned German while a World War I prisoner-of-war. *Hackney Crucible*, p. 93.
310. Review 135, Spring term 1934, p. 19.
311. Review 143, Autumn term 1936, p. 14.
312. Review 103, Summer term 1923, p. 23.
313. Review 126, Spring term 1931, p. 13.
314. Review 146, Autumn term 1937, p. 24.
315. Review 148, Summer term 1938 pp. 18–19.
316. 23–26 February 1932. NA ED 109/3731, pp. 3, 5, 13; Confidential report p. 2.

out inspectors had drawn attention to this issue as far back as 1915. However they suggested letting sleeping dogs lie until Thomas's anticipated retirement in 1935. A further typed note was personal in its criticism:

> [The] Head Master is a man of strong personality and pronounced views, who has been in charge since 1906 or thereabouts and a Head Master since 1896. It is in consequence not surprising to find that the school is in some respects old-fashioned . . . English is probably the worst subject, and Latin and German are rather poor.[317]

William Jenkyn Thomas was not someone who tolerated what he regarded as interference or disrespect. He believed good education required recognition of teachers' (and headteachers') high status and seems to have been able to exercise autocratic authority in negotiations with the L.C.C. In 1926, when the L.C.C. informed him of an imminent school inspection, he wrote indignantly to the Inspector in Charge, Dr. Cloudesley Brereton:

> I was sorry to learn from you yesterday that it is proposed to hold a Full Inspection at this school next term. I have always objected on principle, both publicly and privately, to Full Inspection.... In my opinion they are now unnecessary and undesirable.[318]

Nevertheless, the inspection went ahead. In the surprising context of a commemorative book celebrating Thomas's headmastership, the Assistant Education Officer wrote revealingly:

> Most of us realized that the more he had his own way the better for the school. If anyone at County Hall ever momentarily forgot this they were reminded of it in very trenchant language.

An example of Thomas's petty territoriality is recorded in the Governors' Minutes, where the L.C.C. Education Officer reports:

> The Head Master has complained of what he describes as the increasing custom . . . of persons visiting the school on the Council's business, the legitimacy of whose mission I gather he does not dispute, though he does take exception to their coming to the school without previous arrangement with him so to do . . .[319]

An obituary described Thomas as a 'fearless champion of schools and

---

317. NA ED 109/3731, Confidential report, p. 2.
318. Hackney Archives R/DOW/1/36, 12 December 1925.
319. LMA EO/PS/4/34, f. 259, 24 January 1929.

schoolmasters against bureaucrats, cranks and cheese-paring Governments'.[320]

Between 1913 and 1934, Thomas served as Joint Honorary Secretary of the Incorporated Association of Head Masters (IAH), and was subsequently elected its president. In 1930, he became leader of the Secondary Teachers' Panel of the Burnham Committee, responsible for negotiating salaries, and, from 1929, he chaired the Joint Committee of the associations of Secondary Headmasters, Headmistresses, Assistant Masters and Assistant Mistresses.[321] Thomas became increasingly conservative in his views, attacking what he described as the intrusion of politics into education. In his 1935 presidential address to the IAH he charged the London Labour Party with attempting to remodel textbooks: 'Cooking the books of a business firm is a criminal offence. Cooking the children's books is a grievous sin against the moral code'[322] – remarks widely reported in the national press. Thomas opposed 'progressive' ideas, such as those espoused by the school's first headmaster, Bowen, rejecting the image of pupils' 'unfolding', which his predecessor had derived from Froebel's writings on child development:

> With regard to the methods adopted by the school . . . there is no belief in any 'new' method which claims to revolutionise education, making all things easy and causing every child to *unfold* like a flower . . . the right attitude, in our opinion, is that of progressive conservatism.

Thomas cited in his support the Cambridge classicist W. H. S. Jones:

> Teachers of all grades must resist the attractive but insidious forms in which the doctrine presents itself – interest, self-determination or what not . . . The compelling influence of the categorical imperative, commonly called a sense of duty, is a factor without which education is not only useless but dangerous.[323]

Despite his headship and committee duties, Jenkyn Thomas found time to publish a number of school textbooks, including *The New Latin Delectus*,[324] co-written with Edgar Doughty, a classics master at

---

320. J. E. Medcalf, Review 181, December 1959.
321. Medcalf, p. 51.
322. TCL November 2006, p. 26.
323. In *Disciplina* (1926).
324. Books I and II. London: Horace Marshall, 1908; with F. Reynolds of the Intermediate School, Cardiff. Jenkyn Thomas also edited *Cicero in Catilinam and Vergil* [sic], *Aeneid* (Newport, 1910), an anthology of Sallust and Ovid (1900), for the Central Welsh Board examinations, and two volumes in the Cameos of Literature series: *The Harp of*

Grocers', used at Hackney Downs and other schools; and *Letters to a Young Head Master*, written with Charles W. Bailey, of Holt Secondary School, Liverpool.[325] To fill a gap he noticed for legends of his own country, he published the frequently reprinted *Welsh Fairy Book* in Welsh and English.[326]

After thirty years as Headmaster, Jenkyn Thomas retired in 1935, leaving his successor a major task of reform and reconstruction.[327]

Youth (London: Thomas Nelson, 1907) and *A Book of English Prose* (London: Thomas Nelson, 1909).
325. London and Glasgow: Blackie & Son, 1927.
326. The English edition was originally published by Fisher Unwin, London, 1907. Thomas also published *Cambrensia,* an anthology about Wales (1904), and *Heroes of Wales*.
327. He died on 14 March 1959.

Chapter 4
Weathering the War
Thomas Balk, Headmaster 1936–1952

...a well-ordered and purposeful community, worthily playing an indispensable part in the education of North East London.
HMI Report

When Jenkyn Thomas announced his retirement, ten candidates – all Oxbridge graduates – applied for the post of Headmaster of Hackney Downs, of whom three were shortlisted.[328] The chosen successor was Thomas Oscar Balk M.C., M.A. (1889–1970), a history graduate from Wadham College, Oxford. He came with leadership experience, having been Headmaster successively of Andover Grammar School and Henry Mellish School, Nottingham.[329] During World War II, Hackney Downs encountered many major obstacles: it was in large part due to Balk that it emerged from the war years with positive prospects.

Jenkyn Thomas had instituted limited reforms in the school, which was still running largely upon the framework constructed by his predecessor Charles Gull, though Thomas had successfully managed the transition from an independent educational institution to a local authority school. Balk now proceeded substantially to remodel and reform the school, creating a better organised, educationally more coherent and less rigidly conservative regime. His first year was marked by the retirement of Samuel Richards,[330] a former pupil, one of the original Housemasters and currently senior member of the school staff, signalling the end of an era.

Almost as soon as Balk took up the reins, a team of thirteen L.C.C. educational inspectors descended on Hackney Downs, and between 17 and 21 February 1936 investigated every aspect of the school's life.

---
328. Governors' Minute Book, LMA EO/PS/4/34 f. 344. 26 March 1935.
329. His father, C. G. Balk, had been assistant to James Murray, editor of the *Oxford English Dictionary*, but resigned in 1914 as a result of popular prejudice about his German antecedents. John Hardcastle, TCL, March 2010, p. 17.
330. Like other Hackney Downs teachers, Richards published several school textbooks, including *French Speech and Spelling*. London: Dent, 1922.

During Thomas' headship, the school roll had increased by around 50 percent, from 426 in 1908 to 629 in 1935.[331] Over the same period, the number of boys aged under eleven fell steadily, from 82 in 1915 to a mere 39 in 1935. The vast majority of pupils came from Hackney (67 percent) and Stoke Newington (19.5 percent). In 1936, of 610 boys, 371 held 'special places' – that is, scholarships of some kind. 40 percent of pupils had Jewish heritage, rising to 60 percent in the sixth form:

> almost all destined to become doctors, dentists, lawyers and solicitors. Philosophy, languages, mathematics, and similar subjects only led to teaching, and no-one wanted to enter such an underpaid and unprivileged profession.[332]

In their report, the inspectors judged the school to be decidedly conservative in its teaching methods, singling out for particular criticism the teaching of English, for which there was no Head of Department. They also deplored the poor premises. The inspectors recommended the swimming pool be made available for use all year round rather than solely during the summer term, and argued that a separate gymnasium was essential. They also pointed to serious defects in the main buildings, which dated to the school's foundation in 1873: the classrooms were too small to accommodate thirty boys, let alone thirty-five; in some rooms natural lighting was poor; in eight classrooms some boys could not see the blackboard; corridors were dark, staircases dark, steep and narrow.

> In short, the defects of the 1873 portion of the building render it inadequate for working purposes, and its general style has a depressing effect. A scheme of major improvements is necessary to bring the premises up to modern standards and should be undertaken as soon as practicable.

The Inspectors were particularly critical of the organisation of classes. Boys progressed through the school according to their individual ability and exam results, leading to discontinuity between different boys' paths and the heterogeneous composition of subject groups, making it excessively complicated for teaching and timetabling. The inspectors proposed replacing this confused system with a standard 'steady five year course for all' – allowing variations for particular individuals where necessary – and abolishing the existing non-examination stream for weaker pupils.[333]

---

331. L.C.C. Inspectors' Report, 1936. HDS Archive.
332. Spector, p. 57.
333. In general, the less able pupils were those paying fees.

At this date the school had 30 full-time and four part-time masters – five with first-class honours degrees – plus a French and a German assistant. The inspectors complained that as many as fifteen different masters were teaching English, none of them specialists, and that there was neither consistency nor leadership for this subject – a weakness heavily criticised in previous inspections.[334] The inspectors called for the urgent appointment of an English graduate to take charge of the subject, upon which neither Gull nor Jenkyn Thomas had placed importance. They also called for greater emphasis on speech and drama, for an appropriate syllabus to be drawn up, for up-to-date textbooks and for written work to be systematically organised.

Similarly, the inspectors criticised the dull and out-dated textbooks for geography, history, French, German and Latin, and again called for new and improved teaching materials. They deemed German instruction to be over-reliant on grammar at the expense of developing a 'command of the language as a medium of expression', and were particularly critical of the Spanish master, who lacked both academic qualifications and teaching ability. The inspectors pointed out that a large number of different masters were teaching maths, history and geography – for the last there was no dedicated instructor – and called for greater specialisation in fewer hands. Maths teaching was one of the few areas praised, though even here the report called for modern textbooks. Science – physics, botany and chemistry – still allocated a minor place in the curriculum, was praised for having three full-time, well-qualified teaching specialists, two with first-class honours degrees.

Music was reckoned well taught, as was art, although for the latter the report called for greater freedom in choice of subject matter and execution. The inspectors were unimpressed with workshop arrangements and the time allocated for handicrafts – and highly critical of the equipment available in the commercial department. For the Saturday typewriting course, textbooks were deemed 'very old and out-of-date' and out of fourteen typewriters, two were completely useless and the rest 'in very poor condition'. Even Physical Instruction did not escape criticism: lessons were 'too stiff and formal' and teachers with 'a more intimate knowledge of modern methods' were called for:

> [P]arallel bars and horizontal bars are still used in spite of the fact that it was pointed out in 1926 that such items of equipment were no longer considered suitable for educational gymnastics.

---

334. One English master set pupils to write elegant essays in the style of Joseph Addison and Richard Steele in the eighteenth-century *Spectator*. Julius Alterman, 'School Days', 2009.

The Inspectors also called for funds to supplement the miserly 1,300 books housed in the school library.

Overall, the Inspectors' report amounted to a damning critique of the organisation, methodology, funding and quality of teaching under Jenkyn Thomas' headship, singling out for particular opprobrium the haphazard streaming and progression through the school, old-fashioned and inadequate instruction, the lack of appropriate staff, and the out-dated textbooks and equipment and dark, crowded classrooms.

Balk immediately requested approval for a major purchase of new textbooks: 'For many years the strictest economy had been observed resulting in retaining in use many books which were unserviceable and out-of-date.' He submitted an estimate for providing the books needed:

English	£300
History	50
Geography	97
Latin	10
French	40
German	16
Spanish	5
Mathematics	80
Science	80
	£678[335]

This expenditure was swiftly approved.

Following the Inspectors' report, Balk instituted major organisational changes. The school was henceforth to start earlier in the morning and break later for lunch, leaving enough time for five morning periods rather than the previous four. On two afternoons in the week there were now three periods, on the rest two, allowing more time for after-school clubs and societies, such as play-readings, orchestra and choir. Balk also ended Saturday morning classes, held ever since the school opened: Jews could not attend school on their Shabbat and there were increasing numbers of Jewish boys on the roll. As alternatives to Latin, both Spanish and German were now offered. In response to the Inspectors' criticism, the organisation of forms was now solely on the basis of age, while a monthly report for each pupil replaced the previous weekly or fortnightly versions. Balk also arranged to teach all first-year boys Civics, enabling him to meet every new entrant to the school.

For the first time, the school timetable included games – football or cricket according to the season – with some taking place on Hackney Downs park as well as at the school field in Edmonton. Rowing on the

335. Roughly equivalent to £60,000 in 2024. Governors' Minute Book LMA EO/PS/4/34 f. 380, 23 July 1936.

Thomas Balk, fourth Headmaster.

River Lea was added to winter sports in 1938, as humorously described in the school magazine:

> Winter rowing may be divided into two sections. 'Crew versus barges' provides an apt summary of the first section, with occasional showers to enliven the encounters. A fleet of barges, towed by a tug, which provides an unwanted shower-bath to the already harassed crew, is the enemy's greatest asset, while the wind, ever ready to overturn the boat, is a good second.[336]

A small number of boys were allotted an L.C.C. 'hard case allowance'

336. Review 149, Autumn term 1938, p. 14.

in the form of reduced fees.[337] In one recorded instance, Henrietta Adler, the Vice Chairman of Governors, visited a boy's home to investigate his circumstances, following which he was awarded a grant.[338] A boy who won a Junior County Scholarship and whose father was unemployed was provided with an L.C.C. grant of £9 for his uniform, as well as leather shoes – he possessed only plimsoles.

In 1920 roughly ten percent of Hackney Downs pupils were Jewish; by 1939 this had risen to around fifty percent, remaining at a similar level through the 1950s.[339] Until this date, morning assembly had consisted of Anglican worship for Protestant Christian boys, and Jewish and Roman Catholic pupils could be exempted. After consulting the Chief Rabbi, Dr. Joseph Hertz (1872–1946), about a form of worship acceptable to the Jewish community, Balk conducted a united daily assembly for all boys – Jewish and gentile. In the autumn term, as the nights drew in, Friday afternoon classes were reduced to 30 minutes so that school could finish at 3.30 pm rather than 4.00 pm, allowing Jewish boys to arrive home before sundown, as Sabbath rules required. On the shortest days, the Jewish contingent was allowed to leave at 3.00 pm. Jewish boys were also absent during the major Jewish holy days – particularly Yom Kippur and New Year. During these festivals, some classes shrank to as few as ten or twelve gentile pupils.

In January 1937, Mr Balk suggested to the school Governors that the excessive levels of illness experienced by staff and pupils might be caused by the 'depressing influence' of the school buildings and the harsh conditions under which they worked, which tended to lower their resistance to sickness.[340] At speech day October 1937, Dr. Bernard Homa (1900–1991),[341] who succeeded Major Grantham as Chairman of the Governors in 1936, announced that the original school buildings were to be demolished and replaced with new premises. The Board of Education approved plans for the new buildings in 1938: on the site of the existing Victorian structure there was to be a new three-storey block, comprising staff and administrative rooms, classrooms, and geography, history and maths rooms; behind this a quadrangle, with a hall

---

337. LMA EO/PS/4/35 f. 45, 25 November 1938.
338. Michael Woolfson (1927–2019, later Emeritus Professor of Theoretical Physics at UMIST, Manchester (HDS Archive).
339. Black, pp. 55–56. By comparison, Parmiter's School, Bethnal Green, had 27 percent Jewish pupils, and Coopers' Company School, Bow, 10 percent.
340. LMA EO/PS/4/35 f. 3 28 January 1937.
341. A Hackney GP and elected Labour member of the L.C.C., Homa was regarded as an unofficial leader of the borough's Jewish population. His appointment as Chair of Hackney Downs' governors was recognition of the large proportion of Jewish pupils. Homa (né Deichowsky) self-published his autobiography, *Footsteps on the Sands of Time*, around 1990.

to the west, a two-storey block of classrooms to the east, and a gymnasium and dining-hall to the south. This scheme involved marginally reducing the school roll, from 600 to 560, with a three-form entry.[342] In the House of Commons, 24 November 1938, Fred Watkins, MP for Hackney Central, pushed Kenneth Lindsay, a National Labour MP and Parliamentary Secretary to the Board of Education, for the date reconstruction would begin at this 'very ancient and honourable [school] . . . still lit by gas'.[343] He received an evasive answer, but events in Central Europe put paid to any immediate prospect of rebuilding the school.

Despite Hitler's re-occupation of the Rhineland, the political situation in 1936 was regarded as safe enough for Hackney Downs to arrange an exchange visit with the Oberrealschule, Soest, Westphalia, though no Jewish boys were included in the travel group.[344] During the trip the school party 'had the good fortune to see Herr Hitler who was travelling on the river [Rhine] by steamer . . . ' while at the Youth Hostel at Hohenlimburg 'after a very good lunch [they] were entertained by songs from a band of boys of the Hitler Youth'.[345]

Just two years later, Europe was gripped by the Munich crisis. On Hackney Downs, trenches were dug, air-raid shelters constructed and a searchlight and anti-aircraft gun set up. The L.C.C. called parent meetings to discuss the evacuation of children from London, should war break out. On 29 September 1938, a party of around 400 Hackney Downs boys assembled at the school, prepared to move out of London 'to an unknown destination'. Following Prime Minister Neville Chamberlain's famous dash to Munich, this evacuation was cancelled.

As late as Easter 1939, a small party from the school visited Paris, and another group, led by the Headmaster, travelled to Switzerland in the summer.[346] In June 1939, a party of about 30 German boys from Soest made a return visit to Hackney Downs, hosted by local families, an encounter that caused severe strains.[347] The two schools competed in various sports, including football, athletics and boxing, and Jewish boys faced the dilemma of deciding whether to participate. The stakes were heightened by the fact that the visitors' jerseys apparently featured a 'small red swastika nestling inside a black circle'. At football, the Hackney Downs team, which included several Jewish boys, thrashed the visitors 10–0, while the Hackney heavyweight champion, Alex

342. NA, Records of the Ministry of Education: ED 35/5253.
343. *Hansard*, 24 November 1938, vol. 341: 'Hackney Downs School (Reconstruction)'.
344. Now the Aldegrever-Gymnasium. Beckman: *Hackney Crucible,* p. 94.
345. Review 142, Summer term 1936, p. 15.
346. During the latter trip, sixteen-year-old Clifford Mackenzie drowned in Lake Lucerne (TCL April 2003, p. 11).
347. TCL October 2000, p. 15.

Schwarz, knocked out his German opponent, to the fury of the Grocers' sports master. Morris Beckman recalled, 'It was a relief to everyone when the Soest boys went home.'[348]

On 2 September 1939, just one day before war was declared, 401 pupils, teachers, wives and women helpers – and one young girl[349] – each carrying a suitcase and gas-mask – boarded a special train at Hackney Downs Station, bound for 'somewhere in England'. Several fifth-formers shared a compartment with the Headmaster, who organized a game of cribbage to take their minds off their uncertain future.[350] The same morning, the school's Hackney premises were requisitioned as an Air Raid Report Centre and Fire-Fighting Services Control Point; from the front steps silver barrage balloons could be seen glinting in the sunlit sky.

The evacuees' secret destination turned out to be the fenland villages of Outwell, Upwell and Three Holes, on the banks of the River Nene, Norfolk. Locals complained they had been led to expect junior-age girls, but all the Hackney boys were eventually allocated a billet. At the first assembly in Upwell, the boys listened on the school's radiogram as Neville Chamberlain announced that war had been declared.[351] The school worked hard to integrate with the Norfolk villagers. In their free time, boys acted as runners and telephone operators at First Aid and Air Raid posts, and helped gather the apple and potato harvest. The headmaster was fully occupied, cycling around Fenland, checking on billets and their owners, and ferrying boys in his car from unsuitable hosts to alternative lodgings.

Hackney Downs had been given part-time use of two local schools – the Senior School, Upwell, and the Beaupré Junior School, Outwell – but soon discovered the laboratory at Upwell was not adequately equipped for teaching senior science. Moreover, a number of boys were living in isolated rural digs, making transport, safeguarding and supervision particularly difficult. Within weeks it was arranged to move the entire school to King's Lynn, to share the more appropriate premises of the King Edward VII Grammar School.[352] Reminiscing about the Fenland experience, one former pupil wrote:

> We did not realise how comfortably we had settled down until the day came . . . to say goodbye to all

---

348. *Hackney Crucible*, pp. 94–98.
349. The sister of Len Korn, whose mother would not allow the siblings to be separated, and for whom Balk made an exception.
350. Leonard Elmer (pupil 1935–40): 'Memories', HDS Archive.
351. Wartime, p. 15.
352. See Michael Walker: *King Edward VII School, King's Lynn*, Book Guild, 2005.

> the hospitable people ... to the village school and
> its nettle-infested playing field ... and to the drab
> landscape which had unaccountably grown upon us.

On Friday 13 October 1939, Hackney Downs in exile moved en masse to King's Lynn in fog, having been granted use of the grammar school buildings between 1.15 and 5 p.m in the afternoon, including access to its science laboratories.[353] Some boys deposited their bags on a coach and cycled into the town in a large convoy. In contrast to the basic rural existence encountered in Outwell and Upwell – sometimes without running water, electricity or gas – a number of boys were now lodged with prosperous middle-class families, boasting radiograms and in one case an electrically-operated player-piano.[354] For some, this opened them up to novel experiences. Stanley Dale Harris (1928–1996), later an eminent New York opera and ballet critic, claimed his first exposure to culture came when he was billeted in an eighteenth-century house, with the 'unimaginable luxury and refinement' of conversation during mealtimes. Leon Kossoff[355] was billeted with a Mr and Mrs R. C. Bishop, who encouraged him to paint. At the Lynn Museum he encountered depictions of the town's buildings;[356] his own first known architectural subject was King's Lynn Customs House.[357] In contrast, one boy evacuated to King's Lynn was so appalled by his billet that he cycled the entire distance home to London and changed schools.[358] In an attempt to keep in touch with Hackney, at Christmas 1939 a coach was laid on to bring some parents to Norfolk for a visit.[359] In a duplicated letter to prospective parents, Balk stressed that billets were 'visited each week by the helpers attached to the school', adding it was

> advisable for boys in the school party to have cycles.
> Cycling here is not dangerous and the possession of

---

353. Balk's daughter recorded that the area to which the school was evacuated was in a 'restricted zone'. When she came home for the holidays, she had to be 'vouched for' at the railway station and visited by the village policeman to check the accommodation. (Letter to Willie Watkins, 2 February 2006, HDS Archive.)
354. William H. Greaves, TCL February 2006, p. 121.
355. Born in Islington in 1926 to Jewish parents who had fled the pogroms of tsarist Ukraine. See Paul Moorhouse: *Leon Kossoff*. London: Tate Publishing, 1996, pp. 9–10.
356. By the local brothers Thomas Baines (1820–1875) and Henry Baines (1823–1894).
357. He also sketched St Paul's Cathedral engulfed by flames, based on newspaper photographs. On a visit back to London in 1942, Kossoff discovered his family had been bombed out of his childhood home and moved to a house in the shadow of Christ Church, Spitalfields, later a favourite subject in his work.
358. Philip Bernstein, TCL January 2000, p. 8,
359. There is a detailed account of the first months in Norfolk in *Review* 152, Autumn 1939/ Spring 1940, pp. 3–15.

a cycle allows a boy to go easily from his billet to the
school and to the playing fields . . .³⁶⁰

Life was not easy for the evacuees. William Greaves was allocated poor digs, where he was expected to do housework. Returning there for lunch from a public exam, he was

> handed a bottle of paraffin, cloths and brushes and . . . made to 'do' the bathroom first. This I did, ate a hasty lunch and ran all the way back to the Grammar School only to arrive five minutes late for the written French exam . . . I started writing furiously only to discover I still had paraffin on my hands, making a mess of the paper and had to go out under escort to wash them.³⁶¹

David Ogilvie was billeted with a young woman with a babe in arms and husband away at war; often she did not return home until after eleven p.m., leaving her two hungry evacuees to play football in the street until darkness fell.³⁶² On top of everything else, there was an outbreak of polio in 1942. Two boys were confined to an iron lung; there was one fatality and another boy was permanently affected. Since class sizes were quite small – around fifteen – pupils were able to maintain 'social distance'.³⁶³

Extra-curricular activities were organised for the evacuees. The Hackney Downs orchestra gave a concert in King's Lynn Town Hall, and the school choir found a new conductor in Frederick Bone, organist at nearby Sandringham parish church. A Hackney Downs performance of scenes from *A Midsummer Night's Dream* in 1940 triumphed in a contest for evacuated L.C.C. schools, the production owing much to the newly-appointed English teacher, Joseph Brearley, who left shortly afterwards to serve in the RAF.³⁶⁴ Although the cast consisted entirely of boys, the adjudicator inquired the gender of the cast.³⁶⁵ In 1941, some sixth-formers combined with boys from King Edward VII School to start a rhythm club, listening to jazz records and playing 'a few popular pieces'.³⁶⁶

Hackney Downs boys were not permitted to use the King Edward

---

360. 4 September 1941; HDS Archive.
361. William H. Greaves, TCL, February 2006, p. 122.
362. Wartime, p. 161. Ogilvie (1930–2011) later taught English at the school.
363. Tony Blackburn in Wartime, pp. 90, 149.
364. Brearley (1909–1977), a maverick Yorkshireman, was appointed Deputy Head in 1954. See his edited letters and journals: G. L. Watkins ed.: *Fortune's Fool: The Man Who Taught Harold Pinter*, Dinton: Twig Books, 2008; Joe Brearley: *Seen from the Wings: A Second World War Journal*. Dinton: Twig Books, 2010.
365. Review 153, Summer term 1940, p. 12.
366. *Review* 155, Autumn term 1941, p. 18.

VII School swimming pool,[367] but football and cricket continued. Fixtures were arranged in Wisbech, Spalding, Swaffham and Downham Market, followed by tea and cakes, though everyone had to be back in Lynn before black-out.[368] At first, the Hackney boys were not allowed to use the Grammar School cricket pitches:

> After an extensive search for more playing-fields, the Church Farm ground at South Wootton . . . was obtained for the seniors: the wickets . . . provided all the excitement and unexpected thrills of English village cricket . . . There were other features of village cricket, too: long grass and nettles in the outfield, a thorn hedge to worry the fielder whose job it was to seek the ball hit into the neighbouring orchard, clucking hens and an old white horse that used to remind the last-comer that he had omitted to fasten the crazy gate by wandering off into the lane that bordered our field to search for more tasty food. Later in the season the hens' habit of using the worn patches of the pitch as dust-baths made the wicket even more sporting.[369]

Senior boys organised Jewish Sabbath services and Hebrew lessons at St. James's School.[370] By 1943 these services had moved to the Friends' Meeting House, with numbers bolstered by American servicemen, who often came armed with Hershey bars and gum for distribution. The Headmaster attended Jewish festivals. Occasional Hebrew lessons were given by the peripatetic Rabbi Cohen, who covered large parts of Norfolk on an autocycle, and later by the stricter, bullying Mr. Levene.[371] His efforts to coach boys for Bar Mitzvah were supplemented by observant sixth-formers. There was even a Hanukkah party at Lynn's Pilot Cinema.[372]

During the first year of the war the fearfully anticipated air-raids on London failed to materialise and some evacuees drifted back to the capital.[373] To provide for these pupils, the L.C.C. opened 'emergency' sec-

---

367. Walker, op. cit., p. 82.
368. 'Mrs Buckley' by Ted Patten, 1 January 2018, HDS Archive.
369. J. E. Medcalf, Review 142, p. 15.
370. Two Hackney Downs boys invited a Hackney woman evacuated to King's Lynn to Passover seder, conducted by Rabbi Cohen. She was so impressed that she pledged to send her son to Grocers' after the war. Arnold Rosenbaum, TCL, February 2006, p. 3.
371. Wartime pp. 106, 147.
372. Lionel Lyons, 'Wartime Worship in King's Lynn', HDS Archive; Wartime p. 96.
373. On 13/14 October 1940, in one of the worst wartime incidents, 173 people were killed when a bomb fell on a block of flats known as Coronation Avenue, just off Stoke Newington Road. TCL, January 2001, p. 8.

ondary schools, for which seven Hackney Downs staff had to return to London to teach. Eventually German warplanes appeared over King's Lynn. On 30 June 1942, during public exams, King Edward VII School was hit by incendiary bombs. Most were extinguished, but fires broke out in the laboratories, where flammable materials were stored. When firemen failed to break the windows to douse the flames, the Hackney Downs biology teacher Adrian Gee blew out some glass with a borrowed shotgun. He spent the night in the police cells for the offence of 'discharging a firearm within 25 yards of a public highway'.[374] Although the bombing kept boys awake much of the night – some as firewatchers – next morning's exam started at the required time,[375] while boys uninvolved in exams helped salvage books and other materials. With the exams over, senior boys assisted on nearby farms, 'singling beet, weeding carrot, and ... pea-picking'.[376] Both staff and senior boys assisted in civil defence as Home Guards, Air-raid Wardens, first-aid workers and fire-watchers. When a King's Lynn Squadron of the Air Training Corps was formed in spring 1941, twenty Hackney Downs pupils joined, hoping to enlist in the RAF later. Others joined the Army Cadet Force, the old school battalion in new guise.

During the war, Mr Balk not only ensured evacuated pupils were safe and properly educated, and that arrangements back in Hackney ran as well as possible, he also corresponded with former pupils serving in the armed forces. He wrote several times to an alumnus serving in the air force,[377] and at least twice to a Regimental Signals Instructor at the Catterick School of Signals, describing other former pupils' activities in the armed forces and updating him on exam results.[378]

By the summer of 1943, the King's Lynn contingent numbered only 81 pupils, the rest having returned to London. Hackney Downs in exile now moved to the King's Lynn Technical School, in the town centre. One former pupil remembered hearing the deafening roar of Allied warplanes as they grouped over the Wash before thousand-bomber raids on Germany.[379] As in World War I, the school magazine listed the names of old boys serving in the forces, with a surprising amount of detail as to their activities and locations.

Hackney Downs pupils who returned to London were now attending

---

374. L.C.C. EO/PS/AEO, Ext. 271, 'Note for Mrs Townsend,' HDS Archive; TCL, May 2005, p. 6.
375. Wartime, p. 39.
376. Wartime, p. 40.
377. Stanley Quinn, 'My Years at the "Grocers'", 1994, p. 6; typescript in HDS Archive.
378. Jack Neale. Letters in HDS Archive: 27 October 1942, 14 May 1943.
379. Derek Sheinwald, Letter to Willie Watson, 22 Sept 2011, p. 2. HDS Archive; also Stanley Greenberg in Wartime, p. 110.

one of several emergency schools, including the North East London Emergency Secondary School, based at Parmiter's; the North London School, at William Ellis School, Gospel Oak; Raine's Foundation, Stepney;[380] and Highbury County Grammar School, Islington.[381] In March 1943, the L.C.C. restarted classes for Grocers' boys at the Hackney Downs premises – initially five forms with 135 boys and seven masters, and T. B. Barron, effectively Balk's deputy, as acting Head.[382] The returnees discovered, in the colourful description of one teacher:

> permanently blacked-out windows and flickering gas-lights in gloomy corridors, the swimming-bath a foul, crusted witches' caldron and the back playground a creditable imitation of Pompeii; a food-dump in the theatre and half the classrooms of the middle corridor . . . Little by little the playground was cleared of debris . . . Best of all, we found an admirable collection of boys; boys who had been evacuated and re-evacuated and bombed and bedevilled and consequently knew next to nothing, but boys who were delighted to be at last in a school of their own . . .[383]

A similar picture was painted by a pupil:

> In small classes with windows cross-taped against bomb-blast, we strained our eyes on winter afternoons under the yellow, incandescent gas-light. . . [W]e ploughed through the syllabus, interrupted now and again by the air raid siren, trooping down to the steel-beam reinforced basement rooms to listen to the throb of V1 buzz-bombs, counting when the engine spluttered and stopped overhead: nine, ten, then thump and the ground shaking, and knowing that one had missed us. . .[384]

Plans had been made for all Hackney Downs pupils to return for the start of autumn term 1944, but that summer the much-feared V1 'doodlebug' attacks on London began and many parents despatched their sons back to King's Lynn for safety. In Hackney, the art-master had his

---

380. Closed in 2020.
381. Closed in 1967.
382. Barron suffered chest and respiratory problems caused by poison gas in World War I, as a result of which he spoke in a high-pitched voice. Leonard Elmer, HDS 1935–40, 'Memories', HDS Archive.
383. J. E. Medcalf, Review 158, Autumn term 1944, pp. 5–7.
384. David Merron (Malina), pupil 1942–1949. October 1999, TCL p. 7. Merron published a memoir of his primary school years and wartime evacuation: *Goodbye East End: An Evacuee's Story*. London: Corgi, 2015.

class practise diving under their desks when there was warning of a V1 raid.[385] Harold Pinter, initially evacuated to 'a castle in Cornwall', spent only a short time in King's Lynn, and that during a school holiday.[386] Underlining the perils of wartime London, he reported:

> On the day I got back to London, in 1944, I saw the first flying bomb [V1]. I was in the street and I saw it come over . . . There were times when I could open our back door and find our garden in flames. Our house never burned, but we had to evacuate several times . . .[387]

In his end-of-term letter to parents the following December, Balk asked parents to minimize movement of boys between London and King's Lynn, to avoid unnecessary organisational problems and the interruption of their sons' education.[388] In January 1945, a V2 rocket fell on Hackney Downs park, immediately north of Grocers', leaving the top floor of the school in ruins, the gym roofless and windows smashed.

On the evening of 8 May 1945, pupils playing cricket at King Edward School were interrupted by Balk running onto the field, academic gown flying. He threw his hat in the air and cried, 'Boys – the war is over! We can all go home.'[389] On departing King's Lynn, Balk paid polite tribute to the 'very pleasant connection' with the Headmaster and staff of King Edward VII School 'in the difficult and harassing days of evacuation'. Yet evacuation caused a great deal of upheaval and confusion. Most boys' billets were satisfactory, many very good, but social and class antagonism inevitably arose between the country-dwellers and the boys from working-class London homes. Many pupils thrived in the novel environment and some made lasting local friendships, but others experienced bewilderment and distress. In an interview in *Lynn News*, Balk claimed King's Lynn had not cooperated as helpfully as the villagers of Upwell, and described this as 'unsettling' for some boys.[390] There had been considerable antagonism between Hackney pupils and

---

385. Letter to Willie Watson, 16 November 2014, HDS Archive.
386. William Baker implies mistakenly that Pinter went to 'rural Norfolk' alone with a schoolmaster. William Baker: *A Harold Pinter Chronology*. Basingstoke: Palgrave Macmillan 2013, p. 2.
387. Interview in *The New Yorker*, 25 February 1967. It is doubtful that this was literally 'the first flying bomb'.
388. 7 December 1944; HDS Archive.
389. Les Bentley. At the age of six, Bentley (née Bernstein) had been evacuated from Sigdon Road School, Hackney, to Clenchwarton, a village three miles west of King's Lynn, entering Hackney Downs in exile when he was eleven. Henry Grinberg claimed that on the same date, at the end of sports day, Balk announced solemnly 'Tomorrow is VD Day', hastily correcting himself, 'I should say, VE Day.' Wartime, pp. 70, 116.
390. See Wartime.

those of the King Edward VII School. One Hackney boy recalled:
> The pupils of one school had a generalised dislike of the pupils of the other. Fraternisation was minimal: indeed I cannot recall a single joint enterprise or (for my own part) any exchange of words with any member of the other school.[391]

Another boy recalled the shock of encountering a Black US serviceman for the first time:
> I had never before seen a black person and was struck dumb with fear. My only knowledge of black men came from films and comic strips, where they were pictured as brutal savages, whose principal object in life was to capture white people and boil them in a cooking pot for their dinner. I'm afraid I turned and ran away.[392]

There was a 'half-seen sense of families being torn apart and rebuilt'.[393] Yet one of those who went to Lynn reckoned:
> The evacuated boys of Hackney Downs were better bonded at King's Lynn than we might have been at home in London, for here in Norfolk it was akin to a boarding school existence with our leisure activity close at hand...[394]

With almost all masters and boys living within roughly one mile of King's Lynn town centre, boundaries between teachers and taught were much lower than usual, with frequent informal contact outside the classroom. Some members of staff took boys into their own homes. One pupil recalled that, when – just before his exams – he heard his mother had died back in London, his maths teacher gave him extra tuition at his home on Saturday mornings, resulting in a distinction in his exam.[395]

For the duration of the war, the school had a double identity: King's Lynn and London. Some boys who started at the school in 1939 or 1940 completed their five-year School Certificate course without having entered

---

391. Arnold Allen, CBE (pupil 1932–1942), first Chairman of the UK Atomic Energy Authority. Wartime, p. 54.
392. Roy Barnes, who spent 1943–45 at HDS Kings Lynn. Barnes recalled the English teaching of Stanley Day as a significant influence: '[His] lessons were an exploration of language, philosophy, religion, politics, literature – life itself in short – for which language is a vehicle'. When Barnes' mother decided she should move back from Lynn to South London, Mr. Balk offered to accommodate her son at his own house at no cost to the family, an offer she turned down. Wartime, pp. 64–66.
393. John Kemp, in a letter to Willie Watkins, 17 March 2004, HDS Archive.
394. Ronald Harris, in Wartime, p. 124.
395. Tony Blackburn, in Wartime, p. 93.

a Hackney classroom, while a number of pupils evacuated to King's Lynn from other parts of London were enrolled at Hackney Downs School and became 'Grocers' boys' purely through the accidents of war. Among these was Southwark-born Maurice Micklewhite (Sir Michael Caine, b. 1933), who spent a year at Grocers' School, King's Lynn, before returning to his native south London.[396] By autumn 1945, just four boys on the roll had known pre-war Hackney Downs.

At the end of the summer term 1945, after almost six years' absence, the last batch of pupils returned to London. They discovered:

> ... a desolate scene. The top floor of the school was in ruin; sparrows twittered in the tower and winds blew unchecked through roofless gym and windowless lodge; as the staff sat in conclave before school the ceiling of the class-room above crashed down ... The ground floor alone, newly painted and redecorated, was better than before, but it was filled with bunks and Rest Centre functionaries ...[397]

The premises had been hastily patched up; but with the ground floor still in use as a Rest Centre, boys were unable to have lunch on the premises, and swimming was ruled out because the pool had been requisitioned as an emergency water-supply for fire-fighters.

One former pupil reported that Joseph Brearley called boys who joined the school during the war, experienced evacuation and the Blitz the 'shook up' intake: 'Never was another year like you lot.'[398] Some boys who spent most the war in Norfolk were loath to return home. Les Bentley, who had been away for six years, and saw his mother just three times and his father once during that time, grew to love his foster family and wanted to remain with them on their farm. When he arrived back at London's Liverpool Street Station, his mother took him to a Stoke Newington delicatessen for lunch; unused to Jewish food, he pushed away the chopped liver. So unhappy was he in London that he packed a suitcase, secretly took a train to King's Lynn and returned to his foster family's home, only to be dispatched back to London.[399]

On 20 September 1945, at the first assembly back in Hackney, the

---

396. A blue plaque on the wall of North Runcton Village Hall, where he played Baron Fitznoodle in the school's pantomime, *Cinderella* – 'his first stage appearance' – marks Caine's connection. Caine's publicist, Jerry Pam, six years his senior, was another Old Grocer. (TCL, March 2009, p. 16.) Micklewright was dubbed 'Milkbottle' by a P.E. master, for his pale complexion. Wartime p. 69.
397. Wartime, p. 212.
398. David Merron (Malina), pupil between 1942 and 1949. October 1999, TCL, p. 7.
399. Wartime pp. 70–72. This was just the first of Bentley's three attempts to return to Norfolk.

During World War II, the school grounds were used to store materials salvaged from bomb-damaged buildings.

school paid silent tribute to the former pupils – 64 servicemen and three civilians – who had fallen during the war. Although the war years had been very testing, with pupils and teachers scattered to various locations, a corporate identity was soon re-established. With the passing of the 1944 Education Act, Hackney Downs now operated as a grammar school, with no pupil paying fees. The newly reunited school numbered 530 boys: 110 from King's Lynn, 260 from war-time classes in Hackney, 60 from other secondary schools and 100 newcomers selected by success in the L.C.C. '11-plus' entrance exam. Until 1939, the school had continued to offer a preparatory department, but after 1945 all boys entered the first form at the age of eleven and proceeded at least to the fifth form – School Certificate year – though some left on turning fifteen, before sitting the exams.

The returning school faced a multitude of problems both of accommodation and personnel. The building's poor state of repair prompted the Governors to protest to the L.C.C.; as a result the school was redecorated for the first time since 1926 and essential repairs were put in hand. The back playground, utilised during the war to store materials salvaged from bombed houses, was cleared of debris and resurfaced. The Victorian system of gas-lighting was at last replaced with electric lights, and electrically-operated bells now rang to mark the beginning and end of lessons.

In February 1946, the school Governors registered 'alarm' at the 'high average age of the staff,' urging that, where possible, new appointments should be of men below the age of 30. They were also concerned that many experienced masters were being seconded as instructors for the Emergency Training College scheme, set up to meet the urgent call for qualified teachers.[400] Additionally, a German teacher was appointed to the Control Commission in Germany, and the senior history master transferred to the Ministry of Education. Many senior teachers had retired during the war, and of the younger masters on active service only one – Joseph Brearley – returned permanently to the school, having contracted malaria in North Africa.[401] The music master Philip Henry, on the staff since 1905, retired in 1946, as did T. B. Barron in 1949. Just eight members of staff remained from 1936, 'loyal, experienced, and faithful guardians of tradition'.[402] Capable replacements included Cyril 'Kit' Corner, who taught French.[403] A pupil from this period reported:

> Some of the teachers believed in education in the period after the war as part of regeneration. I cannot imagine . . . that they voted for a Conservative Party. I think most of them were either fairly pink or left-wing.[404]

At a 1946 Governors' meeting, the Head reported the continuing unsatisfactory physical condition of the school buildings:

> ... In some rooms reading and writing were difficult and at times impossible on foggy days ... The natural light in the classrooms was rendered unsatisfactory, except in bright weather, through the high setting of the windows ... and by the failure to reglaze the many windows which were filled with strawboard, substitute glass or linen. 1,403 panes needed reglazing. In high winds the considerable interruption by noise was increased in consequence; in cold weather the

---

400. Governors' Minute Book LMA EO/PS/4/35 f. 90, 16 October 1946.
401. For the next thirty years 'Joe' Brearley was to play a significant role in the life of the school. A Cambridge English graduate, originally from Yorkshire, he was a multi-talented yet restless and disturbed figure who had no time for half-measures. He spoke excellent German and in the pre-war years spent several vacations in Germany, tutoring the children of wealthy, Nazi-supporting families. He also flirted with the Communist Party. Brearley had been taught at Cambridge by F. R. Leavis and I. A. Richards, who 'transformed the young subject of English from a marginal academic discipline into one with a unique aura of excitement, contemporaneity and relevance' Ian Smith: *Pinter in the Theatre*. London: Nick Hern, 2005, p. 15.
402. Report by HMI on London County Council Hackney Downs School. London: HMSO, 1951.
403. Corner (1917–1964) was a graduate of Reading University and the University of Lyons, and served in Burma during World War II.
404. Raoul Sobel. BL oral history: 9b. 19330/John Hardcastle.

temperature of the rooms was necessarily lowered. The gloom in the classroom and the corridors was accentuated by the poor state of decoration. All these factors could not fail to have a depressing effect on staff and boys.[405]

Even after repairs, redecoration and the installation of electric lighting, at Speech Day 1947, the Chairman of Governors could still complain of the 'difficult conditions and limitations caused by the out-dated nature of the School Building'.[406]

Since clothing remained subject to rationing, at this date only a minimal uniform was required, consisting of school cap and tie; the blazer, sportswear and other items of clothing returned in due course. Although the intention was to establish uniformity of dress, differences in the quality and condition of clothing, and extras such as expensive sports gear and overseas visits, could accentuate the divide between the better off and the rest. Evidence of food shortages, even five years after the end of hostilities, is apparent in Balk's note in 1950 that a gift of thirteen cases of apples had been distributed to the pupils, apportioned three apples each.[407]

Many pupils were aware of the events later known as 'the Holocaust'. Some time after VE Day, but before the final return of HDS pupils to Hackney, Henry Grinberg, Henry Woolf and some other boys in Norfolk encountered a group of German prisoners-of war. Grinberg wrote:

> My heart burned with hatred at the sight of them, looking so tanned and healthy from whatever work they had been doing . . . News had been reaching us of mass murders and of the human wreckage discovered in the concentration camps.[408]

The menace of these years is evident in Harold Pinter's plays: he and his group of close friends were aware of the terrors of the Holocaust and the existential threat of the atomic bomb. He wrote: 'It was partly the camps – we were hearing things before ever the government let on.' Boys were all too aware of Hiroshima and Nagasaki.

> And our minds were attuned to horror however much we larked about… Every other day it seemed ghastly new details of the Nazi massacres in the East were being released.[409]

405. LMA EO/PS/4/35 f. 80, 28 February 1946.
406. Review 163, Autumn term 1947, p. 12.
407. School Record, 31 March 1950: HDS Archive.
408. Wartime, p. 117.
409. Henry Woolf, *Barcelona is in Trouble*. Saskatoon: Comet Press, 2017, p. 54.

Closer to home were Mosleyite rallies in Ridley Road, Dalston.

Yet neither the war nor post-war readjustment harmed the school's academic standards: Balk's headship became rich in achievement. One former pupil[410] suggested that for the generation who were at the school during World War II, and who perhaps had to grow up faster than others, relief that the worst hardships and anxieties of the war years were over resulted in a particularly mature and positive response. A fellow pupil recalled that history teachers encouraged class discussion, relating nineteenth-century history to contemporary politics.[411] Another reported, 'We were expected to read widely and constantly – and we did – and when we were not reading, we were expected to be thinking and writing about what we had read'.[412] A peer who was 'critical and rude' at school and negative about much of the teaching, excepted the history teacher, Hooten:

> for whom I wrote 50+ page essays [which] he read and corrected... with witty, apt comments. He treated us like equals and was always available... Most of the rest [of the teachers] can be epitomized by the punishments meted out to Harold Pinter for writing poems and plays in class instead of parroting the teachings of the masters. Nobody asked to see them; we were not supposed to be creative but to perpetuate a dull system.

The same pupil wrote:

> We were all normal, healthy, talented teenagers forced by family circumstances to lead somewhat... austere lives. We had the threat of National Service ahead if we failed [i.e. if they did not gain a university place]. We could not afford to indulge in the youth scene... Our lives were centred around HDS, public libraries and talking things out together.[413]

A glimpse of the school's cultural milieu is afforded by the programme for a symposium on 'Women' conducted by the Senior Debating Society, 3 February 1949:

> Mr Peston:[414] An extract from Schopenhauer's 'Essay on Woman'
> Mr Lefcovitch: Two poems by Elizabeth Browning

410. Harvey Monte, oral recording by John Hardcastle, BL.
411. Harvey Monte/John Hardcastle, BL Recording.
412. Henry Grinberg, 'Pinter at School' in *The Pinter Review: Collected Essays, 1999 and 2000.* Ed. Francis Gillen and Steven H. Gale. Tampa: Tampa University Press, 2000, p. 3.
413. Gerald E. Caiden, 'At Hackney Downs School', pp. 5, 6.
414. Baron Peston of Mile End.

The school prefects, 1947. *Back row, third from right*, Harold Pinter; *third row back, fourth from left*, Maurice Peston; *front row, third from left*, Barry Supple; *fourth from left*, David Ogilvie.

    Mr Ingram: An extract from *Antony and Cleopatra*
    Mr Malina: Three poems by Thomas More
    Mr Schwartz: A Shakespearean sonnet
    Mr Wernick: An extract from Hardy's *Return of the Native*
    Mr Gale: Extract from Tennyson's 'Lady of Shalott'
    Mr Cummins: 'Doris' by Congreve
    Mr de Groot: 'The Female of the Species' by Kipling
    Mr Hooten:[415] Extract from *Pride and Prejudice*
    A quotation from Burton's *Anatomy of Melancholy*, suggested by Mr Medcalf[416]
    Mr Bagul: 'The Prioress' from The Prologue to Chaucer's *Canterbury Tales*
    Mr Law: Wordsworth's 'Three years she grew in sun and shower'
    Mr Supple:[417] Extracts from the *4th Book of Artemas*[418] and James Joyce's *A Portrait of the Artist as a Young Man*
    Mr Rubins: 'Poor but Honest' (author doubtful)

415. History teacher.
416. English teacher.
417. Barry Supple, CBE, FBA.
418. Arthur Telford Mason: *The Book of Artemas Concerning Men and the Things That Men Did Do, At the Time When There Was War* (1917). A satirical view of World War I, written in the style of the King James Version of the Bible.

Mr Hinton: A Shakespeare sonnet
Mr Goldmann: One poem by Byron[419]

A sophisticated cultural diet.[420] Yet, despite such enthusiastic pupils and academic success, a conservative teacher, such as the Head of English, James Medcalf, could write: 'The general standard is lamentably poor: [boys] come from bookless and uncultured homes.'[421]

A piece in the school magazine titled 'Memories of the Tower' conjures up the atmosphere in VI Arts:

> The action takes place in the Tower [the sixth form common room] (which is as noisy as its namesake of Babel) at midnight on a moonlit night. Stanley Harris,[422] in the costume of a ballet dancer, pirouettes gracefully around the room, while his boon companion, 'Dusty' Miller, rummages through the desks and pours ink over all the exercise books. (The reason for this apparent anarchy is that Miller has the reputation of being the only person to obtain Higher School Certificate without doing a stroke of work.) Meanwhile the somnambulant Law bites his nails fastidiously while discussing logical positivism with Geoffrey Arden. In one corner, Harold Pinter is slowly but surely strangling Zwalf, and in another, the god-like Percival is attempting to write poetry, while Henry Woolf[423] whispers witty remarks in his ear. Wernick leans against the window and looks around calmly with a certain 'disinterested curiosity.' At this point John Hubbard enters, is terrified by the bizarre spectacle, and flees into the arms of the on-coming Pugh. Pugh's only reaction is to smile... The substantial figure of Pugh is closely followed by the wraith-like apparition of Henry Grinberg,[424] the famous actor, mystic and literary and musical genius. Unfortunately, Percival does not appreciate this genius, so he promptly sits on the amiable Henry.[425]

---

419. Gerald Caiden, manuscript in HDS archive.
420. A group of six boys, led by Harold Pinter, and later dubbed 'Harold's Gang', argued endlessly, 'quoting plays, poems and novels . . . Samuel Beckett, Henry Miller, John Dos Passos . . . avant-garde films: *Un Chien Andalou, L'Age d'Or, Le Sang d'un Poète* . . .' Henry Woolf, TCL, December 2007, p. 34; Grinberg: 'Pinter at School', pp. 1–4.
421. *English Teachers in a postwar democracy*, p. 58.
422. Dale Harris, later a leading New York ballet critic.
423. Actor and theatre director (1930–2021).
424. Psychoanalyst and author.
425. M. J. Lefford, Review, September 1950, 169, p. 33.

It was in the 1940s and 1950s that the proportion of Jewish boys in the school reached its peak. Barry Supple illustrates this humorously: after the school football team had been soundly beaten a friend suggested 'there's enough of us here for a minyan' – the minimum number (ten) of Jewish men for a legitimate religious ceremony. Many of the Jewish boys' fathers worked in traditional trades, such as tailoring, shopkeeping, the furniture trade and taxi-driving. Politically, most of these boys leaned to the left – to the Communist Party, the Trades Union and the Labour Party – and debated politics endlessly. Supple claims this strong Jewish presence

> did not in any significant way affect relationships within the school, and most school-based friendships were established without serious reference to religion or cultural background. However . . . my out-of-school, home-based, friendships were with Jewish boys.

At the same time, he noted:

> most Jewish boys seemed to me singularly restless with their religion: unobservant and ill-disciplined with the poor souls who were imported to give [Jewish] religious instruction. [426]

His contemporary Harold Pinter recalled:

> There was a tremendous cross-current of people. I cannot remember any problems arising at the school. . . . There was a group of five of us, two non-Jews and three Jews. We used to hang around together and talk about this, that and the other . . . [427]

Another pupil of the post-war period, David Merron, recalled his commitment to left-wing politics and Zionism:

> We'd been . . . shocked by the revelations of Belsen and Auschwitz. Politically, having started from the viewpoint of the then '*Statesman & Nation*',[428] we'd moved further to the left, our perceptions sharpened by the street fights with Mosley's fascists in nearby Ridley Road... [I]n the late '40's, the machinations of the British mandate to prevent the remnants of the holocaust from reaching Palestine, followed by the creation of the State of Israel

---

426. Barry Supple: *Doors Open*. Asher, 2008, p. 93.
427. Often known as 'Harold's gang'. From interview with Barry Davis in Mark Batty: *About Pinter: The Playwright and the Work*. London: Faber and Faber, 2005, p. 99.
428. Now *The New Statesman*.

> in 1948, had awakened strong feelings of Jewish identity. Along with many young Jews... I found a social and ideological home in Zionist youth movements, in our case the Hashomer Hatzair group... [E]nthused by the spirit of the young state and especially of the kibbutzim, we... abandoned out studies and [came] out to join the kibbutz.[429]

The use of corporal punishment at the school continued, though probably with less frequency. Unlike his two immediate predecessors, Balk seems not to have been feared by pupils; sometimes a boy sent to the Head for punishment received a lecture or discussion about their behaviour rather than the anticipated beating. Pinter called out the violence used by one notoriously sadistic teacher, telling Balk he would no longer attend his classes. However tales of blackboard-duster missiles and random assaults with wooden rulers, fingers and fists continue into the headships of Barkway Pye and Williams. One science master, recorded as having repeatedly assaulted boys, on one occasion ordered a pupil to remove his spectacles before repeatedly slapping his head on both sides.[430]

As teaching returned to normal, school clubs and societies began to reappear, with several new groups, such as the Junior and Senior Literary and Debating societies, the latter holding joint meetings with local girls' schools. In 1947, a Jewish Youth Study Group was inaugurated.[431] Cultural life also experienced a renaissance. The Music Society organized lunch-time gramophone record sessions and the school orchestra was re-formed. An Opera-Going Society was founded, with the L.C.C. subsidizing opera tickets at Sadler's Wells. A pupil from this period remembered trips to the Old Vic to see Laurence Olivier in Sheridan's *School for Scandal* and Robert Eddison as Hamlet.[432] A Chess Club, set up in 1947, was affiliated to the London Secondary Schools' Chess League. A Hobbies Club for wood- and metal-work was formed in 1947; an Art Club in 1948; and a Photographic Society and Stamp Club in 1949. A branch of the Council for Education in World Citizenship was launched, where social and political issues were discussed. 1949 also saw the school's first post-war foreign trip – to Switzerland – while

---

429. David Merron: *Collectively Yours: Tales from the Borderline*. Bakewell: Country Books, 1999, p. 38.
430. Brian Gable, Letter in HDS Archive, 2 February 2004.
431. The school produced a number of Jewish ministers, including Dr David Goldstein, associate minister at the Liberal Jewish Synagogue, St John's Wood (1964–1975); Douglas Charing, who founded the Jewish Education Bureau; and Ivan Binstock, in 2022 Rabbi of St John's Wood Synagogue, London.
432. Ian Juniper in TCL , Vol. 9 No. 3, September 2020, p. 13.

Harold Pinter in Joseph Brearley's school production of *Macbeth*, 1947.

in summer 1951 Cyril Corner led the first of many annual school visits to St. Malo, Brittany.

School drama began to build an impressive record of achievement. Joseph Brearley revived school productions in 1947 with *Macbeth*, staged at Dalston County girls' school, in what Barry Supple describes as 'one of the most famous school plays in the history of British state education'.[433] The play was performed in modern costume, the soldiers in cadet-force uniforms, necessitated by the persistence of clothes rationing. The lead role, as in *Romeo and Juliet* the following year, was taken by the future playwright Harold Pinter.[434] Brearley persuaded Alan Dent, critic of the *News Chronicle*, to review *Macbeth*:

> Master Harold Pinter made a more eloquent, more
> obviously nerve-wracked Macbeth than one or two

---

433. *Doors Open*, pp. 102, 116.
434. *The New Yorker*, 25 February 1967, p. 35. For reasons that are unclear, but possibly envy, the following year Brearley vetoed a suggested production of *Hamlet*, with Pinter in the name role. When, in 1949, Pinter refused military service as a conscientious objector, it was to Brearley that his parents turned for counsel. (Michael Billington: *Harold Pinter*. London: Faber, 1996, pp. 11, 13, 22.) Brearley and Pinter reconnected as the latter began his career as a playwright, enjoying a close friendship until Brearley's death. Another professional actor and director, Henry Woolf – First Apparition in *Macbeth* – a close friend at school, commissioned and directed Pinter's first play, *The Room,* in 1957. ('My 60 years in Harold's gang,' *Guardian*, 12 July 2007, G2 section, p. 23.) William Baker: *A Harold Pinter Chronology*. Basingstoke: Palgrave Macmillan 2013 p. 19 passim.

professional grown-ups I have seen in the part of late years.[435]

In the immediate post-war period, school sport prospered. During the war, each year-group had games scheduled on a set afternoon each week, an arrangement continued after 1945. Rowing and badminton clubs were restarted, whilst the foundations were laid for the school's outstanding athletic achievement, largely through the efforts of Leslie Mitchell (1914–2000), who joined the school staff from the army in 1948. Until now the Annual School Sports Day at the school field had been a largely social event, where

> the great and the good gathered in a marquee to partake of refreshments: Mitchell revolutionized school athletics, introducing training, necessary equipment and a professional ethic that concentrated on results.[436]

The charismatic Welshman appears to have been able to discover talent for a particular athletic discipline in unexpected pupils.

The school's swimming pool was not brought back into use until 1951, by which time new changing-rooms and showers had been added. Mitchell decreed that swimming should be 'bollock-naked'[437] – ostensibly because the pool's filtration system was apt to become clogged with fibres from swimming costumes. Nude swimming continued well into the 1960s. Headmaster Balk helped found the North London Grammar Schools' Swimming Association and, in 1949, the North London Grammar Schools' Athletic Association. In 1952 the school magazine reported 'for the last four years the School has walked away with the Grand Challenge Shield of the N.L.G.S.A.A. Championships'.[438] An outstanding athlete was Commonwealth and Olympic Games hurdler Harry Kane, a pupil between 1946 and 1949.

In 1948, Mitchell was asked to start a school Combined Cadet Force (CCF). Initially First 'E' Company, 10th County of London Cadet Battalion, affiliated to the Royal Berkshire Regiment, the Hackney Downs CCF later became an independent unit attached to the same regiment,[439] at its height numbering more than 100 members. During the period of compulsory National Service, possession of War Certificate 'A' offered an easier passage into, and rapid promotion within, the army, so 'Mitchell's Army', with its annual camps and lively social events, enjoyed

435. Billington p. 14.
436. David Ogilvie. TCL, January 2001, p. 9.
437. David Ogilvie's term. TCL, January 2001, p. 9. Teachers too swam naked. Derek Evans, pupil, 1946–1953, 'Recollections from HDS', HDS Archive.
438. Review, 1952.
439. Melvyn Brooks, letter to Col. Digby Thompson, 23 November 1999: HDS Archive.

considerable popularity. The force was disbanded in 1963, in line with government policy. Mitchell also encouraged and expanded boxing – a sport dropped soon after Alec Williams became Headmaster. Like many other teachers, Mitchell was remembered for his personal care: a former pupil recalled the support he received from him when his mother was hospitalized for months.[440]

Balk's headmastership spanned a significant period of transition in English education. The 1944 Education Act replaced the Board of Education with the Ministry of Education, and empowered the Minister to ensure that local authorities adhered to national policy. Elementary education was abolished, replaced by a national two-tier system consisting of primary and secondary education. From 1 April 1945, fees were abolished in all maintained secondary schools, after which Hackney Downs had no fee-paying pupils. Nor did the Headmaster any longer have the authority to select boys solely on the basis of his personal assessment.[441] It had been mainly fee-paying pupils who left early; nationally, the end of fee-paying helped improve academic standards, reduce early leaving and increase the size of sixth forms.[442] In 1947, the school leaving-age in England was raised to fifteen. In 1951, General and Higher School Certificate exams were replaced by the General Certificate of Education, taken at three levels: Ordinary, Advanced and Scholarship. No longer was it necessary to pass a minimum number of subjects simultaneously to gain a certificate. It was now assumed Hackney Downs – a selective grammar school – would aim to prepare boys for continuing study at university or for entry into a profession. In 1952 six pupils were awarded State Scholarships, which paid their university fees.[443]

During this period, education was under wide-ranging discussion nationally and locally. Educational psychologists and teachers were starting to question the validity of the 11-plus exam, which decided a child's future at an early age. Children who 'passed' the 11-plus moved on to grammar school; the rest – often regarded as 'failures' – moved on to a secondary modem school, generally seen by parents, teachers and pupils as inferior. Demand was building to replace the three existing levels of education – grammar, technical or central, and secondary

440. Laurence Field, letter to Willie Watkins, 2 September 1996; HDS Archive.
441. However, successive Heads of Hackney Downs continued to interview applicants. The school was, and remained, oversubscribed, and an interview formed part of the entry process.
442. Maclure, p. 171.
443. Before 1945, there was no entitlement to free university education, though an aspiring student who did not win a State Scholarship might obtain one of a limited number of discretionary awards from their county council.

modern – with multilateral, or 'comprehensive', secondary schools, catering for all types of education, to avoid the socially-divisive effects of the three-level system. There were linked moves to replace single-sex schools with coeducational establishments. Conservatives tended to support the existing system, while the Labour Party, which at this period controlled the L.C.C., backed the comprehensive proposals.

In 1944, with flying-bombs still falling on London, the L.C.C. Education Committee approved plans that included

> a system of comprehensive high schools throughout
> the County of London providing for all pupils equal
> opportunity for physical, intellectual, social and spiritual
> development . . . '.[444]

In June 1945, almost as soon as the war in Europe ended, the L.C.C. formulated secret proposals for a comprehensive high school in the Hackney and Stoke Newington area. They planned to build a new school north of Hackney Downs to accommodate 1,000 boys and 1,000 girls, federated with Hackney Downs and Dalston County schools – each comprising 500 pupils – to create two schools of 1,500, one for boys and one for girls, with mixed classes in some subjects.[445] Hackney Downs' Governors responded defensively, requesting a separate boys' section, the retention of the name 'Hackney Downs School', and that the school should remain on the existing site and retain its own Headteacher.[446]

Hackney Downs presented a particular problem for the L.C.C. The 1944 Education Act provided that:

> . . . secondary schools maintained by a local education
> authority . . . shall, if established by a local educational
> authority. . . be known as county schools and, if
> established otherwise than by such an authority, be
> known as voluntary schools.[447]

Hackney Downs had been established before the L.C.C. was set up, and so was deemed a voluntary school. Such schools 'could not, even if the governors were willing, be converted into comprehensive high schools'.[448] However the school's status was now altered. Although in 1905 the Grocers' Company had gifted the school to the L.C.C., the

---

444. Maclure p. 133.
445. It was probably on the basis of this plan that in 1950 the L.C.C. sought information about a bombed site in Downs Park Road, the road on which Hackney Downs School was situated, though it was deemed unusable.
446. LMA EO/PS/4/35 f. 72, 14 June 1945.
447. Clause 9.
448. London School Plan, February 1947, p. 13.

council was only its trustee; it did not 'own' the school. Any change in the school's status required the written agreement of its Governors.[449] In 1951, anticipating implementation of the London School Plan, the Governors of Hackney Downs agreed the school should be maintained as a 'county school', removing any obstacle to transforming it into a comprehensive.[450] There was controversy over this, and the agreement was later portrayed by some as a 'betrayal'. However Dr. Homa, Chairman of Governors, presented a clear argument in response to a diatribe from the journalist C. H. Rolph, accusing the L.C.C. of forcing the governors to dig 'their own graves' by changing their school's status to that of a County School.[451] Homa wrote:

> The School, which was established by the Grocers' Company in 1876, was handed over for complete maintenance to the L.C.C. in 1906 and it has since been regarded and treated as a County School... [T]he L.C.C. obtained nothing but a building from the Grocers' Company; there were no endowments or other privileges...
>
> When the question of the status of the School arose last summer, the Governors adjourned consideration in order to be more fully informed... It was obvious that we had been functioning as a County School for over 44 years... It was also quite clear to us that to maintain the fiction permitted by the Education Act of 1944 that we were a 'voluntary school' would confer no advantage on anybody. We had no 'voluntary' benefactors to whom to turn. We should still have to rely entirely on the L.C.C. for our existence. On the other hand, this 'voluntary school' status could bring about some disadvantages – it would serve to impede the plans of the Council as the Education Authority for London, and, more important still, it would immediately limit our scope of development. It was no use pretending that we were on a par with Oundle, which was still being

---

449. In 1925 the Governors' permission had been obtained to alter the fees charged to pupils. A handwritten Board of Education minute, 12 January 1923, explained the L.C.C. could not make such amendments without the agreement of the school governors. This document was signed on behalf of the governors by the chairman, Henrietta Adler.
450. The governors of St. Marylebone and George Green schools – both in a similar position to Hackney Downs – refused to become county schools, a decision accepted by the L.C.C. (LMA: ILEA/S/SB/23/02/ 107 & 108). See also a letter from D. Mackinnon Wood, chairman of the L.C.C. Education Committee, in *The Times,* 20 March 1951.
451. In a letter to the *The New Statesman and Nation,* March 17 1951, p. 295.

> maintained by the Grocers' Company. We therefore
> took a realistic view and, deciding to 'call a spade a
> spade', we agreed that the L.C.C. (the legal Trustees of
> the School) should ask the Minister for permission to
> maintain the School as a County School.[452]

In 1951, Labour lost control of the L.C.C. Under the Conservatives, the future of Hackney Downs as a grammar school appeared secure. At the Clove Annual Dinner in 1952, Balk attempted to reassure former pupils, claiming that, though the school

> had now been given the status of a County School by the
> London County Council and could conceivably, therefore,
> be absorbed into a comprehensive school, the Governors
> had been assured that in this eventuality and when the
> School was rebuilt the Grammar School building would
> be erected on the same site as at present.[453]

A new scheme of governance for the school, replacing that agreed in 1906, received government approval on 29 January 1954. However, this controversy was not over.

In 1951, the first school inspection in 19 years took place. There were now 507 boys enrolled; in 1932 there had been 645, though this included 77 boys in the preparatory forms, which no longer existed. Half the pupils were withdrawn from Religious Instruction for Jewish teaching. About 25 peercent of boys entered the sixth form; roughly 16 percent of the boys who had left in the previous three years entered university before or after national service. Once more the English inspector criticised boys' London accents, judging their reading to be 'marred by an uncouthness of utterance which has survived longer than was necessary'. The history inspector noted 'the steadily increasing time allowance' given to Civics which

> seems well calculated to suit the early awareness of
> public affairs which is characteristic of this School where
> fourth and fifth year boys seem to be interested in recent
> political history in a way which is certainly not common.

The inspectors' report concluded:

> The School presents the picture of a well-ordered
> and purposeful community, worthily playing an
> indispensable part in the education of North East
> London. It has successfully weathered the many

---

452. *New Statesman*, March 24 1951, p. 343.
453. *The Clove Review*, Spring 1952, No. 2, p. 17.

difficulties of the war and of the years that followed.[454]

Thomas Balk retired in 1952, aged 62, following 17 tumultuous years as Headmaster. He postponed his retirement for a year to see the wartime group of pupils through their entire seven years at Hackney Downs.[455] He successfully steered the school through the war years and reconstruction that followed, which called for thoughtful leadership, self-confidence and an ability to inspire staff and pupils. Balk exhibited devotion to the school and its pupils, a love of learning, an ability to mix easily with all sorts of people and huge reserves of energy. A former pupil described him as:

> A stern but very fair head [who] as we progressed
> through the school we grew to admire for his love for the
> school and his very real interest in the welfare of current
> pupils and old boys . . . He exerted a considerable in-
> fluence in maintaining the high scholastic and sporting
> success of the school . . .[456]

Another claimed Balk once asserted: 'My job is to send the sons of taxi drivers to university.'[457] This Headmaster's concern for his pupils is aptly conveyed in his reply to a boy who sent him news of his 'A' level success after he retired:

> . . . you have done well & have justified the confidence
> that I had in you . . . I am glad to have your thanks:
> these from a pupil with whom relations have been
> always so friendly and easy make one of the pleasantest
> memories of my headmastership at HDS . . . [458]

When a pupil sent from the classroom by a bullying master was asked by Balk why he was in pain, the Headmaster revealed he shared the boy's tendency to migraines, which freed the pupil to voice other frustrations and, with the head's encouragement, to enjoy a more positive experience in the sixth form.[459] Another former pupil similarly found Balk approachable: having entered the Science Sixth under parental pressure and despite poor science exam results, the boy asked Balk if he could move to the Arts Sixth, to which the Head agreed.[460]

454. Report of HM Inspectors on L.C.C. Hackney Downs School, 29 May–1 June 1951, pp. 2, 6, 7, 16.
455. Harvey Monte/John Hardcastle BL Recording.
456. Stanley Orman (pupil 1946–1954), TCL November 2003, p. 2.
457. Woolf, *Barcelona is in Trouble*, p. 47.
458. Letter to Gerald Levene, 21 August 1954; HDS archive.
459. Gerald E. Caiden, pupil 1947–5: 'At Hackney Downs School', p. 4; typescript in HDS Archive.
460. Harvey Monte/John Hardcastle BL Recording.

Another pupil's outstanding 'O' level results arrived after he had left school and was sweeping floors at a clothing workshop. Balk visited his home and told his father, 'Harold must come back to school – he's university material . . .' The parent replied in a Polish accent, 'We can't afford for him to come back to school – he's got to earn some money.' After Balk promised financial assistance, the boy returned to school, later qualifying as a dentist at King's College Hospital.[461]

Balk exhibited a subtle sense of humour. When a boy was injured during lunchtime cricket, he summoned the batter concerned to agree the wording for his incident report:

> At approximately 1.35, while playing cricket in the back playground, Harvey Monte of Form 4a played a hook to leg and in following through inadvertently hit A. Blutstein on the nose, thereby breaking it. Is that correct?[462]

Rev. Barnett Joseph wrote in *The Jewish Chronicle*:

> Mr. Balk's headmastership was marked by a deep understanding of his pupils, and of their personal academic problems. He was a historian, and the mystique of Jewish history made a particular appeal to him. He often discussed with me the ideals that permeated those who worked in the field of Jewish-Christian relationships. Generations of pupils and especially his Jewish students will remember with real affection and gratitude the help and encouragement he gave them.

---

461. Harold Hersh. Letter from his sister, Jean Taylor, to Willie Watkins, 27 February 2015; HDS Archive.
462. TCL, June 2009, p. 2.

Chapter 5
Steady as she goes . . .
Vernon Barkway Pye, Headmaster 1952–1960

> ...*a well-ordered and purposeful community, worthily playing an indispensable part in the education of North East London.*
> HMI Report

Vernon Barkway Pye (1900–1989), fifth Headmaster of Hackney Downs, took over in September 1952. By coincidence, he had been educated at the King Edward VII Grammar School, King's Lynn, where Hackney Downs had decamped during World War II, before gaining a first in Law at Selwyn College, Cambridge. Pye began his teaching career at Bradford Grammar School, Yorkshire, where – by another co-incidence – T. O. Balk was a colleague.[463] Following war service in the Royal Naval Volunteer Reserve, Pye was appointed Headmaster of Central Foundation School, Cowper Street – where, by further coincidence, Courthope Bowen, first Head of Hackney Downs, had once taught – another grammar school with both Jewish and gentile pupils. After six years at Central Foundation, where he led the necessary post-war reconstruction, Pye moved to Hackney Downs, where he oversaw consolidation and modest expansion rather than innovation, while maintaining academic standards along traditional grammar school lines.

Pye claimed to have received verbal assurances at his appointment that the school's status would not be changed in the foreseeable future. Despite this, in September 1955 the L.C.C. drew up proposals to build a new county secondary school for 1,000 boys on the site of nearby Brooke House (Hackney Central) School to 'work in close association with Hackney Downs'. The Conservative Education Minister opposed turning the grammar school into a comprehensive; hence the council proposed to 'associate' the two schools, rather than combine them. When Pye asked 'in what way schools were expected to work in asso-

---

463. He then worked at the Joint Matriculation Board of the Northern Universities, taught at Clifton College and the Nautical College, Pangbourne, before being appointed senior history master at Portsmouth Grammar School.

ciation', he was informed it would be with separate heads and that 'no particular method of co-operation would be imposed on heads . . . '[464] The governors of Hackney Downs[465] made no objection to this proposal, but suggested additional accommodation might be needed 'to meet the increased demand for grammar school places which will be encountered in the Hackney area in the early 1960s'.[466] To this end, it was decided that a small science block should be built in the school's forecourt and the existing laboratories upgraded.[467] In 1962, it was agreed 'Hackney Downs (SB)[468] school should be rebuilt as a 3-form entry secondary boys' school on its existing site.'[469] It seemed the school was finally to obtain its long-awaited new premises.

Despite the fact that, under the 1944 Act, entry to grammar school was strictly by results in the 11+ exam, Pye continued to interview would-be pupils and their parents. One former pupil, who entered the school in September 1957, recalled being presented with a passage about the 'hero' Clive of India to read, after which he was questioned on it – fortuitously he had read about Clive at his primary school – and was also asked if he could afford the school uniform, presumably to discover whether he would require a grant.[470] Another former pupil, who entered the school in 1953, was requested to read from Dickens' *Pickwick Papers*.[471] At another interview, in 1958, the candidate was asked to read from Harrison Ainsworth's 1843 historical novel *Old Saint Paul's* – a Victorian classic, that contrasted with the books the same boy, on joining the school, discovered in his class library, such as Kingsley Amis' *Lucky Jim*, George Orwell's *1984* and John Wain's *Hurry on Down*, suggesting a headmaster out of touch and sympathy with the times.[472]

When the school's Deputy Head, Mr. Howell, retired in 1952, Barkway Pye appointed Joseph Brearley in his place:

> I had been told of his brilliance as a teacher & his intellectual ability, but it remained to be seen how he would fare as an administrator.[473]

464. L.C.C. EO/DE.1/367, HDS Archive.
465. 5 October 1955. There was a joint governing body for Wilton Way and Hackney Downs schools.
466. Presumably as a result of the post-war population 'bulge'. L.C.C. EO/DE.1/367 L.C.C. Education Committee: D.O. 4 Survey Report Ed. 467 Hackney Downs School. Agenda for Governors Meeting, 28 Sept 1955; D.O.4. KJM/C.
467. May 1959. Ed. 609, report by the Chief Engineer and Architect. AR/S/CASP, CO/B.854.
468. Secondary boys.
469. L.C.C. Ed. 700 in HDS Archive.
470. Melvyn Brooks. Handwritten account in HDS Archive.
471. Alan Ruston, *These Eighty Years*; private printing, 2022, p. 16.
472. The author.
473. Private letter, Vernon Pye to Mara Loytved-Hardeg, 3 December 1977.

This appointment apparently surprised many contemporaries. It was generally felt that Brearley proceeded to take virtual charge of the school, only to feel demoted when Alec Williams took over as Headmaster.[474]

To avoid boys specialising too early, they were offered a general education until the fifth form; many boys sat, and obtained, eight, nine, even ten 'O' Level subjects at a single attempt. During this era, pupils could sit 'O' and 'A'-level exams in a wide range of subjects, including pure and applied maths, physics, chemistry, biology, botany, zoology, English language and literature, French, German, Latin, Greek, history, ancient history, economic history, geography, geology, British Constitution, economics, logic, art and handicraft. Streaming was sharpened in the third, fourth and fifth years, by the addition of a select 'alpha' form of particularly able boys, which allowed smaller teaching groups.[475] Although the senior teachers were not restricted to the alpha forms, this new classification meant those in the 'B' and 'C' – still more the 'Y' and 'Z' forms – could feel disadvantaged. The erratic Joe Brearley even encouraged his 'alpha' English class to stand up and declaim, 'I am an alpha! I am a genius!'[476]

Following the example of his predecessors, Pye tried to convince boys and their parents that the longer a pupil stayed at school the better were his employment prospects. He reported at speech day, November 1954 – guest-speaker Lieut. General Sir Ian Jacob KBE, Director-Gen-

---

474. 'Reminiscences of Joe from David Evison', German teacher. January 1998; HDS Archive.

475. There were experiments in crossing the arts/science divide in the sixth form. One Science 6th pupil of this period remembers the Head of English, John Kemp, taking the form through 'the larger part of the works of T. S. Eliot and Auden – no comments, we just banged our way through poem after poem. I went out immediately and bought those books of poetry and I have enjoyed poetry ever since.' Charles Heller, 8 April 1996.

476. Something of Brearley's mercurial nature is revealed in his 50-line doggerel response (marked 'confidential document') to a versified plea around 1961 from a pupil named Harvey Segal that the date of the school's Speech Day be changed so as not to clash with a football fixture between Arsenal and Tottenham Hotspur (Spurs). One stanza reads:

> A tragic fact that once a year
> The Grocers' pupils must appear
> Together with their hard-worked teachers
> To listen to such dreary speeches –
> And parents, too, be driven barmy
> Within the portals of 'THE ARMY'.*
> But sadder still that this occurs
> When ARSENAL are playing SPURS!
> O woeful day! Who could foresee
> That such a fateful clash would be!

*At this date Speech Day was held at the cavernous Salvation Army Congress Hall in Clapton.

eral of the BBC – that the school had seen a decline in the number of early leavers and a corresponding increase in the number of sixth-formers,[477] with more boys proceeding to university and other forms of higher education. Academic successes for 1959–1960 comprised 523 'O' Level passes – nine boys passed in 10 subjects each – 119 'A' Level passes, an Open Award to Cambridge, 3 State Scholarships and 15 university and college admissions. Pye's concern that pupils stay on was not misplaced: Ivor Stilitz and at least six of his peers came under strong pressure from the Hashomer movement to leave at the end of the fourth year to throw in their lot with this 'evangelical Zionist, Stalinist, atheistic, scouting youth organisation which aimed to capture the hearts and minds of Jewish youth and send them to kibbutz'.[478]

Despite their son's having passed the 11-plus and gaining entrance to the school, some families could not afford the uniform. One boy had to move to a school nearer home, as his parents could not fund the bus fare to Hackney Downs; another continued to wear his blue lower-school blazer in the sixth form, since his parents could not afford the navy jacket required in the upper school. Another pupil, who entered Hackney Downs in 1952, depended on a school cap donated by a fellow pupil, a blazer lent by another boy and a welfare cheque for his shoes and P.E. gear. His father was blind and there was no space for – or recognition of the need of – homework. Although the boy struggled academically, Pye persuaded him to stay on to take his 'O' levels, for which he was coached without charge by a maths master.[479] The same pupil recalled that, although masters amended double negatives in speech, they made no attempt to 'correct' cockney pronunciation.[480] Nevertheless the 1951 HMI Report once more commented: 'in most cases [pupils'] reading is marred by an uncouthness of utterance . . .' adding that 'a little regular practice in the lower forms might eliminate certain unwelcome diphthongs'. In other words, the London accent should be eliminated. Yiddish vocabulary was often heard in the playground.

A pupil later analysed the demographic character of the school:

477. At this date, Jeannette Tawney, wife of the socialist historian R. H. Tawney and sister of William Beveridge, was Vice-Chair of the school's governors. See Ann Oakley, *Forgotten Wives: How Women Get Written Out of History*. Bristol: Bristol University Press, 2021, pp. 101–34. In 1951 the Speech Day guest was the Bishop of London; in 1953 the Chief Rabbi, Dr Israel Brodie.
478. Duplicated typescript 'HDS – The 1951 Intake' (HDS Archive). Stilitz recalled 'Mr Pye talking to a hushed assembly about Stalin's death . . . ' describing it as 'a major historical event'. His contemporary, Michael J. Cohen, who left aged fifteen to become a youth leader with Hashomer, later became Emeritus Professor of History at Bar-Ilan University, Israel, and authored a number of books on Middle East history.
479. Terry Gasking, TCL, November 2003, p. 17.
480. Terry Gasking (b. 1939); Georgina Brewis, BL oral history.

> It's curious that Grocers' was a school with a middle-class ethos, but made up almost entirely of working-class boys... Nobody knew or cared what your father did for a living. It felt like an opening up of things... I remember one friend whose family lived in a prefab, but who was an authority on French existentialism, a genuine intellectual.[481]

Another wrote:

> Some of the teachers were giving mixed messages... They were authority figures in a traditional hierarchy but the sort of things they talked about were quite anti-establishment; left-wing politics, CND and so on.[482]

David Ogilvie, a pupil between 1942 and 1949, returned to the school to teach English in 1957. He later wrote:

> ... this was an extraordinary and quite special school to be in. For a start, it was a real melting-pot of Jew and Gentile, a highly productive mix. Then, I think that nearly all the boys must have been first-time grammar-schoolers, coming, in this unfashionable part of London, from families with few academic precedents, but parents who obviously had intelligence though never the opportunities.[483]

A gentile pupil from this period wrote:

> Mixing with Jewish boys introduced me to Europe and Middle European culture, and to a more sensual, non-Christian attitude to the arts and life generally.

Some Hackney Downs boys were academically qualified for Oxbridge, but not necessarily socially and culturally ready. A pupil who won an Open Exhibition to Cambridge in 1958 reported thirty years later:

> On the whole Cambridge University was an unpleasant experience. I went there, perhaps with the necessary intellectual skills, but woefully unprepared for life, socially gauche and self-critical to the point of abuse. I spent the mornings of my last year in bed (alone), getting up to consume a tin of Nestle's cream and sit in a cinema. I went down with a pass (aegrotat) degree.[484]

---

481. Anonymous essay, c. 1995.
482. Ibid.
483. David Ogilvie, TCL.
484. David Finn, 'HDS – The 1951 Intake'.

Another in the Class of 1951 experienced a narrowing of expectations after an interview with the Headmaster. He said he was keen on medicine, but Pye implied he wasn't clever enough, telling him that career path was not open to him as there were no professionals in his family, he was a poor athlete and didn't play rugby.[485] Several other former pupils reported that Pye refused to give them positive references on leaving, as mean-spirited retribution for some earlier alleged slight or misdemeanour.

By the beginning of the 1960s, with science teaching expanding, John Kemp, Head of English, expressed a fear that English literature was in danger of being marginalised and that 'English in the Sixth would approach extinction by default' unless more boys took GCE in English Literature.[486] A recent research project suggested:

> ... while Hackney Downs by the late 1950s had a majority of pupils who were both urban and working class, the English department didn't see that as a challenge needing to be specifically addressed ... one of the salient characteristics of grammar schools was their dedication to the subject rather than the needs of the pupils ...'[487]

Meanwhile the school continued to attempt to widen pupils' cultural horizons with more foreign trips: to the Netherlands – including a sobering visit to the Military War Cemetery at Arnhem – Belgium, France, Austria, Spain, Switzerland, Yugoslavia and Italy. As the war years became more distant, it became feasible to visit Germany too. In August 1955, Brearley led a trip to Salzburg: one Jewish pupil recalled his parents were unhappy about his participation, as his grandparents had been killed in the Coronation Buildings disaster during the Blitz. The coach took the group past a sign to Dachau; several minutes' silence followed. At Easter 1955, a German teacher[488] took a small group of sixth-formers to stay with families in Cologne, and in July 1960, a Hackney Downs athletics team travelled to nearby Leverkusen, to compete with two German schools. The following year, a party from Freiherr-vom-Stein Gymnasium, Leverkusen, reciprocated, with a week's visit to Hackney.[489]

---

485. Brian Ariel, who later enjoyed a successful career as an ophthalmic optometrist. 'HDS – The 1951 Intake'.
486. John Hardcastle, '"The Rag-bag of All Subjects": English in a London Grammar School, 1945–63', in *Changing English*, Vol. 20 No. 2, June 2013, p. 133; 'Memorandum concerning English Literature', J. Kemp; HDS archive.
487. *English Teachers in a Postwar Democracy*, p. 161.
488. Roy Dunning, a Communist Party member.
489. Stan Posner (1949–1955). In a school with so many Jewish pupils, and only fifteen

The back of the school, viewed from Hackney Downs Station, with an Edmonton branch steam train arriving.

Frequent educational visits were also arranged within the UK. Each year the Economics Sixth undertook a survey of an industrial concern, while in 1959 Brearley took a party of senior boys to the Atomic Energy Research Establishment, Harwell. There were also biology, geography and geology field courses, whilst the Arts Society arranged visits to the opera, theatre, concerts and ballet. New clubs were initiated for the lower school, including geography (1957), stamp-collecting (1958) and junior history (1959) – most requiring teachers to remain after hours to oversee them. A Radio Club, re-formed in 1953, opened the way two years later for a Scientific Society, which featured lectures and films as well as visits. A Hobbies Club, embracing woodwork, metalwork, plastics and light engineering, was supplemented by a Modelling Club. The Art Club was useful for boys hoping to go on to art school or specialise in architecture.[490] The Sixth Form Jewish Study Group was complemented by a Christian Union. In 1954, the Council for Education in World Citizenship branch became the largest school society, with more than 100 members, and debated such subjects as: 'Germany – Quo Vadis?', 'Commercial Television' and 'That the British have no right

years after World War II, the boldness of these German exchanges – for which Pye faced some protests by parents – is noteworthy.
490. The Arts Club owed much of its vitality to the Head of Art, Douglas Fry (1914–2007), a graduate of Hornsey School of Arts & Crafts, who spent much of his teaching career at Hackney Downs.

to be in Suez'. John Kemp initiated a Music Appreciation Society, with lunchtime sessions in the physics lecture theatre (which had a good sound-system), playing Jazz LPs – from the Modern Jazz Quartet and Miles Davis to Dizzy Gillespie and Thelonius Monk.[491]

The Railway Club was re-formed in 1955:[492] it was almost inevitable that a school situated between diverging railway lines would boast such a group. The heyday of the Hackney Downs Railway Club was between 1958 and 1963 – the last years of steam. In 1958, with a subscription of 6d, the club boasted 60 paid-up members, heavily weighted towards the first form. Meticulous financial records were kept: income for autumn term 1958 amounted to £1 16s 6d, with a school subsidy of 10s 6d brought forward from the previous year. Expenses totalled a modest £1, for the Hectograph gelatine and ink required to print the club magazine. An essay competition on 'Travelling on British Railways' attracted a bumper number of entries, with the prospect of a free trip to Swindon Works and Motive Power Depot as first prize. One entry was dismissed by the judges: 'rubbish – do not attempt to summarise texts from books without realizing what they mean'. The winning essay deserves quoting:

> Bridges on British Railways are quite strong. Only
> on rare occasions do you hear about British Railways
> bridges collapsing or falling in any way . . . Sometimes
> you find a platform ticket on the station, you then get a
> platform ticket from the machine (with a little thump),
> march past the ticket collector onto the platform. The
> ticket collector then orders you off the platform, you
> wave your platform ticket in his face. He, perceiving it is
> a platform ticket, throws you off the platform. Needless
> to say, I do not believe in platform tickets.

The club organized trips to railway works such as Eastleigh, Swindon and Ashford. British Railways issued duplicated regulations for such excursions, stipulating in vain, 'An assurance is required that the visit is for educational purposes and not merely for locomotive spotting'. With Dr Beeching's axe about to fall, the Railway Society transmuted into the Transport Society.

School music developed in these years. Senior and junior Gramophone clubs were formed, violin and recorder classes started, and the speech-day choir put on a permanent footing. For 2s 6d per term, younger pupils could obtain a fluorescent membership card for the

---

491. Allan Koop, 'A Tale of Two Brothers – Music at HDS in the 50s and 60s'.
492. There had been a short-lived club in Balk's time: he was a train enthusiast.

newly-formed 'Sound Club', licensing them to experiment on a range of instruments and participate in improvisational music-making. This unique society was set up by the eccentric, but brilliant, maths teacher and composer, Kenneth Payne,[493] whose results drew praise from an L.C.C. Music Inspector and the Director of the London College of Music. Something of its ethos is conveyed in his account:

> This Club, of Fifth and Sixth Formers, which meets at irregular intervals, seeks to make odd sounds by means of the weirdest instruments, ranging from glass tubing, wood blocks and Meccano plates to pianoforte, cymbals and drums. We then attempt to record, playback on magnetic tape, and criticise our own efforts with a view to obtaining the maximum satisfactory effect from each example... The atmosphere of recorded examples ranges from *Musique Concrete Reinforcé* to *Symphonique Sèriale Serieux*, but a boisterous wind sweeps through all our sessions, often turning aesthetic gems into jokes, and vice versa. But the ultimate hope is that our research into the effects of (more or less!) musical sounds and rhythms on the emotions of the listener, will prove to be basic, vital and far-reaching, as well as entertaining.[494]

The following year Payne issued a further report:

> Ukulele, Guitar, Toy Clarinet and Recorder arrive at School from homes where unsuspected talent has been developing, almost simultaneously with the arrival from the London Music Shop of Psaltery, Gong, Drum and Chimes, and – from the L.C.C. – Violins, Clarinets, Trumpet and 'Tenor Saxhorn in E flat'...
>
> As an illustration of what can happen, 'Example 1' for Toy Clarinet, Recorder and Guitar was thought out, tried, scrapped, re-composed, rehearsed, played upside-down and backwards and finally 'prepared for recording on

---

493. In February 1963, two educational psychologists visited the school to investigate Payne's 'teaching machine for mathematics' (School Record, 14 March 1963). Kenneth Ashe Payne (1925–2006) took composition lessons with Delius' amanuensis, Eric Fenby (1906–97). Geoffrey Hole (HDS pupil 1951–1958) recalled Payne's exceptional maths teaching: 'We calculated escape velocities, using Newton's laws of motion [and] orbits . . . He was far ahead of his time in getting us to tackle such an interesting topic. (Email to Willie Watson, 5 May 2006). 16 April 1963, Payne informed the Headmaster he would leave within the next ten days, which he proceeded to do, possibly to work on perfecting teaching machines (Letter from Alan Koop to Willie Watkins, 4 June 1996).
494. Review, 18 December 1959, p. 30.

to tape'... all in the space of one day – between 1.30 and 5.00 p.m., with a short break for work from 2.00 till 4.00...[495]

A school hymnbook was published in 1958, compiled specifically for use at the combined Jewish and Christian assemblies. The task of editing the hymnbook fell to the practising Christian Classics master and assembly organist, W. G. 'Billy' Boyd, in retirement ordained an Anglican priest. His selection required the approval of the Jewish Chair of Governors, Dr. Homa.[496] Boyd's task was to compile a selection of hymns that would cause no offence to Jewish pupils, for instance by reference to Christ, the Holy Trinity, the cross, saints or any other Christian topic or dogma. The book contains some 120 Christian hymns, in some instances altered, shortened or reworded for this usage. For example, Hymn 18 substitutes 'Father' for 'Saviour'; 19 'Lord' for 'Saviour'; 23 'holy' for 'Christian'; while in No. 29, the Christian hymnwriter's original and crucial penultimate verse was completely omitted.[497] So successful was Boyd in editing the hymns that it never occurred to one Jewish pupil 'that these hymns were part of Christian tradition'.[498] Hymn No. 114 never failed to attract ribald sniggering and furtive nudges at assembly, since it included the perilous line 'in intercourse at hearth or board with my beloved ones'. The innuendo did not pass unnoticed: in a second edition this was adjusted to the more innocent 'fellowship at hearth or board'. There were no Jewish texts, but several secular poems masquerade as hymns. Jesus is, of course, not named, though God is. When boys sang Mendelssohn's *Elijah* with girls from nearby John Howard School, the name 'Jehovah' was supplanted by the more acceptable 'Almighty'.

Whilst the daily assembly was interfaith in this period, there were separate Christian and Jewish religious education lessons. The former were taught by Christian staff – not religious specialists – while a local rabbi taught the Jewish classes, which were often ill-disciplined. The Head of German recalled: 'The [Jewish] RI classes were usually in chaos... And nobody even bothered, because it wasn't anything to do with the rest of us'.[499] In the 1950s and 1960s, Jewish boys could have kosher

---

495. Review 182, December 1960, pp. 37–38.
496. Dr. Geoffrey Alderman reports a rumour that the Chief Rabbi, Dr Israel Brodie, was also consulted.
497. 'We read thee best in him who came/and bore for us the cross of shame,/sent by the Father from on high,/our life to live, our death to die.'
498. Charles Heller, April 1996, author of *What to Listen for in Jewish Music*. Toronto: Ecanthus Press, 2006.
499. Roy Dunning, interview with John Hardcastle, BL recording.

lunch in nearby Shacklewell Lane, at the New Dalston Synagogue.[500]

The school's greatest cultural achievement of this period was drama. Joseph Brearley produced Sheridan's *The Critic* in 1950, with girls from John Howard School; *A Midsummer Night's Dream* in 1951; and J. B. Priestley's *The Good Companions*, with its huge cast, with girls from Dalston County in their school theatre. David Ogilvie remembered rehearsing in 'all sorts of places', including the West End flat of the screen actor Basil Radford.[501] Next came Labiche's farce *An Italian Straw Hat* at Dalston County School, with several staff in the production, among them geography teacher Albert Calland.[502] When Brearley became the school's Deputy Head, Calland took over production of the school play, on condition it be staged in the school amphitheatre, with the audience surrounding the stage on three sides. When he visited the school for interview, he assumed plays were staged in the assembly theatre: 'Good God, no!,' replied Joe Brearley, 'Can't stand open stages. Proscenium arch, curtains. Box of magic for me.' Pye agreed to Calland's requested use and the transformation of the school theatre 'as long as he had a clear walkway for assembly . . . and didn't fall over scenery.'[503] There followed

> a series of plays rarely equalled in any school . . . plays in their own right, not just school plays; not just well-meaning social occasions, or embarrassing attempts to be instructive. Rather . . . an artistic activity, undertaken in the conviction that plays are not just entertainment, but that they project and define important truths.[504]

This series commenced with Ibsen's *An Enemy of the People* (1955), in a style derived from European Expressionist and Constructivist theatre. Calland argued 'if we could stage a 19th century realist play in a Greco-Roman theatre, anything could be done'. This was followed by Shakespeare's *Julius Caesar* in modern dress (1956); Shaw's *Caesar and Cleopatra* (1957); Thornton Wilder's *Our Town* (1958); Sophocles' *Oedipus Rex* (1959)[505] – pronounced a 'magnificent production' by the *Times Educational Supplement*; Eliot's *Murder in the Cathedral* (1960); and Brecht's *Galileo Galilei* (1961) – the first amateur production of the

---

500. Now Shacklewell Lane Mosque, the first Turkish mosque in the UK.
501. Brearley had connexions with several leading actors, including Michael Redgrave.
502. Calland (1928–2016), a Birmingham University graduate, left Hackney Downs in 1961.
503. Albert Calland, TCL , December 2007, pp. 9–10.
504. John Kemp.
505. A former pupil reminisced: 'I remember coming out of a performance of *Oedipus Rex* and being so stirred by it that I unwittingly lit up a fag in the corridor! I was carpeted by the Headmaster next day.'

English version of the play.[506] All these productions were distinctive for their scenic design and construction, undertaken by Douglas Fry,[507] head of art, and William 'Woodie' Warburton, woodwork teacher.

For many boys, these exceptional productions opened up the world of theatre. A pupil who saw *An Enemy of the People* aged thirteen claims it 'helped to create my strong interest in the serious professional theatre, at which I have been a regular attender since the early 1960s.'[508] Another wrote that the experience of acting in Calland's productions led to years of 'acting, directing, box-officing, anything...'[509] Calland's departure in 1961 was a severe blow to school drama.

During this period, athletics dominated sports just as drama did cultural activities, although a wide range of activities was on offer, including football, cricket, rugby-fives, soft-shoe soccer, five-a-side football, cross-country, basketball, tennis, badminton and table tennis. The Hackney fives team won the London Grammar Schools' Marchant Cup in 1955, 1956 and 1960; and in 1957 and 1959 Hackney Downs won the London Grammar Schools' Swimming Association's Grand Challenge Shield. Yet athletics took precedence. Notwithstanding individual victories, success was a team effort, the school gaining the NLGSAA Grand Challenge Shield every year between its inauguration in 1949 and 1966. John Kemp recalled:

> The White City steam-rollering of other schools in
> athletics was not entirely to their liking... Especially
> since we [Hackney Downs] developed a kind of
> American cheer-leader style in the audience. A row of
> HDS boys would have a string of placards, G R O C
> E R S, which they would turn to face the track, with
> the accompanying chant at intervals... Result, formal
> complaints from other schools about unsporting or
> ungentlemanly conduct...[510]

Much of this athletic success was due to the coaching of Leslie Mitchell, who was, as mentioned above, also responsible for the Cadet

---

506. Hans Eisler's score had to be copied by hand from manuscripts in the British Museum Reading Room. (Tony Wibberley, geography teacher, TCL, November 2005, p. 24.) Charles Heller remembered 'the actor playing one of the Cardinals was a Hasid from Stamford Hill, and he kept a Talmudic volume under his Cardinal's robes which he read while waiting in the wings...' (HDS Archive).
507. Douglas Rackley Fry (1914–), a conscientious objector during World War II, attempted to broaden school art beyond flat paintings to design and 3D work.
508. Alan Ruston (1953–60), 'HDS Remembered: An Enemy of the People' (March 1996, HDS Archive).
509. Edward Thomas, pupil 1954–1959, 'Play Time', April 1996, HDS Archive.
510. Letter to Willie Watson, 4 September 2000; HDS Archive.

Corps, which continued to offer a range of activities, including shooting, camps and military inspections. Benefiting from the school's athletics prowess, the corps' athletes achieved their own series of victories in the County of London Championships, and provided many members of the County of London Army Cadet Force team, which competed successfully for the National Trophy.

Other school sports were subordinated to the demands of athletics, a notable casualty being rugby football. In 1958 a teacher[511] started rugby practice on Hackney Marshes, following which a school team was formed, achieving a record of eight games played and won – much of its success due to leading athletes. The following spring, athletes were barred from rugby, as it was alleged risk of injury might threaten the school's success at the crucial White City meeting. Lacking some of its best players, the rugby team suffered a series of humiliating defeats; when Edwards left the school in 1962, rugby vanished too.

Vernon Barkway Pye retired at the end of the summer term 1960. His patrician-sounding name was apt for a patrician-seeming individual. He was by no stretch a reforming head, although perhaps he quietly achieved more than he has been given credit for. He seemed to allow his subordinate, Joseph Brearley, leeway to express his boundless energy and passions, which could prove destabilizing and irritating to his fellow teachers. A number of members of staff experienced Pye as distant, inflexible and unsympathetic. An incident is recorded when, three years after having taken up the headship, Barkway Pye required the help of the Head Boy to guide him to the VI Economics classroom. Some thought Pye 'saw his time in Hackney as one leading to retirement', avoiding risk to his health and his pension.[512] Comparing him unfavourably with Balk, another former pupil recorded his contemporaries felt Pye 'never properly understood us at all or some of the staff who openly rebelled at his stiff manner'.[513]

---

511. Modern languages specialist David Edwards.
512. Former pupil Melvyn Brooks, in TCL, November 2009, p. 18.
513. Gerald E. Caiden, 'At Hackney Downs School', p. 5; typescript in HDS Archive. Another pupil called him 'the closest thing to a sneer on legs'.

Chapter 6

Fire! Fire!

Alexander Ernest Williams, Headmaster 1960–1974

The new school will still be Hackney Downs.
The Review, December 1963.

Alexander Ernest Williams (1914–2006), with a Cambridge first in Classics and an Oxford Theology degree, was appointed sixth Head of Hackney Downs School, overseeing yet another testing period in the school's story. Having served in the RAF, where he learned Japanese, in 1957 Williams was appointed Headmaster of Archbishop Temple's School, Lambeth.[514] He held a relatively elitist view of education in a period when such opinions were under increasing political pressure. A practising Christian,[515] Williams became Chairman of the North London Branch of the Council of Christians and Jews. Although under his headship morning assembly continued to include all pupils – Jewish and gentile – Williams introduced separate assemblies on Friday mornings, with gentiles housed in the school theatre and Jewish boys in the dining hall. Jewish assembly was overseen by biology teacher Malcolm Jacobs, a former pupil. Williams attended every other week, wearing his mortar board in place of a Jewish kippah.[516]

At the beginning of Williams' headship, the future of Hackney Downs as a selective-entry grammar school seemed assured. The school roll stood at well over 600; the existing buildings – old and overdue for replacement – were supplemented in 1961 with the promised pair of new physics laboratories[517] in the front playground. The school's final link with the Grocers' Company was severed in October 1961 when the L.C.C. purchased the Edmonton sports field from the Livery.[518] School

---

514. He features briefly, conducting school assembly, in the 1959 social-realist documentary *We Are the Lambeth Boys*, directed by Karel Reisz.
515. Originally a Baptist, Williams was ordained an Anglican priest after retirement.
516. Letter from Melvyn Brooks to Glyndwr Watkins, 27 March 2000.
517. One was named after Dr. Homa, longstanding Chairman of Governors.
518. As a parting gesture, in 1962 the company presented the school with a new Best Boy casket to contain the Roll of Best Boys, with £100 to endow the prize.

Athletics training in the school's front playground.

football and cricket continued there, each year-group travelling from the school by Grey-Green coach on a set afternoon.

The school's athletics success continued, and school clubs and societies proved as popular as ever. The pompously named 'Literary & Debating Society and Arts Group' discussed such contemporary issues as obscenity in literature – this was the era of the *Lady Chatterley's Lover* trial – and the Beat Generation. A Jazz Society was formed, and the pop musician Michael Vogel – professional name 'Zack Laurence' – began his career as pianist and composer while at Hackney Downs. After the abortive Hungarian uprising of 1956, two Hungarian exiles entered the school, one a pianist named Endre Stuber.[519] In 1961 the sixth form organized a St. Valentine's Day dance in the school dining-room, to raise money for Congo Relief.[520] The wide range of school visits and journeys also continued, with regular skiing holidays in Switzerland. A group of teachers from the Soviet Union visited the school in 1961, and the following year Hackney Downs boys joined a combined Hackney schools' trip to Moscow and Leningrad – claimed to be the first from the area, and the largest school party, to have visited the country.

During the early years of Williams' headship there were several sig-

519. Edward Thomas (1954–1959), 'Play Time'; HDS Archive.
520. This was the time of the Congo Civil War (1960–64).

nificant staff changes. 1961 saw the retirement of Adrian Gee, Head of Science since 1948: the successful expansion of science teaching was largely due to his efforts. The sudden death in 1964 of the senior French master Cyril Corner shocked the school. The appointment of younger heads of department seemed to promise progressive development, without – in Williams' words – 'either violent upheaval or stagnation'. In some instances teaching was innovative, even immersive. The Head of German, Roy Dunning, recalled interrupting a history lesson to stop 'what sounded like a terrific row', only to be told later by the history teacher William Lamont[521] that 'they were enacting the discussions of the Levellers'.[522]

John Kemp, who joined as Head of English in 1956, described the Jewish contribution to the school's ethos:

> You could not think of very intelligent Jewish kids as people simply who were going to take and to pass exams. You thought of them also in terms of various types of Art and Culture, and political discussion, of deep human suffering; and to sense the suffering of somebody whose parents went into the concentration camps or somebody most of whose relatives had been wiped out or somebody who'd got that load of grief right behind him . . .[523]

The Holocaust was ever-present. In the later 1950s, paperback copies of Lord Russell of Liverpool's *The Scourge of the Swastika* (1954),[524] with graphic photographic evidence, were passed around the playground. In June 1962, a public exhibition at Hackney Town Hall, attended by some boys, commemorated the Warsaw Ghetto, with photographs and disturbing objects such as discarded spectacle frames and children's shoes. When Joseph Brearley led a school trip to Prague in 1964, Jewish boys identified relatives among the Holocaust victims commemorated on the walls of the Pinkas Synagogue.

In a school so sensitive to wider political issues the Cuban Missile Crisis of October 1962 was taken very seriously:

> [T]he world was on edge as the USA and USSR came face to face over missiles in Cuba. We were all sure that the world was going to end. Walking home we discussed how we would spend our last minutes on Earth. Many had no doubt, they would go round to their girlfriends

---

521. Subsequently Professor of History at Sussex University.
522. Roy Dunning interview, John Hardcastle; BL oral history.
523. Review July 1975, p. 17.
524. Sub-title: *A Short History of Nazi War Crimes*.

and fornicate as best they could; while my Orthodox Jewish friends claimed they would go to their synagogue and pray fervently ... Next day, Mr. Marr said to us in his most portentous voice: 'Always remember that this day we came to the brink of destruction.'[525]

During this period the staff-room housed teachers with a wide range of personalities and backgrounds. The French master Ormond Uren (?1919–2015) – falsely alleged by the writer Nigel West to have belonged to the Philby spy-ring – had been jailed in 1943 for passing information from the Hungarian section of the Special Operations Executive to Douglas Springhall, national organiser of the Communist Party and a Soviet agent.[526] He was released from prison in 1947, but remained on a government blacklist.[527]

The post-war population 'bulge' brought to the school many boys with high academic ability, who responded positively to the expanding opportunities in universities. The sixth form increased in size, and a handful of boys stayed on after the two-year 'A' Level course, creating a seventh form. In 1961, 27 boys were accepted for degree and other further education courses; in 1962, 32. The same year, Williams introduced a Sixth Form Teaching Week in the summer term, when senior boys who had finished their 'A' Level exams taught junior forms.

As the school reassembled after the summer holiday in September 1962, its future seemed secure. Earlier that year the L.C.C. had published a revised school plan: of all London boys' county grammar schools, only Hackney Downs and Bec Grammar School, Tooting, were exempt from expansion or amalgamation under the council's comprehensive school policy. It is unclear why. In the same year it was confirmed Hackney Downs would be rebuilt ... at some point.

A new, young geography master,[528] took over school drama and planned to produce Anouilh's *Antigone* in the school theatre. The final dress-rehearsal took place on the evening of Monday 18 March 1963; next morning, following an extensive fire, much of the school lay in ruins. The conflagration began soon after 2 a.m., with flames spreading rapidly through the building's top floor and tower. More than 100 fire-

---

525. Charles Heller, TCL, Vol. 8 No. 2, October 2018, p. 41.
526. Uren learned Hungarian in 1937 when, aged 18, he spent the summer on the estate of a Hungarian countess, with whom he had an affair. For a recent reappraisal of case see: Roderick Bailey, 'The Trials of Ormond Uren: A Study in Security and Spy Mania' in *International Journal of Intelligence and Counterintelligence*, Vol. 36, 2023, Issue 1, pp 109–140.
527. Frances Williams, *The Guardian*, 23 July 2015. See also website of Birkbeck, University of London.
528. Colin Harris.

men took nearly four hours to bring the fire under control. The police response had something of the Keystone Cops about it: in the small hours the teleprinter at nearby Dalston Police Station began to chatter: 'Hackney Downs School, serious fire, LFB in attendance, all available officers make way to assist.' Dalston had neither vehicles nor radio, so the officers went outside and stopped a car. When they opened its door, the driver fell out drunk. He was a colleague; after putting him to bed in the surgeon's room, they drove to the school in his commandeered vehicle.[529]

A former pupil described arriving at school next morning:

> As I turned into Bodney Road . . . I saw what I thought were feathers laying around all over the road and pavement. Groups of boys were walking up the hill to school and a woman was coming the opposite way and stopping at each group as she reached them. She said something that made each group run up the hill at full pelt. When she reached our group she said: 'You can go home now your school's burnt down.' We thought she was a crank, but just to be sure we raced up the hill to see for ourselves . . . we were suddenly confronted by the sight of blackened, charred timbers that were all that remained of the school tower. What I thought was the result of a pillow-fight in the street was in fact the fine ash . . . My immediate concern was for my brand new tracksuit, bought the previous weekend and left in my locker overnight.[530]

600 boys arrived for school and assembled in the playground, before being told to return home.[531] The school reassembled the following day in the gymnasium, where the headmaster promised that Hackney Downs School would remain together, as a single unit. Although the fire brigade saved the gym, the library and science block, the school theatre and the roof and top floor of the main building were all destroyed. The rest of the building was saturated with water and no classrooms were usable. The fire was probably caused by the theatre-lighting rheostat dimmer overheating.[532]

---

529. The son of woodwork teacher William Warburton was a serving officer at Dalston. TCL, December 2007, p. 36.
530. Stewart Shaller, TCL, November 1996, p. 3.
531. Three months later a fire destroyed the memorial pavilion at the school field.
532. A pupil who was operating the dimmer the previous day recalled the rheostat as too hot to touch when he failed to shut it off completely. Letter from Alan Koop to Willie Watkins, 4 June 1996.

A senior school group on a field-trip pose for a photograph, c. 1962. *Far right*: Charles Heller.

An evocative account of the damage appeared in the school magazine:

> The bottom corridor a river-bed of dark silt; the entrance hall a black funnel, with spidery timbers creaking overhead; books, desks and papers turning to pulp as the water dripped and splashed incessantly as if from the roof of a cave; everywhere the soft, penetrating smell of wet plaster and charred wood, sickly sweet and deathly: in the face of all this, nobody had the heart for jokes about extra holidays, and most of us just stood in little groups and stared glumly, all the more disheartened as the demolition men hitched their lorry to our tottering gables and brought them thudding down ... The gymnasium was piled high with tea-chests; the fives-court became a kind of casualty clearing-station for personal property; and Melvyn Brooks, firmly and properly ignoring danger signals, suborned firemen, demolition men, anybody within reach, and preserved a whole museum-ful [sic] of relics.[533]

On 22 March, Mr. Williams sent a lengthy letter to parents confirming no boys would be transferred to other schools and outlining his plans for continuing lessons. A second letter, on 22 April, stated 'arrangements for the rebuilding of the school are going ahead with all

---

533. Review, 18 December 1963, p. 3. Brooks became unofficial school archivist.

possible speed ... on the present site, which ... is fully capable of accommodating a grammar school that meets all present day requirements.' In a further letter at the end of the summer term Williams was anxious to squash

> one or two alarmist rumours about the size and siting of the new school... [T]he new school will be built for 600 boys (our present numbers), and it will be on our present site ... [T]he character and work of the school will be unchanged.[534]

During the difficult months that followed, staff and pupils alike demonstrated impressive resilience. *Antigone* went ahead, in borrowed costumes and on the stage of neighbouring John Howard girls' school, in Lower Clapton. The most immediate requirement was for classroom space. Science, handicraft and P.E. lessons could continue on the main site. L.C.C. divisional officers quickly located accommodation for the three lower-year groups in ten classrooms at the Jewish Victoria Youth Club and adjacent synagogue in Egerton Road, Stamford Hill,[535] where the Deputy Head, Joseph Brearley, took charge. The middle school was housed in the few usable rooms on the main school site. Senior forms were allocated six classrooms at nearby Wilton Way Secondary Modern School, with Cyril Corner in charge, and one form was based at Hackney Technical College. By the end of the week of the fire, every boy had been accommodated, with school lunch provided at nearby Craven Park and Amhurst schools. Some textbooks and stationery were salvaged from the burnt-out school, whilst other books were requisitioned.

By the beginning of summer term, the situation had eased somewhat. Four classrooms and a lecture theatre on the west side of the school had been restored to use, and the school library converted into a temporary office and staffroom. By reducing the number of teaching periods to seven per day, and introducing a longer morning break, it was possible for pupils and teachers to move between the various sites as the timetable required. Twice-weekly assemblies were held in the playground. The headmaster notified staff:

> I shall take the Assembly from the doorway of the Metalwork Shop, and I shall be glad if masters will group themselves on each side of the doorway. Since the time taken is likely to be no more than ten minutes, I assume that masters will not mind standing.[536]

534. 25 July 1963, HDS Archive.
535. Now owned by the Bobov community, one of the largest Chasidic sects of ultra-Orthodox Jews. See Elks, pp. 104–106.
536. Hackney Archives R/DOW/1/36, May 1963.

The catastrophic school fire, 18/19 March 1963.

The hasty improvisation, rescheduling and requirement for patience and goodwill were reminiscent of the wartime evacuation, less than twenty years earlier.

Longer-term planning was immediately put in hand. As early as 26 March, a meeting of L.C.C. education officers agreed to recommend to the Governors the complete replacement of the central section of the school with a new building. It was suggested that meanwhile the ground and first floors of the school's central section be temporarily reinstated, protected by a 'metal umbrella', with some forms accommodated in temporary huts.[537] During the summer term, the first two of eight prefabricated classrooms were erected in the front playground, enabling the forms temporarily accommodated at Wilton Way to return to the main site. The two surviving floors of the main building were re-roofed, though there was no further mention of a 'metal umbrella'. By the time autumn term 1963 began, the entire school had returned to the site.

As early as 30 April 1963, a schedule was drawn up for a completely new main building, situated in the front playground, replacing the original building erected by the Grocers' Company. This was to include an assembly hall designed for staging plays, a dining hall with a Kosher meals servery,[538] a library, twelve classrooms, a sixth-form suite,

537. Minutes of meeting at County Hall, 26 March 1963; HDS Archive.
538. L.C.C. Ext. 403, Ref. EO/DE.7a. HDS Archive. Many Jewish boys had Kosher lunch at Shacklewell Kosher Centre, provided by the Kosher School Meals Service. In 1964 Williams requested that Kosher meals be transported from Shacklewell Lane to the school, as it was 'desirable, educationally and socially, for arrangements to be made, if practicable,

music room and art rooms.[539] The Council architect was instructed to prepare plans,[540] which were approved on 4 June 1964,[541] and the site handed over to contractors in July 1965. During the summer term, the swimming pool was unavailable for use, and at the end of term the chemistry and biology laboratories were handed over to the builders. It was anticipated the new buildings would be ready for use by the end of 1966. The fire seemed almost a blessing in disguise: the long-desired rebuilding, sanctioned in 1938, but postponed by the outbreak of war, was finally to be put in hand. James Young, Chairman of the Education Committee of the Inner London Education Authority (ILEA)[542] laid the commemorative stone on 17 March 1966.

At Speech Day 1965, Williams quoted a recent newspaper headline, 'The knell tolls for grammar schools' – but went on to claim 'he did not feel this was true of Hackney Downs, for its new building was an earnest indication of an even brighter future.' Everything seemed normal: for the seventeenth successive year, the school won the Grand Challenge Shield of the North London Grammar Schools' Athletic Association, while the school's swimmers emerged winners in the London Grammar Schools' swimming gala. However, just three months after rebuilding commenced, the ILEA started to plan the comprehensive reorganisation of all its grammar schools; Hackney Downs was no longer exempt.

On 9 February 1966, Alec Williams met the Assistant Education Officer at County Hall to discuss 'proposals for expansion of school on comprehensive lines'.[543] The plan was for Hackney Downs to expand from a three-form entry school taking ninety boys a year selected by examination to a six-form entry school taking 180 boys of all abilities, about one-quarter of whom would previously have been reckoned of grammar school potential, and one-quarter below average ability. On 4 April the Education Officer, Dr. Eric Briault, Deputy Education Officer, Mr. Kingdom, Divisional Officer, and Miss Goss, District Inspector, discussed their proposals with the school staff, while a special Governors' meeting addressed them on 19 April. There were strong opinions:

for all the boys concerned to be able to dine on the school premises and that this would help to promote the corporate spirit of the school.' L.C.C. EIO/FS.1/6046, SM/MAN/6649. 2 July 1964. HDS Archive.
539. L.C.C. Ext. 403, Ref. EO/DE.7a. HDS Archive.
540. L.C.C. 4 July 1963 AR/S/8419; EO/DE.7a/403. HDS Archive.
541. L.C.C. EO/DE.7a/403; AR/S/422/6503.
542. The London County Council was abolished in 1965 under the London Government Act of 1963. Although the new Greater London Council took over most of its functions, a new education authority for London, the Inner London Education Authority, succeeded the L.C.C. Education Committee. Maclure p. 146.
543. School Record, HDS Archive.

Geography lesson, c. 1962, with Anthony Wibberley.

> [M]any of the staff would prefer to see us continuing to do the work which we already do so well, in the atmosphere of educational adventurousness on which we pride ourselves. We are particularly saddened that, having looked forward to taking over a new building designed for a specific community of 600 boys, we shall not be able to take advantage of it in the ways we had hoped.[544]

Having said this, the teachers' statement continued more positively:

> Our interest now is in the development of a comprehensive school which can maintain the reputation of the existing school and build upon it, and can be thought of in terms of modern educational principles.

However they pointed out the new premises had been specified for the needs of the existing grammar school, and that the plan would result in 'an average Comprehensive in below-average quality of accommodation'.[545] They also pointed out that many of the staff were highly

---

544. 'Memorandum from the Staff of Hackney Downs School concerning the Proposed Reorganisation', undated duplicated document, but evidently published between February and June 1966.
545. The Memorandum included an 'Addendum on Accommodation', with detailed measurements and calculations demonstrating that the existing accommodation fell short of

academic and not equipped to teach less able pupils, though they determined 'to avoid divisions between academic and non-academic staff in future years'. They requested training in teaching the less able and a delay in the re-organisation, so that both staff and premises were ready for the change, also expressing scepticism about the building contractors' timetable.

A second staff memorandum was considerably more forceful, pleading for implementation to be delayed until 1969, and expressing a sense of having been betrayed by the ILEA:

> when large numbers of Grammar Schools seem likely after all to survive in London, our hopes for the quality of our proposed Comprehensive School are somewhat dimmed... In a sense, circumstances have betrayed us, with our own co-operation.

Alec Williams made a belated plea to the ILEA, urging 're-consideration of the fundamental question whether such a reorganisation of the school is necessary or desirable in the existing situation in London,' and arguing 'the existence of a small homogeneous school with a strongly academic bias need not be regarded as undesirable or anomalous.' He added:

> Unlike most other maintained grammar schools in London Hackney Downs has not been included in previous schemes of reorganisation, and the staff has been led to assume that the school's status and character would remain unaltered.[546]

Pressed to voice publicly his disapproval of the ILEA plan, Bernard Homa refused, possibly out of personal loyalty to the Labour Party.

An elite concept was at the heart of the Victorian school, something strengthened by the 1944 Education Act and the 11-plus exam, designed to grade pupils according to their perceived intellectual capacities. The existence of an alpha form – an elite within an elite – reinforced hierarchy and competition, which many of the staff felt to be morally damaging. John Kemp argued:

> What happened from 1963, after the fire, was roughly this. We knew it was a good grammar school. It was a rich, exciting place to teach in, and I think to learn in. It

---

the needs of a six-form entry school; and 'that to introduce the scheme in 1967 would make overall planning impossible; prevent a proper overhaul of the old buildings; and condemn us to a succession of makeshifts' (HDS Archive). Much of this proved to be prophetic.
546. 'Comment by Head Master', undated duplicated document, evidently published between February and June 1966; HDS Archive.

was specially enriched because the tone was set to a fair extent by the Jewish boys – about half the total – and by their families' strengths and attitudes to education. But though it was good, many of the staff felt uneasy at the cost to other schools; once we had creamed off the ablest boys in the area, what sort of deal did the rest have? The atmosphere of the time was moving in favour of comprehensives; equal opportunities for all; and the fire, oddly, reinforced this feeling for some staff. For a time, the senior school shared premises with a half-empty, run-down secondary modern [Wilton Way]; and the HDS staff could observe 'how the other half lived'. We saw often lively and alert children in a pretty depressing and limited place, and tended to say, 'We could give a lot to that kid, if only we had him at Hackney Downs.'[547]

Kemp claimed the ILEA were 'amazed' when the teachers agreed to expand the school into a comprehensive, but added 'some staff were doubtful. Some were rather scared. Some pointed out the special value of a grammar school in the inner city . . .'[548]

Summing up his view of the school, and why it was open to becoming comprehensive, Kemp wrote in the centenary edition of the school magazine:

> It used to be a good, rather exciting, very open grammar school, as grammar schools go. There was a great deal of intellectual but also what you might call moral/social ferment. Starting from a more intellectual basis the children have always been very concerned about social and political matters, and there's always been a great deal of argument going on in the school. Around the school and in English lessons and after school in various societies and in the way children talked to each other it has always been a vociferous and energetic and very lively place. Because it always used to give the staff who were sensitive to it the idea that the children were open, that there were many lively minds among the children who could be accepted by the staff as equals, and because somehow this made the staff more enterprising than they might have been in a quiet suburban grammar school, I think that there were more

547. Kemp, pp. ii-iii.
548. Kemp, p. iii.

people open to change and open to the challenges of becoming comprehensive than there might have been in many grammar schools.[549]

Lord Peston later justified in similar terms his support for turning the grammar school he attended into a comprehensive:

> [Hackney Downs in the 1940s] was a highly selective world, in sporting as well as academic life . . . This was the crux of the case for comprehensive education. In my mind, three propositions underpinned it. First, as R. H. Tawney put it, if a school was not good enough for my child, it was not good enough for anybody's child. Second, educational success, however it was evaluated, depended on family background, and social and economic circumstances, as well as on the individual. Third, and most important of all, the 11-plus was inefficient, socially harmful and morally wrong . . . It took virtually no account of separate speeds of individual development. Worse still was the divisiveness, which so many people still hanker after, based on the bright being separated for their secondary education from the majority.[550]

The ILEA now sent a letter inviting parents to a meeting on 21 June 1965 at John Howard School (the new Hackney Downs assembly hall was not yet ready), chaired by Dr. Homa, with Lou Sherman (1914–2001),[551] Hackney representative on the ILEA, and Dr. Briault, when the scheme was made public.[552] Alec Williams told a restive audience that, though he originally believed the plans should be re-considered, he now accepted them: the question was no longer whether the school should turn comprehensive, but how it should do so. The Labour-controlled ILEA was committed to comprehensive schools and fewer than ten parents attended a meeting called by Conservatives to form a Parents' Association to fight the Hackney Downs proposal.[553] In 1965, the Labour government decided to approve only schemes providing for comprehensive education, allowing Williams and Homa to argue that the ILEA had moral and legal justification for its plan. Williams commented later:

549. Review, July 1975, p. 16.
550. Maurice Peston, 'Hackney Downs: why it had to fail,' *Independent on Sunday*, 30 July 1995.
551. Sherman had been a pupil at Hackney Downs.
552. HDS Archive.
553. *Review* 188, December 1966.

the staff generally were more enthusiastic about the change than I was at first. The London Director of Education pointedly congratulated the staff for their attitude, and I had to point out that I too meant to make it work . . . [554]

German teacher Roy Dunning had a low view of Williams' commitment, believing the Head had ambitions to

be offered a kind of Troika, which would have been Hackney Downs and then two of the other comprehensive schools, with him not really doing anything except sort of manipulating the money for each of the three.[555]

A letter to a former pupil seems to betray Williams' lack of enthusiasm for the change: ' . . . [W]e can do nothing to change government and ILEA policy, and we must therefore do our best to make the new scheme work.'[556]

In March 1967, Labour Minister of Education Anthony Crosland approved the ILEA plan for Hackney Downs.[557] Although the 1967 local elections ceded control of the ILEA to the Conservatives and Homa was ousted as Chairman of Governors, it was argued comprehensive reorganisation of the school had already gone too far for it to be reversed. It was also argued, based on population statistics, that there was urgent need for additional secondary school places in Hackney. Christopher Chataway, Conservative leader of the ILEA, claimed Hackney Downs was the appropriate school to meet this demand, with its partially-restored original building and new buildings shortly due for completion.

The approved architectural scheme for the new buildings consisted of two main structures on the north and south side of the site, connected by covered ways and arranged around a central quadrangle:[558]

North side: Stage 1 teaching block of three storeys, linked at the east end of the assembly hall.

North-east corner: Block A of Stage II, a three-storey building containing four house rooms, class rooms and specialist rooms, youth service accommodation, a kitchen extension and new boiler house.

---

554. TCL, November 2003, p. 9.
555. Roy Dunning/John Hardcastle BL recording
556. Alec Williams to Melvin Brooks, 27 June 1966; HDS Archive.
557. Crosland's Circular 10/65 famously requested all education authorities to submit comprehensive schemes to the government (Maclure p. 180).
558. Overall, the plans were not dissimilar to those drawn up before World War II.

> *East Side*: Swimming bath (built 1889), formerly the east wing of the school.
>
> *South side*: Block B of Stage II, a two-storey building, containing workshop, technical drawing offices and art rooms, linked to the gym by a roof terrace over a covered play area.
>
> *West side*: Science laboratories, formerly the west wing of the old school.[559]

Work had already started on what was now labelled Stage I, but halted on 21 March 1967 when the contractor went into liquidation.[560] Construction did not restart until June, when a new firm took over. The new teaching block was ready for occupation in September, and the new buildings were officially opened by Sir Edward Boyle on 1 February 1968.[561] The upbeat programme for the opening ceremony affirmed:

> the school is now adequately equipped for its traditional grammar school course. Indeed, it now possesses in its specially designed theatre, its pottery craft room, its Mathematics Laboratory and other specialist rooms, its Sixth Form common room and group teaching rooms, facilities which, but for the fire are not likely to have been available for many years. When, in the next two or three years, the additional buildings now projected are completed, the School will be ready to offer not only its present academic courses but the much wider range which a comprehensive school must provide.

The new buildings cost around £260,000.[562]

On 20 November 1967, the Headmaster, Deputy Head and Head of English, John Kemp, with a deputation of governors, met the Chair of the ILEA Schools Committee to 'press for delay in reorganisation owing to doubt about timing of new buildings [i.e. Stage II],' concerned that the school was not yet ready to accommodate 900 pupils.[563] After a second meeting, the ILEA agreed to postpone implementation until September 1969.[564] In October 1968, work began on the Stage II Buildings,

---

559. L.C.C. EO/PS/AEO, Ext.271, 'Note for Mrs Townsend.' HDS Archive.
560. School record; HDS Archive.
561. Boyle (1923–81), a maverick Conservative, who held posts in the Treasury and Department for Education and Science. Possibly his ambivalence in the grammar/comprehensive debate suggested his suitability to open the new buildings.
562. About £4.5M in 2025.
563. School Record.
564. Alec Williams was on Sabbatical Leave for the spring term 1968, part of it on a study tour of Swedish schools, which seems odd, considering the huge changes both structural and

the additional accommodation needed for the 180-entry comprehensive school. By 17 April 1970, the original Grocers' Company School building had been completely demolished;[565] the old gym – now a year-round swimming pool – together with the science block, were the only parts remaining of the old structure. On 11 December 1970, the headmaster noted 'School rebuilding now complete (since March 19, 1963 . . .).[566]

Despite these administrative, organisational and structural challenges, teachers and pupils maintained the life and work of the school. The wide range of clubs and societies was extended by the addition of a French Club, an Astronomical Society, a Mathematical Society and a Pottery Club, with a kiln incorporated in the new buildings. The only activity discontinued was the Cadet Corps, disbanded by Alec Williams in December 1963. With the ending of National Service, there had been a decline in its popularity, though boys continued to achieve success in the new Duke of Edinburgh's Award Scheme.

The school continued to offer a wide range of sports. In 1967, the LGSAA's Grand Challenge Shield, won for 18 consecutive years, was finally relinquished. However, a running club was started in 1968, the school coming first in the new North London Schools Running League. The school's rugby-fives team won the Marchant Cup every year between 1964 and 1968, and swimming teams won the Hackney Schools' Gala Grand Challenge Shield in 1964 and 1965, and the London Grammar Schools Swimming Gala between 1965 and 1967.

Within four months of the fire, a party set off on a geography fieldcourse in the Rhine Valley; another group travelled to the Baltic a month later. Over the next six years, school groups visited Switzerland, Austria, Czechoslovakia – still behind the Iron Curtain – France, Belgium, Holland, West Germany, Denmark, Sweden and Israel, while in 1964 and 1968 boys enjoyed an educational cruise in the Mediterranean.

Music and drama continued to play a significant role in school life. The orchestra staged concerts, and the organ destroyed in the fire was replaced with a new pipe organ. School plays continued almost without a break: in 1964 Thornton Wilder's *The Skin of our Teeth*, and the following year Shakespeare's *The Winter's Tale*. English teacher Gordon Gledhill produced Brecht's *The Caucasian Chalk Circle* in the new theatre in 1968, and in 1969 a powerful presentation of Arthur Miller's *The Crucible*, with John Howard School.

organizational currently taking place (School Record). In his absence, Joseph Brearley was Acting Head, which led to considerable unnecessary turmoil.
565. 'Rebuilding and Reorganisation', duplicated paper in HDS Archive.
566. School Record. In the middle of the quadrangle, were placed stone slabs incorporating the arms of the Grocers' Company, originally located above the entrance to the school.

Academic success was sustained between 1965 and 1970, despite the upheaval caused by the fire and rebuilding; more boys than ever proceeded to university or college. In 1966 the school began to offer the academically less-gifted the opportunity to sit the new Certificate of Secondary Education (CSE) exams. Additional subjects were offered, including Classical Hebrew, Italian and Russian, and the innovative Nuffield Science course was introduced. Along with the larger, better equipped, library the school appointed its first dedicated librarian. 1968 saw possibly the first woman form-teacher, the American Marjorie Lueck.[567] A contemporary pupil had the impression 'most of the teachers were centre left or left'.[568]

The school received its first comprehensive intake in September 1969. 150 boys entered the first form in six classes of 25 boys each, together with 15 new full- and part-time members of staff, who included six women. In September 1970, the first-form intake increased to 180. 'Remedial' teachers were recruited and a well-equipped technical department created. The six old Houses were replaced with four new Houses – the new building had only four suitable rooms. The previous bright blue uniform, with its yellow camel badge, was jettisoned for a less conspicuous black version. In September 1972, pupil numbers rose to 870, of whom fewer than 200 had been admitted while Hackney Downs was still a grammar school. By this date, the school had outgrown its premises: laboratories and workshops had to be used as 'form bases' and no longer could the whole school be accommodated in the theatre.

Between the first comprehensive intake in 1969 and his retirement in 1974, Williams presided over a school that was still largely 'grammar', since the ILEA had agreed, as a sop, to weight the initial new intakes in favour of more academic pupils. Many parents with sons at Hackney Downs during the late 1960s were furious about the decision to change the school's status, though many Jewish parents had already left Hackney for more agreeable districts such as Redbridge, Barnet and Harrow. The result was a shift in the school's demography: whereas, in 1962, 250 in a roll of 600 were Jewish, by 1972 there were only 118 Jewish boys and the Kosher meals service had ceased.[569] At this time a number of staff left, unhappy about the changes.[570]

567. Barry Levene, (HDS 1966–73); Letter to Willie Watkins; HDS Archive. Another teacher between 1969 and 1973 was Ken Worpole, later a community publisher at Centerprise community centre and bookshop in Kingsland Road, Dalston. The shop had been set up in 1970 by Glenn Thompson, a black American draft-resister, and his partner, Margaret Gosley, who worked at Hackney Downs School as librarian (Elks, p. 29).
568. Ralph Levinson, interview with Georgina Brewis; BL recording.
569. See also Elks, p. 105.
570. Review, 194, December 1972.

Further education admissions 1958–1974[1]	
1958	20
1959	20
1960	15
1961	27
1962	35
1963	23
1964	43
1965	42
1966	40
1967	27
1968	34
1969	41

1. Source: *Review*.

One pupil of the late 1960s, the period during which the school was transmuting from grammar to comprehensive, claimed 'most of the kids in the school were actually quite racist . . . I remember there being some real anti-Semitism from some kids'. He also recalled 'at the time of the Six Day War [June 1967], we had an Egyptian kid come to the school,' whom Jewish boys wanted to send to Coventry. When the first fully comprehensive intake started at the school in 1970, it included a number of boys of Afro-Caribbean background: 'I remember kids around me saying . . . "Look at these coons coming into school . . . "'[571]

Inspired by the student unrest of the late 1960s and counter-cultural publications such as *The Little Red School Book*, a smattering of school pupils across the country staged strikes. The school librarian, Margaret Gosley, recalled a pupil strike at Hackney Downs:

> They decided to have a protest and they all went and sat on the playing fields, with their arms folded, singing 'We shall overcome'. But they timed it all wrong, because they started at the beginning of the dinner hour so by the end of the dinner hour they were all worn out, tired, and they'd missed their dinner. And it was really easy to get them back in to school again.[572]

571. Ralph Levinson interview with Georgina Brewis; BL recording.
572. Margaret Gosley, https://www.ahackneyautobiography.org.uk/trails/education/1

The school magazine published a short introduction to most of the subjects offered at the school, setting out how they would be taught to CSE (Certificate of Secondary Education) and GCE standards. The geography department jettisoned textbooks and taught A level, O level and CSE in a 'home-made programme'. The Technical Studies department also prepared boys for O level, A level and CSE. For the first two year-groups, the science department followed the Nuffield Combined Science scheme, but then taught the separate branches of science. There was also a two-year Social Studies course for the fourth and fifth forms, which included academic work and visits to playgroups, primary schools and old peoples' homes. Some sixth formers assisted in the school's Remedial Department.[573] During the summer holiday 1973, a Headstart project was introduced, offering 40 pupils due to start in September a specially designed induction week. During the year, the school was disrupted by a series of National Union of Teachers' strikes[574] and at least five break-ins and thefts of school property.

In 1972, Joseph Brearley took early retirement, aged 62.[575] In a farewell speech, John Kemp, who took over as Deputy Head, enlarged upon Brearley's need to 'live big':

> ... the school has often been nearly big enough, never just an East London school. It has been in a sense European, in a sense classless, and much of its quality and strength has lain in its Jewishness.... [A] sense of a deep past and suffering were somewhere there; and a sense of energy, curiosity and argument. Poland and Russia were there, and Yiddish and Hebrew, and it was right for Joe; his temperament could be 'met,' and it could often be free. He has said that anyone who has taught at Hackney Downs becomes an 'honorary Jew'; and Yorkshireman as he is, he is an honorary Jew, too. Such paradoxes for someone who, I think, is also an honorary German.[576]

573. Review, December 1972.
574. Teaching staff turnover in London schools was at a record high of 30 percent annually, and young teachers were finding it practically impossible to find affordable accommodation in the capital. In 1973, a series of controversial strikes were called to press for an increase in teachers' London Allowance.
575. A former pupil reported Brearley saying: 'I'll soon be retiring. I'm not spending my time teaching a bunch of dimwits.' TCL.
576. John Kemp, June 1968, responding to Brearley's journal, *The Search for the Golden Flower*. HDS Archive. He added '[Joe] wrestled with ideas of God that have got in the way. Ideas of God are elusive opponents, so battle has tended to be joined with their visible manifestations, in the person of teachers of R.I., organists, and Headmasters... Yet something in his mind allowed him to pace the corridor, chanting ... "*Libera me, Domine, de mortua aeterna, in die illa tremenda*".'

Deputy Head Joseph Brearley in the school library.

Many former pupils' views were less nuanced: one recalled: 'I have this picture of [Brearley], always raging about school, raging…'[577]

Many traditions continued in the new Hackney Downs. Annual plays resumed: *Andorra* by Max Frisch in 1971; Robert Bolt's *The Thwarting of Baron Bolligrew* in 1972; and *Indians*, by Arthur Kopit, in 1973 – all produced by English teacher Frances Magee. She also produced *The Tempest* in the new theatre in 1975, to mark the retirement of Alec Williams; and, with a huge cast, Brecht's *The Resistible Rise of Arturo Ui* in 1976.

A small group of boys produced a subversive magazine called *The Hackney Miscarriage: The Irresponsible Generation Bites Deeper*, printed on a Gestetner with the support of the radical bookshop Centerprise. One of those involved recalled:

> The magazine was very badly received at the school and seen as a dig at everything it stood for. The humour was irreverent and the articles were often anti-police and anti-authority. We were just testing the limits and probably influenced by publications such as *Oz* and *International Times* etc.… When the first magazine came out, a storm erupted at the school – absolute mayhem. It was banned.[578]

577. Ralph Levinson interview with Georgina Brewis: BL recording.
578. Neil Littman, pupil. https://www.ahackneyautobiography.org.uk/trails/education/5

Centerprise also published a collection of 50 poems by a Hackney Downs pupil, 12-year-old Jamaican-born Vivian Usherwood. His poem 'The Earth has opened its mouth' opens:

> As the earth rumbles I cry.
> The earth opens up like an alligator.
> And eats the people and the buildings
> Without even showing.
> It suddenly opens without giving a warning...[579]

At Easter 1974, when Williams retired, John Kemp voiced little doubt about his achievement:

> There can be few Headmasters who have combined to quite the same degree the capacity to solve problems quickly and economically; shrewdness over both personalities and finances; foresight; consideration for others; and fairmindedness . . . Buildings rose and fell in complicated succession, so that the use of accommodation had to be replanned, not once or twice, but every year for several years, and sometimes several times in a year. To make complexity still more complex, the decision to develop as a Comprehensive School was taken as the new Grammar School was being built, so that as soon as some new rooms were occupied, we had to think about tearing the insides out to turn them into something different. Throughout all this Mr Williams remained clear-sighted and dependable . . . As a result, the school . . . never lost a sense of identity, staff morale has remained high, and a spirit of co-operation and goodwill has been kept up . . . [580]

This for public consumption. On the other hand, a left-leaning senior teacher reckoned Williams 'had no idea what he was doing' during the transition to comprehensive, and recalled that, when Williams had to go into hospital and John Kemp asked what needed doing, Williams replied 'There's not a lot – there's just canoeing certificates to issue . . . '[581]

---

579. Vivian Usherwood: *Poems*, Dalston: Centerprise, 1972. Usherwood died in a housefire in 1982, aged 21.
580. *Review* 195, December 1973.
581. Roy Dunning/John Hardcastle; BL oral history.

Chapter 7
Hopes and Fears
John Kemp, Headmaster 1974–1989

> *Hackney is an unusually underprivileged place. It has by far the highest proportion of dwellings unfit for human habitation . . . and by far the lowest educational attainments in London. Incomes in Hackney are the lowest in London, and well below the national averages . . .*
> From *Inside the Inner City: Life Under the Cutting Edge*
> Paul Harrison, 1983

At the very time Hackney Downs Grammar school was being converted into a comprehensive, a survey revealed that Hackney had a disturbing profile of low-attainment in primary schools, low staying-on rates at secondary level and a high proportion of children from immigrant families. All this in an area with high population density, high rates of illegitimate births and mental health referrals, dangerously high air pollution and large numbers of poor and unfit dwellings.[582] In addition, from the early 1980s Hackney's Labour-run council was riven with factional disputes:

> Hackney Council has a uniquely dreadful reputation. In-fighting amongst the permanent but faction-ridden Labour majority, waste and inefficiency, political-correctness policing, extensive fraud and internal corruption . . .[583]

It was against this context that the leaders of Hackney Downs strove to run a safe, effective school.

Eight candidates applied to succeed Williams as Head, four of whom were shortlisted.[584] The successful candidate was John Kemp,[585]

---
582. *Social Atlas of London*, 1974.
583. Jake Arnold-Foster, *New Statesman*, July 1996. See also Elks, pp. 84–5.
584. School Report.
585. Kemp ceased editing the annual school magazine, the *Review*, when he became head. It was replaced in July 1975 with a larger-format, illustrated version, edited and produced by English teacher Robin Chambers, then in 1976 by a spiral-bound version, edited by Peter

the Deputy Head, and the first internal appointment to the post. Kemp (1929–2009), son of a London post-office manager, graduated with first-class honours in English at King's College London, where he also completed a Master's degree.[586] He taught at Minchenden Grammar School, Southgate, for a few months before moving in January 1954 to become Head of English at Hackney Downs, where he spent the remainder of his working life.[587] Kemp was a sensitive man, with a strong egalitarian impulse; he recruited women teachers in an all-boys school, and refused to resign from the National Union of Teachers after his appointment as Headmaster.

By this date – 1974 – the school roll had risen to 985. Kemp's first term as Head was marked by a series of unofficial strikes by NUT members on the staff. At the end of the summer term, 19 teachers left, which added to the organisational disruption.[588] The autumn term saw a number of break-ins at the school premises, the responsibility for which was traced to pupils. In September 1975, staff expressed concern about the new first-form: 'our first impression had been of a wilder, more difficult intake. Later modified'. At a staff meeting on 25 October, 'increasing aggressiveness in the school' was noted, while a similar meeting on 3 December addressed the subject of 'Black children in school, & Black Community in Hackney'.[589] In November 1977, news of the death after a heart attack of the former Deputy Head, Brearley, aged just 68, came as a shock to many. In 1978, there was another fire at the school, which resulted in the destruction, among other things, of much of the school archive.

The proportion of 'old grammar school' standard pupils now fell, and non-streamed, mixed-ability classes were introduced, which Kemp later said:

> may have taken the edge off the highest academic achievement in some subjects, at some times. . . .
> Nevertheless, a lot of 'average' pupils achieved far more than the arbitrary categories might have suggested . . .[590].

In an undated document for new members of staff, John Kemp attempted to outline the school's profile and modus operandi:

Hollamby. There was no subsequent printed annual review of the school's affairs.
586. *The Times*, 4 May 2009; Kemp was the first Head of Hackney Downs to be accorded a full-length obituary in this newspaper.
587. He acquired the nickname 'Neddie' after he let slip his fondness for the Goon Show, in which Harry Secombe played the hapless Neddie Seagoon.
588. A crisis of teacher supply in London at this period was exacerbated by the raising of the school leaving age in 1973. Maclure p. 199.
589. John Kemp's notes, in the School Record.
590. Kemp, p. v.

> The school is inclined to democratic processes, and there are various Committees dealing with such matters as curriculum, resources and expenditure, as well as meetings to consider cooperation between departments, Common Room matters, and whatever else arises.[591]

Regarding 'Homework', he explained:

> We want children of all abilities to do some work at home, whatever suits them best... Obviously in an area with so many social problems, children may have great difficulty in working at home, and we have to allow for that.[592]

There remained a strong emphasis on drama, with school productions of politically-themed plays, such as Brecht's *The Resistible Rise of Arturo Ui* and Nigel Williams' *Class Enemy* – attended by the playwright[593] – and a revival of Thornton Wilder's *Our Town* (1980). In the new buildings, provision had been made for a wider range of art activities. The Head of Art[594] had been invited to advise the architect on equipping his studio, which included a pottery room and kiln. The school recruited optimistic young teachers, often left-leaning, some of whom attempted to transform the curriculum.[595]

With these apparently progressive and successful developments, Hackney Downs became 'one of the apples of the ILEA's eye,'[596] with overseas visitors who wished to observe education frequently directed to the school. 'We became a "media school"...' Kemp wrote later. 'It was, really, too much, and I think we began to rely on our own P.R. ... We were carried along by a real belief in ourselves.'[597] He reported hubristically to the school Governors:

> In the past year, the reputation of the school... has led to members of staff – particularly from the English and Modern Languages Departments – being in demand for lecturing and to run courses... I have myself been invited to lecture and run seminars at the London and Cambridge Education Departments, and

---

591. Hackney Downs School: Introductory Notes; HDS Archive.
592. Ibid. An ILEA Inspector's Report, 10–12 November 1989, objected to the 'implication that Hackney children cannot be expected to do [homework].' Hackney Downs School Review, 1–2 November 1989, Yvonne Beecham.
593. Brian Capaloff: *Eggs, Chips & Leo's Café*. Amazon, n.d., pp. 112–113.
594. Douglas Fry.
595. John Hardcastle, personal communication.
596. Kemp, p. v. This was due in part to Kemp's personal charisma.
597. Kemp, p. v.

at the Royal College of Defence Studies. . . . Thames Television spent two days here in November . . . filming a programme to demonstrate how a school can use the media of cine-film, video-film and printing in its own educational work. Large parties of students from London, Leicester and Cambridge have visited us; we are told that the lecturer from the Cambridge Education Department's English section announced . . . that given our circumstances and what we are trying to do, we must be one of the best Comprehensives in England.[598]

However a number of factors over which the school had little or no influence conspired to undermine this optimistic view. Among these were changes in the demography of north London – particularly Hackney. As we have seen, upwardly mobile Jewish families, whose forebears had moved into the borough half a century earlier from East End slums, now moved on to the semi-detached suburbia of north-west and north-east London. In the mid-1950s, more than half the pupils were Jewish; by 1970, less than a third; by the end of the 1970s, scarcely any.[599] As Jews moved out of the borough other groups moved in. First came immigrants from the Caribbean, then those from Bangladesh, Vietnam, Turkey (including Kurdish Turkey) and Somalia, as well as a minority from Eastern Europe.

By 1976, roughly half the school's pupils were people of colour, and by 1990 pupils spoke some 27 different languages. For the first time, Hackney Downs had a majority of pupils who lacked a basic grasp of English, and the school had to develop a policy to meet this problem, appointing specialist staff to teach English as a Second Language.[600] Significant cultural issues and challenges also surfaced: for example, some Muslim parents objected to their sons being taught by women, and – like some Afro-Caribbean parents – expected the school to foster a regime of corporal punishment, which became illegal in all ILEA

---

598. *Centenary Review*, December 1976, p. 6. Not all publicity was positive. *The Daily Mail* education correspondent Christopher Rowlands visited the school to report on an exchange visit by a Russian teacher and followed up with an article mentioning 'pornographic drawings in text books, disturbances in class, a guest teacher upset to the extent that she was in tears'. Capaloff: *Eggs*, pp. 109–110.
599. One pupil in the mid-1970s recalled having been bullied for being Jewish. He also recorded that naked swimming was still the practice and experienced bullying from two PE teachers. (Brian Capaloff: *Eggs*, pp. 70, 78). By 1989 the school had only two Jewish pupils (Black, p. 60). Although many Jews still lived in the borough, fundamentalist beliefs led many to reject secular schools in favour of faith-based academies.
600. The Hackney Downs Staff Handbook (September 1986) contains a section devoted to English as a Second Language (ESL) and bilingual pupils.

schools in 1981.[601]

In September 1983, as part of the ILEA anti-racist policy to improve provision for bilingual pupils, a pioneering project was set up at Hackney Downs for pupils to be taught English as a second language within the school, rather than – as hitherto – at a local language centre. Hackney Downs was selected because 'the school has been sensitive to its changing population' and

> there is . . . a conscious fostering of cultural and linguistic awareness in the pupils . . . Concerned teachers from maths, modern languages, humanities and English formed an ESL working party to keep consciousness of bilingual pupils' needs on the whole-staff agenda.[602]

Kemp attempted to address racism within the school:

> ...initiatives included a 'racist incident monitoring group', which included staff and pupils, and various staff-pupil discussions. This helped us to deal with, and moderate, all sorts of potential clashes; notably when large numbers of Vietnamese boys ('boat people') arrived in a few weeks. The older Afro-Caribbean pupils felt challenged in their 'manor', and conflicts in the school were associated with street clashes. Lengthy discussion with the black pupils, individually and in groups, worked through the crisis (made stickier by the Vietnamese having almost no English)...[603]

In the 1970s the move towards multiculturalism began in Britain, challenging previous educational policies of assimilation and integration. The ILEA circulated its initial papers on multi-ethnic education in 1977. A long-gestated Department of Education and Science report *Education for All*, finally published in 1985, defined the task of education as:

601. As early as 1976, Kemp had identified such a tendency in 'black parents': Kemp to the District Inspector, ILEA, 9 December 1976 [typescript carbon copy in the possession of the Clove Club]; his letter was triggered by a fifth-former having slapped a woman teacher.
602. Sylvia Riley and Jean Bleach, 'Three Moves in the Initiating of Mainstreaming at Secondary Level' in edd. Christopher Brumfit, Rod Ellis and Josie Levine, *English as a Second Language in the United Kingdom*. Oxford: Pergamon, 1985, pp. 79–80.
603. Letter from John Kemp to Sally Tomlinson, 7 June 1999; UCL IoE Archive HD. On the Vietnamese community see also Elks, pp. 87–89. John Hardcastle claims 'boat people' was a clumsy and unhelpful label. Some of these pupils were Hong Kong Chinese or Sino Vietnamese, often middle-class, and in some cases already speaking both English and French – yet the Senior Management Team felt it would be 'too much to expect them to learn English and French from the beginning'. ESL lessons and Vietnamese reading books were inappropriate for these boys. Personal communication.

meeting the needs of ethnic minority pupils and preparing all pupils, both ethnic majority and ethnic minority, for life in a society which is both multi-racial and culturally diverse.[604]

The report claimed that West Indian children were:

underachieving in relation to their peers ... There is no single cause ... but rather a network of widely differing attitudes and expectations on the part of the teachers and the education system as a whole, and on the part of the West Indian child to have particular difficulties and face particular hurdles in achieving his or her full potential.[605]

Despite the new immigrant influx, the Hackney child population fell during the 1970s, whilst increasing numbers of parents opted for coeducational secondary schools. Ever since the headmastership of Gull, Hackney Downs had been oversubscribed; but by the mid-1980s, with 180 places on offer, the school was receiving only around 120 applicants for admission. Although at the start of Hackney Downs' life as a comprehensive school there was a disproportionately large high-achieving intake, by the 1980s this imbalance had been reversed, as the school gradually lost its high-ability intake, becoming – in all but name – a secondary modern school. Smaller numbers of pupils led in turn to reductions in staff numbers, financial cuts and attempts by ILEA officials to increase the school's falling roll by transferring from other schools boys with learning and behavioural problems or who had been expelled. The full impact of these developments was felt only after Kemp retired, though the rapid turnover of staff was already having a deleterious effect.[606]

In March 1982, the ILEA instigated a Quinquennial Review of Hackney Downs; its glowing report concluded:

The unanimous opinion of the visiting team of inspectors was that rarely does one visit a school where the staff seem so valued, so involved in decision-making and so consulted in a meaningful way. The lessons seen and the atmosphere experienced around the school suggests a very good staff-pupil relationship. All agreed that pupils really are known by the staff and every effort is made to meet their needs. A great deal of credit, it seems, must

---

604. Race, pp. 181, 183.
605. Race, p. 183.
606. The French department 'suffered a 100% turnover within the last three years.' Quinquennial Review 1980-81, May 1982, p. 74.

go to the Head and his effective style of leadership. The overwhelming impression of the school during the two days spent there was one of admiration for what was going on.[607]

The inspectors singled out for praise the Humanities course – which combined English, history, geography, social studies and drama – as a positive example of inter-departmental collaboration. Teaching this programme in 1982, John Hardcastle worked with a group of four black and three white students, considering the place of Afro-Caribbean history in the school's curriculum, with discussion extending to racism, class, slavery and cultural history. One pupil completed a 23-page report, suggesting this type of work offered 'The possibility of taking control of our own lives, our own education, and becoming our own experts . . .'[608] Attempts were made to create a new A-level literature course, concentrating on Caribbean and African literature, for 'pupils . . . dissatisfied with the more traditional approach', and including proposals to introduce multi-cultural literature and coursework.[609]

However this approach cut across the curriculum and assessment policies proposed by ILEA Chief Inspector Dr David Hargreaves in a report[610] intended to address 'falling standards' and long-standing questions about achievement vis à vis social class. This resulted in a meeting at the school, when Hargreaves asked Hardcastle: 'If you teach [the Caribbean poet Derek] Walcott, how do I reply to ILEA members who ask why you're not teaching Milton' and 'Can I tell ILEA members that Black students' attainment levels improve if they study Black literature?' Hardcastle responded that Walcott was included for his literary merit, for his symbolic importance as a Black writer – and because many Hackney pupils' families originated in St Lucia.[611] To the

---

607. ILEA Hackney Downs Quinquennial Review: Supplement: Inspectors' Visit, 30–31 March 1982; HDS Archive.
608. Alex McLeod: 'Critical Literacy: Taking Control of Our Own Lives', *Language Arts*, January 1986, Vol. 63, 1, p. 49.
609. Peter Traves, 'A better A level', in ed. Jane Miller, *Eccentric Propositions: Essays on literature and the curriculum*. London: Routledge & Kegan Paul, 1984, pp. 243–54. Some students participated with the author of a BBC World Service radio programme text. Staff/student relationships were informal, with teachers known by their forenames, feeling no need to conceal their left-wing allegiances – for instance to the Anarchist and Socialist Workers' Party – and recommending the works of such authors as Wilhelm Reich, Karl Marx and Ralph Miliband. Capaloff: *Eggs*, pp. 111, 118.
610. 'The first independent committee of inquiry to consider comprehensive schools and to do so within the specific context of a single... local education authority.' *Improving Secondary Schools*. Londin: ILEA, 1984, p. iii.
611. The Swann Report into the education of children from ethnic minorities – *Education for All*. London: HMSO, 1985 – endorsed the teaching of Black texts.

second question, Hardcastle had no evidence to offer. This was all in the context of the Brixton uprising of April 1981, when staff were 'asking ourselves why the riot didn't spread to Hackney.'[612]

The inspectors were also impressed with the school's sanctuary and remedial department, and encouraged the introduction in September 1982 of the ground-breaking 'Skills for Living' course. In the late 1970s an autonomous women's group, comprising teachers and support staff, had been set up to combat sexism and sexual harassment within the school. Arising out of this, a course developed by Claire Widgery and Mike Davies, aiming to combat sexist attitudes, was initiated – something quite exceptional in a boys' school at this date. This innovative scheme included food-work, childcare and domestic crafts such as sewing, and was intended to prepare boys for domestic responsibility, helping them to 'develop a repertoire of expression and ways of relating which included intimacy, trust, cooperation, mutual supportiveness . . .'.[613] It was also hoped the course might foster a collaborative approach:

> Home economics used to be very individualistic, but the boys here [at Hackney Downs] work in groups, and make a meal together: the emphasis is less on skills than on how they work together.[614]

This new curriculum also covered sexuality – 'previously cornered into the plumbing facts about human bodies in the science curriculum' – focussing on friendship and intimacy rather than sexual relationships.[615] These initiatives gained

> the involvement and positive support [of] pupils, parents, governors, the headteacher, John Kemp, and the majority of staff . . . The enthusiasm of the pupils spread around the whole school and older pupils were asking to join in.[616]

The ILEA held up this course as exemplary:

Hackney Downs is the first of the Authority's all boys'

---

612. Personal communication. In 1978 some boys leafleted and demonstrated on Hackney Downs as part of the protest group 'Hackney School Kids Against the Nazis', opposing the racism of the National Front. Capaloff: *Eggs*, p. 115.
613. Magee, p. 158.
614. Sue Askew, quoted in Anne Karpf, 'Boys won't always be boys', *The Guardian*, 12 March 1985, p. 23.
615. Magee, pp. 163–164. Two Hackney Downs women teachers published a booklet intended as a resource for in-service teacher training, covering such issues as how women experience sexism in boys' schools, sexual harassment and responses to sexism. Sue Askew and Carol Ross: *Sexism in Boys' Schools*. London: ILEA, 1985.
616. Magee, p. 161.

schools to make the issue of gender explicit in the curriculum ... Hackney Downs sets an example of attitudinal education which, while raising issues, is not coercive but which extends positively the range of choices the pupils have ...[617]

David Torn, a pupil at HDS in the 1980s, and later a much-lauded secondary school teacher, wrote glowingly of his experience of the school:

> Growing up in Hackney in the 1980s was tough. Even tougher when my mother died in 1981. I was 10 and my dad regularly spent all of his wages in the betting shop or the pub every Friday. However, there was a place I could go where I knew hope would reign supreme... Hackney Downs... was [a school] where students were genuinely cared for and encouraged to believe that they could make something of their lives. ... I am a teacher because of the passion that my teachers displayed. Their desire to bring about a fairer society moved me and inspired me to become one of them...[618]

In 1982, Hackney Downs staff presented the first local authority sponsored conference on programmes for boys, the ILEA's 'Equal Opportunities – What's in it for Boys'.[619]

Despite their lavish praise, the school inspectors noted areas which they believed needed attention, including religious and social education – especially comparative religion, health, careers and politics. They also called for better provision for 16–19 year-olds who were not taking A-levels, a greater focus on design and technology, greater consistency in marking pupils' work and stricter standards for homework, punctuality and attendance – all harbingers of future problems. Finally, they expressed concern about discipline, claiming some staff were ignoring or accepting

> noisy factious behaviour in the classrooms and corridors ... [which] could possibly lead to a borderline group whose non-integrated behaviour is reinforced by being ignored

---

617. Frances Morrell, Chair, Schools Sub-Committee, ILEA, 1985, quoted in 'Hackney Downs School, defence of the school'; HDS Archive.
618. David Torn, 'Wanted: heads who will fight to change the world', *tes magazine*, 7 March 2008. With Peter Bennett, Torn authored *Brilliant Secondary School Teacher.* Harlow: Prentice Hall, 2011.
619. Jane Martin: *Gender and Education in England since 1770*. Basingstoke: Palgrave Macmillan, 2021, p. 257.

and who will test out boundaries more and more.[620]

One of the school's deputy heads took a more nuanced view of discipline:

> The school was an orderly community, although a number of teachers believed that some of the order was based on traditional male values of competition, strength and power and a conventional, authoritarian approach to 'discipline'. In many ways the school was liberal and progressive, but pastoral care was unstructured and tended to respond to individual problems rather than the creation of a culture and ethos in which such problems might be minimized.[621]

Certainly serious issues of pupil behaviour were occurring as early as 1975. The Head of English reported:

> Last year we left all the rooms open for forms to use during break and lunchtimes, but there was so much damage to clocks, ceilings, wall displays, and furniture that after trying everything we could think of, short of denying teachers any break at all, we decided we must, for the time being at least, go back to locking doors.[622]

In an attempt to understand the context of this problem, the same teacher profiled current pupils' background:

> Most of the children come from high rise flats. Many have only one parent. Hardly any will have had playgroup or nursery experience... 70 boys out of our first year intake of 180 [aged 11] have reading ages below 8.5 years.[623]

Truancy and vandalism were growing problems in the school. By the early 1980s, while attendance in the first year averaged 90 percent, by the fifth year it could fall as low as 70 percent – occasionally even 50 percent. In his study of Hackney, Paul Harrison reported: 'Truants play video games in cafes, sniff glue, wander the streets, and, not infrequently, break the law'. John Kemp commented: 'Hackney kids bring into school the style of surviving on the street.'[624] Vandalism meant around ten door panels needed replacement every week, while classroom ceil-

---

620. ILEA Hackney Downs Quinquennial Review: Supplement: Inspectors' Visit, 30–31 March 1982; HDS Archive.
621. Magee, p. 157.
622. Robin Chambers, 'In Another Country: Hackney Downs', *English in Education*, Vol. 9 No. 1, Spring 1975.
623. Robin Chambers, 'In Another Country...'.
624. Harrison, p. 289.

ings had holes poked in them. Petty theft, both by pupils and intruders, was endemic: anything from handbags and dinner money to lab equipment and calculators was stolen, while extortion rackets – extracting pocket-money with menaces – were common.

In the mid-1970s, shortly after the school became comprehensive, Kemp and his staff attempted to clamp down on violence and disorder:

> but the result was a number of very dramatic confrontations. You can't screw these kids down. You have to talk through and defuse tensions, so you don't get explosions. But that means, inevitably, that we have to accept a less orderly and demure, more rough and ready atmosphere . .

Harrison noted the results of this policy while researching his book:

> Inside the building, one boy is strangling another on the stairs below the head's room. Another pair have each other in half-nelsons in the entrance. Teachers pass by without reacting. In the playground, boys push in front of teachers, trample over the shrubberies, and in whatever direction you look, there are half a dozen fights going on, of every degree of seriousness from horseplay to vicious sadism.[625]

A 1976 speech by Prime Minister James Callaghan at Ruskin College, Oxford, launched a major national debate on education and a government campaign to reduce the powers of local authorities, make teachers more accountable, give greater power to parents and increase public control of school curricula.[626] This rebalancing took a decade to implement, but resulted in new pressures on local authorities such as the ILEA:

> the view came to be held in government that the education service was not providing value for the money spent on it . . . [and] the education service found itself increasingly on the defensive.[627]

The left-leaning politics of the ILEA fuelled a gathering storm. In 1981, the Greater London Council, of which the ILEA was a committee,[628] was controlled by a left-wing Labour group led by Ken Livingstone. The ILEA now banned streaming by ability in addition to selection by ability, and – in

---

625. Harrison, p. 290.
626. Maclure, p. 193.
627. Sir Peter Newsam, Chief Education Officer of the ILEA 1975–81, in 1981. Maclure, p. 193.
628. From 1986, the ILEA was directly elected.

an attempt to meet problems of recruitment – implemented a policy of compulsory redeployment of teachers. Kemp was no longer able to appoint the teachers he considered most suitable; instead he was constrained to accept 'a diet of unwilling recruits, temporary appointments and a high proportion of "supply" staff.'[629]

The ethos of Hackney Downs teaching staff changed too. The Hargreaves report highlighted the fact that 'the state of teacher morale has proved to be a recurring theme' in London schools.[630] During the 1980s, semi-formal groups and alliances began to form among the school's teachers, who identified with various different socio-political movements outside of school. Kemp regarded this as 'the idealism you needed to teach in the city' which he believed 'often went with left-wing politics.'[631] Others were more specific in their analysis:

> [in the 1980s] Hackney Downs attracted . . . a high proportion of politically idealistic teachers. At various times it employed some of the most high-profile Left-wingers in East London, who were disliked at the ILEA and at the National Union of Teachers HQ.[632]

This group became involved in a series of local salary disputes, which made the school unpopular with both parents and the education authority, and so less likely to attract new pupils. When twelve teachers were arrested for demonstrating outside an ILEA divisional office, protesting against the authority's failure to challenge racism in their schools, two were from Hackney Downs.[633] The ILEA ruled that the school, with its declining popularity and falling roll, had to make do with fewer resources. Essential repairs and maintenance were hugely delayed, or not carried out all, with the result that the buildings deteriorated into an eyesore. In 1985, following a break-in, two of the science rooms were damaged by fire; it was two years before they were repaired.

Until about 1985, the school continued to provide a good standard of education as a comprehensive. However, following the 1982 inspection, classed as a 'specimen' operation, a second inspection was carried out in July 1985. Kemp reckoned:

> those two years had seen a big change in the ILEA, with 'rigour' becoming the buzz-word, especially as the ILEA

629. O'Connor, p. 16.
630. *Improving Secondary Schools*. London: ILEA, 1984, p. 98.
631. Kemp, p. viii.
632. O'Connor, p. 19.
633. L. R. Reed, '"Zero tolerance": gender performance and school failure,' in ed. Debbie Epstein, Jannette Elwood, Valerie Hey and Janet Maw: *Failing Boys? Issues in gender and achievement*. Buckingham: Open University, p. 69.

was facing a hostile government, and trying to prove that it, too, could demand 'standards.'[634]

Nevertheless, the 1985 report remained largely complimentary:

> The school has much to recommend it. Its policies have been consistent with the principles of comprehensive education. Mixed ability teaching operates across the 11–16 age-range, group sizes are small, pupils have the opportunity to negotiate some of their learning and there has been considerable curriculum development in many areas of the curriculum. Much of the teaching is distinguished, a variety of appropriate styles being used. The school has played a leading role in implementing the Authority's initiatives.
>
> The school is to be congratulated upon developing highly positive relationships between pupils and staff and also within the staff. This is testimony to the deep commitment the staff feel towards pupils and is apparent in the mutual respect that was shown.[635]

The inspectors added, 'This is a school with a most civilised and humane working environment…'[636] For the first time adjectives such as 'disappointing', 'unsatisfactory' and 'rigorous' appeared:

> … there are grounds for concern based on measurable indices of performance. The school has had difficulty in recruiting pupils for the coming school year, public examination performance has been disappointing and the staying-on rate is low. Attendance, though improving, is still unsatisfactory, particularly in the fourth and fifth years. It is essential for the school to retain its present humane and liberal atmosphere but there are indications that a more rigorous approach to whole school policies is needed as a prerequisite to further development.[637]

This perceptive verdict identifies the negative trends that were, in part, to prove the school's eventual undoing.

However, after a further visit in November 1987, 'to concentrate upon evidence in the form of documentation, work done and work in progress' one inspector, who wished to see the school succeed, noted:

---

634. Kemp, p. viii.
635. O'Connor, pp. 17–18. This report was written by David Hargreaves, subsequently Professor of Education at the University of Cambridge.
636. Jane Martin, op cit, p. 257.
637. O'Connor, pp. 17–18.

'The lessons I saw were particularly well structured and all pupils engaged in their work.' He stressed his findings ought to be considered alongside those of other inspectors, who were less impressed. He noted that unemployment among Hackney Downs school leavers – 5 percent – was among the lowest in the division, and that a much higher number of pupils were achieving Grade A at O/GCSE level than elsewhere. 'I think the school should be supported . . .'[638]

From 1987 onwards, Hackney Downs was regarded negatively by the ILEA. In 1983–84 it lost control of its curriculum to the authority.[639] For a time Hackney Downs shared a sixth form with John Howard girls' school, but by the mid-1980s no secondary school in Hackney had a sufficient number of academically qualified pupils to justify a sixth form. In 1986–87 the ILEA abolished school-based sixth forms and set up sixth-form colleges in their place. The loss of a sixth form deprived Hackney Downs of the kudos of pupils who progressed to higher education. The policy made economic sense, but dealt a heavy blow to a school which had previously attracted highly-qualified teachers enthused by the challenge of preparing pupils for university entrance: 'Suddenly, with an increasing proportion of low-ability juniors, the place looked far more like a "secondary modern," less attractive to new teachers.'[640]

In 1986 a group led by a hard-left NUT geography teacher[641] fought for the removal of the asbestos used in rebuilding the school twenty years earlier.[642] This resulted in closure of the affected building for more than a year, and the use of unsuitable alternative premises, such as portakabins in the front playground. 'Temporary timetable after temporary timetable was drawn up, imposed and discarded. The school descended into organizational chaos.'[643] In a bitterly cold winter, with the heating system failing, almost every school building was out of action: most

638. Russell David to John Kemp, 19 November 1987; HDS Archive.
639. This development should not be confused with the imposition of a National Curriculum, under the Education Reform Act of 1988. However the advent of the National Curriculum, and the need to comply with it, imposed stresses on Hackney Downs at a time when the school was least able to cope with additional bureaucratic burdens.
640. Kemp, p. ix. The virtual end of pupils entering higher managerial and professional careers contributed to the demise of the Clove Club, which effectively ceased to exist in 1986. It was revived in 1995, mainly in response to the impending closure of the school. For the next two decades it published a successful newsletter, *The Clove's Lines*, sharing news and memories of former pupils, and creating an active network. The considerable exodus of former pupils to Israel meant successful reunions were held there in 1988 and 1999.
641. Richard Rieser, who became Director of Disability Equality in Education.
642. Kemp claimed this crisis 'reinforced the long-held ILEA view that HDS had a troublesome union.' Kemp, p. viii.
643. O'Connor, p. 19.

teaching – including drama, art and the humanities – took place in the science labs.[644] John Kemp reported: 'lessons went on in one or two remaining oddments of building, pupils coming in in shifts to work or to receive homework.'[645] An ILEA Inspector noted:

> the prolonged asbestos-related disruption is causing considerable strain which has been aggravated by the absence of technical support . . . the year has, physically, mentally and emotionally, been the hardest yet . . . The virtual exodus of your mathematics department is another bitter blow. . .[646]

Writing in September 1987, John Kemp looked back on the previous twelve months:

> . . . a terrible year: closed buildings, bad conditions, cramped space, car park full of huts, dust, mess. Science block. Gas, water, electricity. Felt it would never be over.[647]

In an emotional letter written shortly before his death Kemp summarised the deteriorating situation:

> As the 80s went on, and the intake became more and more difficult, the tensions in London, Hackney, and the school involved Union rivalries; various left-wing groups in the Union; racial tensions between neighbourhood groups; rivalries within the ILEA and in Hackney; a crude sort of 'black power' ideology affecting many local councillors; feminist cross-currents as the staff changed; and others.[648]

By the end of the decade, the school roll had fallen to fewer than 700. Many of the new entrants were, in Kemp's words, 'awkward customers,' forced into the school whether the Head approved or not.[649] A document entitled 'Discipline Problems – Who to refer to' details how members of staff were to deal with poor behaviour, 'emergencies' and 'serious misbehaviour outside lesson-time'. A document for pupils entitled 'School Rules' lists basic regulations, such as not interfering with other people's property, not scattering litter, spitting or writing or

---

644. John Kemp, 'Sylvia Chatwin', HDS Archive.
645. John Kemp to Sally Tomlinson, 7 June 1999. UCL IoE Archive.
646. Russell David, Acting Divisional Inspector, ILEA, to John Kemp, 8 June 1987; HDS Archive.
647. Handwritten note; HDS Archive.
648. Handwritten letter to Willie Watkins; HDS Archive.
649. O'Connor, p. 24.

scratching on walls. The Head felt it necessary spell out a ban on 'fireworks, matches and lighters, and of course weapons' and on climbing 'out of the playground onto surrounding property or roofs'.[650]

John Kemp's energy and devotion to duty cannot be doubted: among his papers he left a five-page single-spaced account of 'A typical day for me at Hackney Downs', which included an in-tray of 27 items awaiting him on arrival at school at 8.40 am, countless phone-calls, conversations and unanticipated meetings throughout the day, including a 'cover' lesson that he had agreed to teach. He left school at 5.55 pm, discussing problems with the Head of English on his train journey home, and taking with him work on pupil references and assembly preparation.[651] Kemp took his role very seriously, making detailed notes for school assembly talks, which covered behaviour, events in the news and ethical and faith themes. The wide range of topics he addressed included town-planning, religion and morality, the Red Cross, homework, waste and recycling, the school environment, fighting, taking responsibility, noise, Chernobyl, the Hillsborough Stadium disaster, religious festivals, smoking, road safety, Advent, Christmas and Yule, the moon – and even memories of the closure of the school field in July 1968, with Joseph Brearley playing Wagner over the PA system.[652]

In 1988, Margaret Thatcher's Education Reform Act – 'ERA' – demolished the post-war educational settlement, shifting power to central government and decreasing the role of local education authorities. These reforms introduced a national curriculum, initiated parental choice and began the policy of monitoring school performance by means of regular testing and inspection, publishing results and encouraging competition.

In May 1989 the Labour-run ILEA – abolished twelve months later – became the first local authority to name its worst performing comprehensive schools: Battersea Park; St Richard of Chichester, Camden; and Hackney Downs. The school was shocked and angered. There had been no warning that the ILEA had identified the school as a 'cause for concern' before the arrival of a letter from the Education Officer[653] asserting: 'Hackney Downs became a source of real concern following the publication of an ILEA Inspection Report back in 1985.' As we have seen, that report was generally positive, while recommending improvements. Mallen claimed the nub of the problem was that the school had failed to recruit enough pupils.[654] He seems to have hung the school out

650. Undated duplicated documents issued by John Kemp; HDS archive.
651. 'Head's Log' 1986; HDS Archive.
652. Handwritten notes in HDS Archive
653. David Mallen, appointed in 1988. The letter was dated 27 April 1989.
654. Mallen to Kemp, 27 April 1989, quoted in a duplicated defence of the school; HDS Archive.

to dry, advising the Headmaster to prepare a press statement because the press might pick up the story – which it did, and not just locally. The *Daily Telegraph* headline was: 'ILEA enrages staff by naming worst schools'.[655] With hindsight it seems, from this date, the school's future was in doubt.

In a defensive response, the school argued that the opening nearby of the large coeducational Kingsland School, and the high staffing levels at Kingsland and Homerton House boys' school, had brought about the falling roll at Hackney Downs – and that the school's first-year intake for September 1989 was double that of the previous year. The school argued further that the Muslim community, with a preference for single-sex education, placed growing confidence in the school, which offered a carpeted prayer-room and hosted Eid festivities and other Muslim cultural events. The school also maintained that, 'given our current intake' – some of the most disadvantaged children in Hackney, with 61 percent awarded free school meals and 45 percent having English as a second language – 'we are still achieving comparative success at examination level' and that 'maths results in 1988 were the best in Hackney . . . '. Despite falling rolls and staff shortages, Hackney Downs claimed to be 'way ahead of most other schools in the Division, in having "Broad and Balanced" science on offer for all pupils', and that 'this recent representation of our work and our school by the ILEA [was] casual, inaccurate and insulting'.[656]

The politics of Hackney began to enter the school. In the early 1980s, a Hackney Black Teachers Group had been set up, with Hackney Downs at its centre.[657] By 1985, a combined Hackney Black Parents and Teachers Group had been formed, organising a conference on 'The Impact of the Schools Psychological Service on Black Children', to address such issues as language diversity and testing.[658]

By the late 1980s, independent groups within the school included a women's staff group, a Black staff group and a Black parents group, with the rare situation of the Black Chief Education Officer, Gus John, attempting to mediate between Black and white staff and the school

---

655. *The Daily Telegraph*, May 5 1989, p. 2.
656. Hackney Downs School, duplicated defence of the school; HDS Archive.
657. A working conference of Ethnic Minority Teachers within the ILEA was held on 28 March 1983, organized by the Hackney Black Teachers Group and supported by Hackney NUT. 52 black teachers from Hackney attended, the first time black staff had been released to attend such a conference during school time. The conference 'overwhelmingly demonstrated that racism permeates the entire [London] educational system'. 'Report of Working Conference and Minutes of Black Teachers Group', UCL IoE Archive MF/8/42.
658. 1 June 1985, held at Hackney Free and Parochial School. Leaflet; UCL IoE Archive HD.

Governors.⁶⁵⁹ At an in-service training day in 1989, the staff Women's Group listed a number of grievances about the treatment of female staff by both pupils and male teachers, and complained about the use of aggression to manage pupils.⁶⁶⁰ Eventually the Black Staff Group and Black Parents' Group coalesced into a Black Staff and Parents' Group (BSPG). A printed leaflet was circulated, explaining the group 'was formed to deal with issues in education which affect Black pupils, Black parents and Black Teachers', and listing their concerns, which included racism, suspension/expulsion, school transfer, cultural/historical education and interpersonal relationships with teachers/headteachers.⁶⁶¹

Fed by the discrimination and violence that Hackney's Afro-Caribbean population was experiencing, Black activism expanded, with calls to emulate black-power groups in the USA calling for equality separation. One local group campaigned for Hackney Downs to be turned into a Black-only school, arguing that if Jewish faith schools could be established so should a school catering solely for boys of Afro-Caribbean background. In a 'racist incident book', Black teachers and parents started to record alleged under-achievement by Black pupils in classes taught by white teachers. Kemp's successor as Head, John Douglas, argued that any such record should be kept 'as a whole school document . . . by a member of the Senior Management Team,' and asserted 'its . . . existence can only cause pupils to believe that Hackney Downs is a divided school with a divided staff...'⁶⁶² Black staff argued the school had damagingly low expectations of black pupils, stereotyping them as low achievers. In fact, exam results indicated that Black and Asian boys did better at Hackney Downs than in the borough as a whole and nationally, and it was the minority of white pupils who were underachieving.⁶⁶³ Some Black parents argued lack of discipline at the school caused their sons to underachieve, and that Black boys did not respond well to being taught by women. The Skills for Living course was attacked, as were 'approaches around doing work on gender that fail our male youth'.⁶⁶⁴

During the second half of 1989, increasing amounts of the Headmaster's time were occupied with attempts to contain factions within the school. In November came another ILEA inspection report, which lamented that 'the school [had] been allowed to fall into a state of such

---

659. Tomlinson, p. 92.
660. O'Connor, p. 21.
661. Copy in UCL IoE Archive MF/8/42.
662. Letter from John Douglas to The Black Parent/Staff Group, 26 March 1990; UCL IoE Archive MF/8/42.
663. O'Connor, p. 21.
664. L. R. Reed, '"Zero tolerance": gender performance and school failure,' in *Failing Boys?*, p. 70.

disrepair'. The inspectors criticised the school's homework policy and teachers' marking practice, yet all observed lessons were rated satisfactory – one very good. This new review concluded with 14 recommendations, some of which must have served further to demoralise staff – for instance: 'At least one Inset day should send at least all heads of department and preferably all teachers to observe good teaching in a high achieving department elsewhere.'

Understandably exhausted, John Kemp opted for early retirement in December 1989, just before the ILEA was wound down, not wishing to be employed by the London Borough of Hackney, 'a pretty Keystone Cop outfit at the best of times!'[665] Perhaps he stayed too long. He believed in the comprehensive ethos and was determined to make it succeed at Hackney Downs – and for a time it did so. Generously resourced, with a complement of able and supportive staff and a significant proportion of grammar-stream pupils, the teaching of mixed-ability classes had been successful. Although Hackney Downs no longer boasted the glittering roll-call of university entrances achieved formerly, exam results remained good.

In his leaving speech, John Kemp wrestled with the conundrum of the class and cultural implications of educationally empowering working-class pupils. He confessed to a love of 'the sharpness of London kids', but posed a paradox:

> a school in a working class area which must tend to
> be an instrument of class control, aiming to be a place
> giving power to working class children. But how were
> we going to do that without recreating them in the
> image of 'high culture'? Yet if we didn't recreate them
> so, weren't we trapping them in what we saw as their
> limitations?[666]

In the same address, Kemp told pupils that he had wanted their education to empower them to run their own lives, to choose how they did so, to be wise and not be pushed around. One of the joys of working at Hackney Downs, he said, was 'there was always the chance that any class might have somebody in it cleverer than you were.'[667]

---

665. John Kemp letter to 'Alan', 26 November 1992; HDS Archive.
666. Ibid.
667. Handwritten notes, HDS Archive.

Chapter 8
Endgame: 1990–1995

1989 was not only the year John Kemp departed but also the year that the ILEA was abolished, a result of the Thatcherite assault on London's government. As from 1 April 1990, the education authority's functions were delegated to the various London boroughs. The London Borough of Hackney now set up its own autonomous education authority, with Hackney Downs School under its control. At the time the school was transferred to the care of Hackney, it was one of eight in the borough 'giving cause for concern'. The break-up of the ILEA, and the budget cuts forced on the boroughs by the Conservative national government, inhibited the new education authority from the outset.

Formed in 1965 from the old boroughs of Hackney, Stoke Newington and Shoreditch, Hackney was controlled by Labour at the outset. In 1968, power in Hackney shifted to the Conservatives – then three years later back to Labour. However, the 1990 local elections left no party in overall control, reflecting the political turmoil in the area, with the Hackney Labour Party itself deeply fractured. After retirement, John Kemp harboured perhaps paranoid suspicions 'that some of the former ILEA officials who took up office in the new Hackney authority brought with them some sort of hostility-residue to the school'.[668]

By the end of the 1980s, Hackney had become one of the most densely populated, culturally diverse and economically deprived boroughs in the country. More than 50 percent of families in the borough were single parent, while 50 percent were on low wages or no earned income. By 1990, 90 percent of Hackney Downs pupils came from ethnic minority families, 80 percent of them speaking English as a second language and 75 percent eligible for free school meals. 60 percent of pupils were registered as having Special Educational Needs, and a further 20 percent were awaiting assessment for similar problems. Immediately neighbouring the school were the notorious Pembury and Nightingale

668. Kemp, p. x.

estates,[669] home to crack-cocaine dens, heightening levels of drug usage and related problems in the borough. Between 1985 and 1995, more than 66 percent of the school's intake lived in these estates.[670]

Policing in Hackney had for some time been corrupt and racist: Ernie Roberts, Labour MP for Hackney North and Stoke Newington, claimed there was 'a complete breakdown of faith and credibility in the police'. The death of 21-year-old Black British Colin Roach at Stoke Newington police station in 1983 led to protests and demonstrations and a powerful report indicting the policing of Hackney. Another report described incidents involving police and schoolchildren, such as the following:

> A teacher from Hackney Downs School witnessed 12 and 13 year old boys [sic] in their lunch hour being stopped, spread-eagled and searched by a squad of Special Patrol Group officers.[671]

At another Hackney school, a teacher who intervened when some boys were frisked outside their school was arrested and charged with assault, but subsequently acquitted.[672]

In January 1990, the Department of Education and Science published a report entitled *Schools in Hackney: Some Issues*, deeming Hackney to be among those local authorities facing the greatest educational problems. This report judged that, across all the borough's secondary schools, only 20 percent of lessons were good/very good, and 50 percent of science and maths lessons and 40 percent of English lessons unsatisfactory or poor. The report concluded 'the scale of difficulties requires a radically different approach' – but offered no solutions apart from asserting 'Nothing will be achieved ... unless ... teacher recruitment and retention can be resolved. All the rest is dependent on that.'[673] Starting from basics, in autumn 1990 Hackney Education Authority published an attendance survey of its secondary schools, reviewing the monitoring of registration and emphasizing the legal and practical importance of regular and accurate attendance and punctuality records.[674]

---

669. The Pembury Estate was partly made up of 1930s L.C.C. 'walk-up' blocks of flats and partly of 1960s maisonettes and bungalows. The Nightingale Estate consisted of six 22-storey tower blocks, built in 1968 by the Greater London Council, which fell into disrepair in the late 1980s.
670. Neurath, p. 19.
671. *Policing in Hackney 1945–1984*. London: Karia Press, 1989; Elks, pp. 91–93; *Police Out of Schools*. Hackney Teachers Association, 1985.
672. Police Out of Schools.
673. *Schools in Hackney: Some Issues: A Report by HMI*. Department of Education and Science, January 1990. HDS Archive.
674. Hackney Secondary Schools Attendance Survey Autumn 1990, Hackney Education.

Between 1990 and 1995 the school had four different Headteachers, the last three 'Acting Heads'.[675] John Douglas, the immediate successor to John Kemp, left at the end of 1993.[676] Kemp noted that several good teachers left when he retired.[677] In the school's Prospectus,[678] Douglas claimed the school was 'once again proud of its latest examination results', with one third of GCSE entrants obtaining grades A C, the equivalent of an 'O' level pass. This Prospectus set out the school's current teaching practice and curriculum. Maths was taught under the SMILE scheme, with pupils organising work for themselves, using materials available in the classroom. Science and Humanities were taught as integrated studies, with the traditional sciences of biology, chemistry and physics combined as a single subject. The five-year integrated Humanities course covered 'History, Geography, Social Science and elements of Religious Education' and was based around 'four central themes . . . power, ideas, space and change'. Personal, Social and Health Education (PSHE) aimed to provide 'practical skills (foodwork, childcare, domestic crafts, etc.) to help boys learn to take domestic responsibility and not regard this as a woman's realm' – presumably developed from the earlier Skills for Living course.

By this date many serious structural and maintenance problems were evident in the school buildings, since the premises had long been neglected. An 8-page survey in January 1990 listed broken windows, leaking roofs, cracked walls in the science block and serious decay to the Victorian swimming pool. Despite years of complaints, Hackney offered neither funding nor resources to resolve these problems.[679]

The discipline book kept by Mr Douglas reveals continuing – or

---

675. The account that follows is a summary of the almost constant cycle of events, inspections, reports and controversies that occurred between the resignation of John Kemp and the school's closure in 1995. A detailed and documented account was published shortly after, written by a team consisting of the Acting Headteacher for the final period, Elizabeth Hales; Jeffrey Davies, Deputy Head in the same period; Maureen O'Connor, an educational journalist; and Professor Sally Tomlinson, an educational academic. The book argued that the school was wrongly closed, with many of the teachers, governors, parents and pupils feeling aggrieved – even betrayed. (Maureen O'Connor, Elizabeth Hales, Jeffrey Davies and Sally Tomlinson: *Hackney Downs: The School that Dared to Fight*. London: Cassell, 1999.) The book was originally to have been published by Falmer Press, who withdrew for legal reasons early in 1998 (IoE HD). See also Sally Tomlinson, 'A Tale of One School in One City,' in R. Slee, G. Weiner and S. Tomlinson (eds.): *School Effectiveness For Whom?* London: Falmer Press, 1999, pp. 157–69.
676. John Kemp claimed this was a 'virtual sacking': Letter to Howard Cohen, 5 June 1993; HDS Archive.
677. Kemp, p. x.
678. Undated, but probably 1991; HDS Archive.
679. Sally Tomlinson, 'Failing Schools: the case of Hackney Downs'. *Forum*, Vol. 40, No. 3, 1998, p. 83.

worsening – pupil behaviour problems, with numerous reports of violence, disrupted lessons, swearing and bullying. One boy was accused of exposing himself to a female teacher; another of bringing a knife to school; one pupil burned another's backside with a Bunsen burner; another was found with 200 cigarettes and yet another set fire to a fellow pupil's hair with a lighter. One group of boys was accused of causing a fire under the railway lines.[680]

Early in 1990, a first-form tutor wrote an in-depth pastoral profile of a 'problem class'. This form included nine boys for whom English was a second language, six known to be experiencing family difficulties, five who had accidents or medical conditions that interfered with schooling and six who found it difficult interacting with their peers. Many came to school late or were frequently absent. Soon after joining the school, the class split into two antagonistic groups. The tutor argued that the social environment of Hackney Downs – for instance being kept waiting for their subject teacher to arrive and the large number of 'cover' teachers, along with lessons that didn't happen, particularly swimming and games – contributed to the bad behaviour. He finished the report by excoriating the 'insane' 'softly softly' policy for failing to protect boys from assault by fellow pupils.[681]

Elizabeth Hales, who joined the staff in May 1990 as the third Deputy Head, and who had wide experience in education, described her first impressions of the school:

> When I first arrived at Hackney Downs I could not quite believe what I had come to. So many pupils far more challenging than I had ever encountered before across all cultural and racial groups. Those who would not sit in a seat, let alone do any work, but simply wandered around the room chatting to their friends, who sneered if you tried to get them to take notice ... The little Kurdish boys who threw themselves to the ground the day that the police helicopter came low over the playground. (The last time they had seen a helicopter it turned out that a man in a uniform leaned out of the side and fired a machine gun at the people below.) Those same children when autumn came cramming their pockets full of berries 'in case they ever got hungry and needed something to eat.' Two new Somali boys who took handfuls of food that had been discarded into the pig bin and crammed them into their pockets for the same reason.[682]

---

680. Loose pages; HDS Archive.
681. Gordon Gilchrist, 'IGG: a half year pastoral report,' February 1990; HDS Archive.
682. O'Connor, pp. 33–34.

In May 1990 the Head of the English for Speakers of Other Languages (ESOL) department produced a report that defined the school's population as 'multicultural, multiracial, and bilingual (in some cases multilingual), with four main languages being Turkish, Bengali, Punjabi and Urdu.'[683] She stressed the negative experience of non-English speaking pupils on arriving at the school, often mid-term, and called for bi-lingual education to help address this problem.

In November 1990, Hackney's Education Development Adviser, Teresa Johns, visited the school to monitor the school's policy and records for attendance and punctuality.[684] The following January, Gus John, Director of Education for Hackney, issued a report following a further inspection of Hackney Downs.[685] He pointed out that by September 1991 the school roll would be a mere 400, for a school built to accommodate 1,000, and that 2,500 surplus secondary places were currently available in the borough. One consequence of the low school roll was that between September 1991 and July 1992 more than 30 percent of the 'casual' intake were pupils excluded from, or truanting at, other Hackney schools.[686] Gus John's report on Hackney Downs began: 'The roots of the present difficulties . . . may lie, paradoxically, in its earlier successes', and praised the school's

> fine record of consistently welcoming successive arrivals in the neighbourhood from other cultures . . . As a part of the change to a comprehensive system the headteacher and staff adopted a whole-school mixed-ability approach to the curriculum . . . showing themselves to be forerunners in educational practice . . .

He commented that, despite this earlier success,

> the school seemed to lose . . . its impetus. Hackney Downs, although retaining an ethos of gentleness and respect for all its pupils, was perceived by some outsiders as being arrested in a time warp.

John's report claimed that the 1985 ILEA inspection 'while congratulating [the school] on its ethos reported some impatience from representatives of the Afro-Caribbean pupils about what they saw as the failure of the staff to push them' and 'perceived a lack of direction and rigour about the school's delivery of the curriculum.' He also repeated

---

683. C. F. Sayarer, Hackney Downs School SESOL Departmental Report, May 1990; HDS Archive.
684. 27 November 1990, letter to John Douglas reporting on the visit.
685. Review Visit to Hackney Downs Secondary Boys' School on 29, 30 and 31 January 1991; HDS Archive.
686. Tomlinson, 'Failing Schools', p. 83.

earlier criticism of the built environment, which

> ... as a whole gives an appearance of neglect and disrepair. Advisers witnessed broken windows; major structural damage inside classrooms; leaking ceilings and roofs ... The pupil number shrinkage has created an impression of emptiness in the buildings ... in nearly all the blocks only a few rooms were in use ...[687]

By this time the school comprised 33 percent 'boys of Afro-Caribbean origins'; 33 percent Asian and 33 percent Turkish, Kurdish and white pupils. Although the ethnic mix of staff largely reflected that of pupils, only three Black people held management positions. The report concluded ominously: 'There can be no doubt that Hackney Downs school is at a critical stage in its development', and called for clearer structures and accountability on both curriculum and disciplinary issues.[688] John's report made a total of 27 recommendations, noting defensively 'It is predictable that staff will say that there is no time to carry out all these duties ... ' In June, in response to the report, John Douglas drew up an Action Plan that covered schemes of work, homework and work programmes. He also produced a revised Code of Conduct, restating procedures for dealing with pupil misbehaviour and setting out a draft set of Disciplinary Procedures.[689]

There followed over the next couple of years an endless succession of inspections, reviews, reports and recommendations. In June 1991, Hackney Education's General Advisor, Sport & Health sent the school a 9-page 'Curriculum Statement', a 3-page 'Review of the Physical Education Department' and 2-page outline of his required aims and objectives for the school: 'better correlation between stated aims, objectives and learning experience of all pupils' and 'better balance in the range and type of activities on offer'. He requested a response by the beginning of autumn term.[690]

In October 1991 came a 'Follow-up Review' by the Senior Advisor, Secondary at Hackney Education, to 'assess how the school has positively addressed the recommendations made in the review undertaken during the spring term'. Prior to this, the Inspector requested a comprehensive list of materials she required for her investigation: copies of current timetables, a plan of the school, the school handbook and parents' prospectus, a curriculum statement, policy documents, job de-

687. Review Visit to Hackney Downs Secondary Boys' School on 29, 30 and 31 January 1991; HDS Archive, p. 5.
688. Ibid, p. 47.
689. Duplicated document; HDS Archive.
690. 28 June, 10 July 1991; HDS Archive.

scriptions, exam results for summer 1991, copies of referral and late slips, the school's examination entry policy, the school's development plan, the INSET plan for 1991/92, the financial statement for INSET and departmental allowances, staff allowances and structures and the Curriculum Analysis for 1991/92. In addition, during the review, the Inspector demanded to see all Schemes of Work, attendance monitoring documents, all class registers and mark books, Senior Management and Departmental monitoring files and the patrol book, as well as selected pupils' work for assessment.[691] On 27 September in preparation for this review, Douglas issued a document to staff, preparing his defence in advance:

> I do not regard [the Inspector's] lists as exhaustive and there is other information which we will make available
> – for instance:
> Various profiles of the school population e.g.:
> Linguistic diversity
> Learning needs
> Pupil 'turnover'
> Pupil destinations

He finished rather forlornly, 'I hope this paper will spur enthusiasm to "shine" in the forthcoming review: there is no reason to feel overwhelmed by these lists.'

The planned review took place in October, involving a team of ten specialist subject advisers, led by the Senior Secondary Adviser.[692] It lasted three and a half days, the Advisers observing 51 lessons, interviewing 12 members of staff, assessing 26 registration periods and attending three assemblies. Inevitably the preparation for, and the conduct of, such an intensive inspection, while there was urgent pressure to improve things severely interrupte the regular running of the school. Verbal feedback immediately following the review was that the Inspectors were more positive than in the spring, that recommendations had been taken seriously, but some practice was still inconsistent with policies and official procedures – especially regarding attendance and punctuality, discipline, classroom management and cohesion. The full Report, when released, recognized that many of the recommendations made in the spring were being addressed, but found

> many pupils displayed a lack of involvement in the classroom . . . The deterioration of pupil behaviour is a question which members of the school, staff, parents

---

691. 23 September 1991, Letter to John Douglas; HDS Archive.
692. Yvonne Beecham.

and governors alike must address . . . Many pupils at Hackney Downs are seriously underachieving.

The review listed 24 recommendations, some for immediate implementation, others to be implemented by April 1992, plus an appendix totalling 39 further recommendations by subject area.[693] Following this review, John Douglas met the Staff Association, who were concerned about 'the general state of discipline within the school' – for example a pupil who 'in a fit of temper . . . threw the drill chuck key across the room with great force and then proceeded to attack his work and the bench with a hammer in a very uncontrolled manner'.[694] The report was followed up in January 1992 with a letter from the Chief Inspector at Hackney Education,[695] noting '. . . there are still the major concerns of management and pupil behaviour . . . in need of urgent and vigorous attention.'[696] John Douglas wrote a strongly worded letter to Gus John, Hackney's Director of Education, on 16 January 1992, accusing 'the LEA [of] washing its hands of the school' and questioning the report's claim that the school had 'received all the support we could have. . . .'. Douglas angrily described parts of the report as 'almost inflammatory, [with] sweeping statements regarding attendance, examination results, exclusions and pupil basic-skill development, all of which are major issues confronting the school but complex issues...' He also expressed concern that the absence of praise in the report would result in 'staff feeling aggrieved or defeated and giving up, the danger of committed hardworking staff losing confidence in the LEA's commitment to the school and deciding to "bail out".'[697]

Hardly had this review been considered before a one-day HMI inspection took place, on 5 February 1992. Verbal feedback following this inspection was not dissimilar to previous reviews: although teaching was judged satisfactory – sometimes good – it was claimed teachers had low expectations of pupils, lessons needed clearer aims and goals, pupils' response was 'sometimes lackadaisical' and attendance and punctuality remained poor. Younger pupils were said to be 'fractious and volatile', needing tighter organisation.[698] By the end of February, Douglas had issued another Action Plan, with targeted and dated outcomes.[699] In March the LEA Inspector, Design Technology, reported on

693. Hackney Downs School Follow-up Review, October 1991. Hackney Education. HDS Archive.
694. 15 and 28 October 1991; HDS Archive.
695. Dr. Morgan Dalphinis.
696. Letter to John Douglas, 10 January 1992; HDS Archive.
697. Letter to Gus John, 16 January 1992; HDS Archive.
698. Summary by John Douglas, 6 February 1992; HDS Archive.
699. Action Plan 'For EMT 27/2/92'; HDS Archive.

his visit to the school on 26 February, with yet another set of recommendations.[700]

Meanwhile teachers' reports of violent and destructive pupil behaviour continued. On 30 March 1992, the Heads of Year sent Douglas a round robin, claiming the behaviour of a large number of pupils was 'at crisis point' and complaining that 'a large proportion of staff... seem to be "passing the buck"... not taking responsibility for the basic structure and control of their lessons.'[701] Elizabeth Hales, one of two Deputy Heads, wrote a forceful report on the behaviour of a Year 7 class, demanding the exclusion of two boys,[702] amidst general concern about Year 7. Hackney's Development Adviser [703] reported 'this particular year group is very difficult to handle' and 'establishing effective classroom control was extremely difficult'. He was critical of the induction programme for the new intake, particularly as boys came from a large number of different feeder schools. For many boys, Hackney Downs was not their first choice, and the school was unlikely to attract a balanced intake as its reputation had plummeted. The report ended, inevitably, with 16 further proposals for reorganisation and action.[704]

In autumn 1992, Hackney Education Authority implemented yet another inspection. This time 4 lessons were rated good, 19 satisfactory and 22 poor, and concern was raised about the physical safety of science teaching. The report concluded that the school was at risk, since in four different areas it failed to conform to the Department of Education 'Framework for Inspections': teaching and learning, management, pupil behaviour and pupil safety.[705] Hackney Downs was now added to the 'at risk' register of local schools.

On top of all this, on 22 October the DfE sent two HMIs to follow up their February inspection. They summarised their findings:

> In a significant number of classrooms pupils are barely under control and staff struggle to maintain order. Noise levels are intolerable. Aggressive behaviour among pupils is widespread and ranges from physical jostling to actual assault... Standards of learning and achievement in the fourteen lessons observed... were either unsatisfactory (3) or very poor (11)... The quality of teaching is generally poor to unsatisfactory with work

700. Letter from Jack Haslam to John Douglas, 10 March 1992.
701. Copy in HDS Archive. Six senior teachers' names were attached.
702. 24 March 1992.
703. Barry Taafe.
704. Duplicated five-page report, April 1992; HDS Archive.
705. Report on Inspection Visit to Hackney Downs School, Autumn 1992, Dr Morgan Dalphinis, 18 November 1992; HDS Archive.

often unplanned, as well as inappropriate for the ability, age and language fluency of pupils . . . The school's physical environment is grim; some rooms are unfit for teaching purposes; the social areas are squalid. Many areas are unoccupied. The buildings are dirty . . . This latest visit provided evidence of a marked deterioration since February – to the point where immediate action is required.[706]

School rules spelt out a number of behaviours that were forbidden, but clearly occurring frequently:

anything which is potentially dangerous or likely to cause damage or nuisance within the school is banned. This includes any sort of weapon, matches, lighters, cigarettes, fireworks. Throwing things is also forbidden. . . . Pupils should not climb across desks, or lean out of windows. School walls must not be climbed, school roofs must not be climbed on to . . . . Gambling, selling and 'trading' are forbidden.[707]

In November 1992 an internal report was drawn up of the ethnic profile of the school. Of 429 boys on the school roll, 54 percent were from the 'New Commonwealth', comprising 32 Africans, 125 Afro-Caribbeans, 44 Asians and 25 Bengalis; another 25 percent were Kurdish, Turkish, Chinese, Somali, Arab or Vietnamese. 52 percent of pupils were bilingual; reported second languages including Amharic, Arabic, Bengali, Cantonese, Dutch, Yoruba, Twi, French, German, Greek, Hindi, Italian, Urdu, Turkish, Ga, Gujarati, Kurdish, Malay, Mende, Patois, Punjabi, Wolof, Somali, Viet and several Caribbean Creole dialects. 30 percent of pupils were Muslim[708] – at this time a school mosque was provided, open to boys of all years. A Hackney Parents Centre was also based at the school, providing information and advice. The swimming pool was utilised by three local primary schools, the nearby Stormont House special school, a Parent and Toddlers Group and a Jewish boys' group, in addition to Hackney Downs pupils.[709]

In a downbeat report for the Governors' meeting on 11 November, John Douglas, wrote:

The feeling of the school . . . is too often one of being overwhelmed by problems. The number of pupils being

---

706. DfE to Gus John, Governors and Headteacher, November 1992, NA ED 289/140.
707. 1993 Annual Parents Information Booklet; HDS Archive.
708. Hackney Downs Language and Learning Service (S11); HDS Archive.
709. Governors' Report 1992/3, 23 June 1993; HDS Archive.

sent out of lessons is too high, the number of pupils causing disruption and unpleasantness around the school is too large . . .[710]

In December 1992, Douglas issued a paper titled 'Focusing our efforts', setting out urgent priorities for the school, which included enhancing classroom effectiveness, rewarding pupils and clarifying staff roles.[711] At Christmas, John Douglas left the school 'to start a professional secondment with Hackney LEA';[712] John Kemp claimed he was in effect sacked. Douglas was succeeded by Peter Hepburn, seconded from Homerton House, Hackney's only other boys' secondary school, where he had been Deputy Head.

Hackney Council was meanwhile in chaos. Seventeen council staff were dismissed for fraud, and in February 1993 the Chief Executive revealed allegations of corruption in the Housing Department. Following a review of secondary school provision in the borough, the Director of Education[713] issued a twelve-page report recommending that Hackney Downs be reorganized as a co-educational school, 'to help meet the overall need for additional mixed places in Hackney,' admitting its first mixed entry in September 1995.[714]

This public report was soon followed by a report to the school Governors, dated 20 May, setting out detailed plans for this change, 'if the Educational Committee agree to it'. It suggested that, though the school roll was low – 441 in September 1992, roughly half the building's capacity – it would assist the building alterations and maintenance necessary for the change to a coeducational school if the number of pupils on site was temporarily reduced still further. To this end it was proposed there be no pupil intake in September 1994, and that the first mixed intake should arrive in September 1995.[715] The planned work was to include converting some toilets for girls' use and providing additional changing rooms, while also upgrading the science laboratories, making structural repairs and redecorating the buildings internally and externally. It was suggested Homerton House and Hackney Downs should share

---

710. Headteacher's Report to Governors for 11 November 1992; HDS Archive.
711. 'Focusing our efforts', 4 December 1992; HDS Archive.
712. Report to the Governors, 23 June 1993; HDS Archive.
713. Gus John. Born in Grenada in 1945, and appointed in 1989 as Hackney's first Director of Education, the first person of colour to hold such an appointment in the UK. Subsequently Associate Professor of Education and Honorary Fellow, Institute of Education, University of London.
714. 'Review of Secondary School Provision in Hackney', 12 May 1993; HDS Archive.
715. To reduce pupil numbers still further, it was suggested some boys be transferred to Homerton House School, which had replaced Brooke House and Upton House schools and was accommodated in a tower block.

facilities and teaching, although only Hackney Downs would have coeducational provision.[716] These proposals worried Hackney Downs staff, who feared Homerton House might take control of their school. At a staff consultation on 27 May, addressed by Hackney's Deputy Director of Education, one teacher asked pertinently how girls might experience this predominantly boys' school, and how the school could hope to attract pupils when it had such a poor reputation.[717] In the event, the Department for Education rejected the coeducation proposals on the grounds that there was 'no certainty that the school could provide an adequate environment for girls, or that it could recruit a sufficient number of girls for a balanced intake.'[718]

An anonymous and undated internal report, apparently dating to the summer term 1993, summarised the current state of the school.[719] It stated that the foyer and ground-floor corridors of the main building had been painted, giving the school 'an enormous lift'. Staff committees had met, Governors committees were busy, a Student Council established, a School Development Plan finalised and an appraisal process put in in hand, while a Steering Group was discussing how to provide for 'students who find it difficult to cope with mainstream teaching'. A pastoral weekend was organised for Heads of Year and Senior Management at the University of Essex, with Gus John joining for a day.

In June 1993, the Deputy Head of Maths resigned, in protest at the department's lack of facilities; when she attempted to reverse her decision, she was not restored to her post. The Head of Maths left shortly afterwards, in controversial circumstances. Both teachers belonged to the Hackney Black Parents and Teachers Group, and a large group of pupils staged a protest outside the school about the 'unfair dismissal' of the Head of Department.[720] Looking back several years later, the General Secretary of the Secondary Heads Association commented:

> The school's mathematics department serves as an
> example of how there were no small problems at
> Hackney Downs, only crises and impossible situations.
> Even small incidents frequently exploded into major
> difficulties, often overlaid with accusations of racism and
> tensions between groups of staff.[721]

716. 'Review of Secondary Education Provision in Hackney: Director's Proposals', 19 May 1993; HDS Archive.
717. Hackney Downs Staff Consultation Meeting, 27 May 1993; HDS Archive.
718. O'Connor, p. 92.
719. Acting Headteacher's Report, presumably by Peter Hepburn; HDS Archive.
720. O'Connor, p. 86.
721. John Dunford, General Secretary of the Secondary Heads Association, *Times Education Supplement Magazine*, 3 September 1999, reviewing O'Connor et al, *Hackney Downs*.

In March 1994, the Hackney Black Parents & Teachers Group distributed a duplicated leaflet titled 'Things You Should Know About Hackney Downs School!', which included the demand (in capital letters): 'All parents should remove their children from Hackney Downs School and place them in other schools.' They also organised a meeting under the slogan 'Parents against low educational standards action group'.[722] By this date, the school Governors, largely political appointees, were no longer actually in charge of the school. Direction was in the hands of Hackney's education department and its Director of Education, Gus John, who was strongly invested in the role of education in raising the aspirations of Black children, yet openly critical of the conduct of some of the Black teachers at the school.[723]

By September 1993, the school's staff included two coordinators of Learning Support, three teachers responsible for Personal, Social and Health Education (PSHE) and four Language Support and TESOL[724] teachers. A review around the same time showed that of 467 pupils, 101 exhibited behavioural problems, 99 had special educational needs and 41 were persistent truants.[725] Violent behaviour continued: in October, one boy stabbed another with a pair of scissors.[726]

After the departure of Peter Hepburn in January 1994, Ken Russell, one of two Deputy Heads, became Temporary Head, but took sick leave at the beginning of February, never to return.[727] Russell's successor as acting head, Elizabeth 'Betty' Hales,[728] immediately encountered serious staffing issues due to the rapid turnover caused by stress-related sickness among teachers, and also faced the ongoing problem of the school's dilapidated fabric.[729] Hackney Downs was now characterised by drug-taking, vandalism and gratuitous violence by a significant proportion of pupils, many of whom had been excluded from other schools.

The Schools Act of 1993 had introduced a new framework for school inspections, now to be conducted by Ofsted, with reports and exam reports for the first time made public, leading to the appearance in the national press of annual league-tables ranking schools, singling

722. The meeting was held at the United Reformed Church, Clapton, 16 March 1994. UCL IoE Archive HD.
723. Fran Abrams, 'This is Gus John,' *Independent on Sunday*, 21 July 1996.
724. Teaching English to Speakers of Other Languages.
725. Carried out by Deputy head Ken Russell. O'Connor, p. 66.
726. Letter from Elizabeth Hales, 7 October 1993; HDS Archive.
727. O'Connor et al, *Hackney Downs*, p. 82; see also Memo from Danny Silverstone, LB Hackney, 3 March 1994. UCL IoE Archive HD.
728. On Hales, a physicist by training, see Gerald Haigh, 'Redemption in NW1,' *Times Education Supplement Magazine*, 10 November 2000.
729. Tony Burgess, 'Death of a School,' *London Quarterly*, April–May 1996, p. 34. Dr Burgess was the last Chair of Governors, ousted when the Education Association was set up.

out for public opprobrium and humiliation those with poor results. In May 1994, an Ofsted inspection of Hackney Downs School was put in hand. The resulting report highlighted underachievement by the majority of pupils, regular disruptive behaviour and physical bullying, racial tension and an unacceptable level of poor teaching,[730] and claimed 'a constant undertow of poor and bizarre behaviour makes all classes difficult to teach'. The only exception to the general criticism was in English and Drama, where: 'Results are above the national average ... Pupils can speak well and listen attentively.' This report summed up the problems facing the school:

> There is overwhelming evidence that the school faces a rare mix of socio-economic, financial and professional issues. The area served by the school has some of the highest indices of need in the country. In the last two years, the school had had four headteachers, and nearly 68% of the staff hold acting or temporary posts.[731]

Although the report praised the 'very effective and thoughtful' leadership of the newly-promoted Acting Head, Mrs Hales, in improving staff morale, the Inspectors adjudged that the school now required 'Special Measures'.[732] Yet in 1994, although only 11 percent of 15-year-olds achieved five GCSE passes at grades A to C, 65 percent achieved passes at grades A* to G and 82 percent left the school with at least one GCSE pass; additionally, 55 percent achieved a vocational qualification. In the 1994 'league table' of secondary schools in the borough, Hackney Downs achieved fifth place out of fourteen, ahead of Hackney Free and Parochial and Homerton House schools.[733]

No single party now controlled Hackney Council. In search of political leverage, Labour factions vied with one another in prescribing radical solutions for Hackney Downs. In 1994, the right-wing Conservative Secretary of State for Education, Gillian Shephard, embarked on a policy of 'naming and shaming' failing schools: Hackney Downs was an easy target.[734] Singling out a school for punitive purposes could prove

730. Tony Burgess, 'Death of a School,' p. 101.
731. Summary of the Inspection Report, 16–23 May 1994, Mrs S. R. Richardson. UCL IoE Archive HD.
732. Even delivery of the much-delayed Ofsted report was marked by incompetence and carelessness. The courier arrived after the school had closed for the day, so he opened the package, unpacked the confidential documents and crammed them into a disused post-box at the school gate. The soggy, wet papers were discovered a few days later. O'Connor, p. 109.
733. http://www.education.gov.uk/performancetables/archives/schools_94/h204/lb204.shtml.
734. See Pamela Sammons, 'Zero tolerance of failure and New Labour approaches to school improvement in England,' *Oxford Review of Education*, Vol. 34, No. 6 (December 2008), pp. 651–64; specific mention of Hackney Downs, pp. 654–5.

useful to the Conservative political agenda of appearing to bear down on poor educational practice and results and improving standards. As Sally Tomlinson pointed out in 1998:

> Individual schools and their personnel were discussed as though divorced from an historical position, from basic social, economic and educational structures, and from the pernicious effects of 'market forces' which have moved more 'desirable' pupils out of particular schools and ensured that other schools take in large numbers of those children considered 'undesirable'. Children with special needs, migrant and minority children, second language speakers, children living in poverty and deprived circumstances are now concentrated more than ever in smaller numbers of urban and estate schools.[735]

At a special meeting, on 18 October 1994, the school Governors 'expressed concern about the lack of trust between themselves and the LEA' caused by 'speculation about the LEA's plans to consult on a proposal to close the school'. The Chair of Governors, Pat Corrigan,[736] resigned and Dr Tony Burgess, an academic from the Institute of Education and long-time Governor, was elected in his place.

By late autumn 1994, the state of the school buildings had become an urgent safety concern. The Deputy Head, Jeffrey Davies, reported to Hackney Education Authority:

> I have given instructions for the music block to be closed due to serious flooding on the stairwells which meant that I could not guarantee the health and safety of students in that area . . . I have also closed the gym for the same reason. There are other areas of the school which will constitute health and safety risks if the heavy rain persists. These include classrooms . . . technical workshops, art studios and the top floor of the science block. . . [I]f the bad weather persists . . . it will be difficult to find sufficient teaching space for all classes or to guarantee the safety of large areas of the site.[737]

By October 1994 the school roll had fallen as low as 300, partly because there had been no Year 7 intake, halted to prepare for the mooted change to co-education, and partly because parents were concerned by the stories of racial conflict at the school. Despite a noisy Hackney

---

735. Tomlinson, Failing Schools, p. 92.
736. Corrigan was also Chair of the Hackney Education Committee.
737. O'Connor, p. 146. These buildings were still only twenty-five years old.

Town Hall demonstration by teachers, the Education Committee voted unanimously to commence school closure consultation.[738] On 16 January 1995, at a public meeting attended by 107 parents and staff, Diane Abbott, MP for Hackney North and Stoke Newington since 1987, argued:

> It would be tragic if a labour [sic] authority clashed with [parents and teachers]. . . The least that the labour politicians owed them was a real explanation. One thing was very clear: the educational case for closing Hackney Downs had not been made to the parents . . . If it was only due to money, then they should also be told that . . . [739]

Hackney now announced plans to close the school, transferring the remaining pupils to Homerton House. Early in 1995, with a school roll numbering fewer than 200, the Hackney Education Committee endorsed this scheme, and on 23 March gave public notice that the school would close in July. This triggered a community campaign to 'Save Our School', with the governors and staff presenting statutory objections to the Department of Education. The same month, a further HMI visit found 'significant improvements' at the school, and argued Elizabeth Hales was 'turning the school around, and – despite lack of support from the LEA – it was an "improving school"'.[740] In March 1995, Ofsted made yet another inspection, to investigate the implementation of their May 1994 Action Plan. They found that the 1994 GCSE exams had seen an increase in the percentage of pupils gaining five or more Grades A to G; lessons were rated between satisfactory and unsatisfactory; lesson planning had improved; there was clear direction and leadership from the [acting] Headteacher and significant improvement in pupils' classroom behaviour.[741]

On 8 June 1995, following a dispute between Hackney Labour councillors and a change in committee chairs, the decision to close the school was reversed. The ensuing media frenzy resulted in an upsurge of public support for the school.[742] On 28 June, Hackney Council rejected the closure proposal and Hackney Downs announced: 'The school is staying open with Local Authority Support', inviting parents to a

---

738. Andy Beckett, 'Scenes from the classroom war,' *The Independent on Sunday*, 27 November 1994, p. 18.
739. Minutes of meeting. UCL IoE Archive HD.
740. Tomlinson, p. 92.
741. Letter from A. J. Rose, Ofsted Director of Inspection, to Elizabeth Hales, 17 March 1995. UCL IoE Archive HD.
742. Barber wrote cynically, 'once the decision was taken to close Hackney Downs, people suddenly discovered they loved it', and suggested that much of the support generated at this point was political opportunism. Michael Barber, *The Learning Game*, p. 114.

meeting on 13 July to recruit boys for 'Year 7 and all other years'.[743] On 7 July, Gillian Shephard indicated she had no further interest in the matter. Then, astonishingly, just seven days later, and having received no new information or briefing, the Secretary of State announced that she intended to set up an Education Association. She cited four grounds for concern: poor GCSE results, variable lesson quality, poor attendance and unsatisfactory attitudes to work on the part of some pupils.[744] Accordingly, the 'North East London Education Association' took over management of the school on 27 July.

An Education Association[745] allowed the government to hand over control of a school regarded as failing to an 'Education Association', with members appointed by the Minister. Such a task-force was now rapidly set up. It consisted of Richard Painter, senior executive with ADT electronics and security; Michael Barber, adviser to David Blunkett, the Labour Shadow Education Minister; Bryan Bass, outgoing Head of City of London School; James Aston, Education Group Manager at the accountants Kidson Empey; Richard Davies, former Director of Education, London Borough of Merton; and Joan Farrelly, former Chief Inspector, London Borough of Hammersmith and Fulham. In an internal Department of Education and Science memo about the Association members, Michael Barber was described as 'a considerable catch ... As a former chairman of Hackney's Education Committee, his presence will wrong-foot the LEA' – revealing that the department was manoeuvring to outwit the Hackney Education Authority.[746] A letter from Michael Collier, Chief Executive of the Funding Agency for Schools, to John Hedger, at the Department for Education and Employment, mentions 'your and [Michael Barber's] view that the most likely outcome will be the closure of the school'.[747] It appears minds had already been made up. In their book, Maureen O'Connor and her co-authors characterized the North East London Education Association as a 'hit squad'.

In a briefing note for the Education Association, the Chairman, Richard Painter was instructed to

assess whether the school is viable ... and decide whether it is possible for the school to return to viable

---

743. Leaflet in HDS Archive.
744. O'Connor, p. 192.
745. Authorised under sections 218–28 of the Education Act, 1993.
746. Barber was a Hackney resident and first Chair of Hackney's Education Committee. After the closure, Tomlinson and Barber conducted a lively debate in the *Times Education Supplement*. 'Creation of Education Association at Hackney Downs', 21 July 1995. NRA ED 289/161 p. 3. O'Connor, p. 226. Hales' book was in part a response to the seven-page account (pp. 113–19) of the school's closure in Barber's *The Learning Game*.
747. NRA ED 289/161, 21 July 1995.

numbers and for the standard of education to be raised to a satisfactory level. But if you conclude that this would not be possible within – say – 2 years, it would be in the best interests of the pupils if the school closed as quickly as possible.[748]

The briefing included background notes, noting:

> There is currently a dispute between Hackney's officers, who feel that the school is now too small and should close, and the new controlling political group on the Council who want it to remain open. The governors campaigned vigorously to retain the school.[749]

One of the school Governors, R. N. Philipson-Stow, of Guinness Mahon Holdings,[750] wrote confidentially to Shephard saying he had 'become increasingly disappointed with the conduct of the LEA, in particular its senior officers, in its relationship with the school and the destabilizing effect these have had', while welcoming the Education Association and offering 'the fullest confidence in the current Senior Management and staff team of the school'.[751]

The animosity within the school itself is revealed in a crudely typed, undated and anonymous document addressed to one of the Department of Education civil servants involved in the review:

> MS COSTIGAN,
>
> WE ARE A GROUP OF CONCERNED STAFF AT HACKNEY DOWNS SCHOOL WHO FEEL YOU OUGHT TO KNOW THAT THERE IS A DEFINITE SPLIT BETWEEN THE LEA AND THE COUNCIL AND BETWEEN THE LEA AND THE SCHOOL. THE SCHOOL CANNOT MOVE FORWARD AND BE ABLE TO TURN AROUND. THE PRESENT STRUCTURE MUST CHANGE BY THE E.A.
>
> THE GOVERNING BODY IS INEFFECTIVE AND IS A SUPPORTERS, [sic] CLUB FOR THE HEAD AGAINST THE DIRECTOR OF EDUCATION IN OPEN CONFLICT. THEY SPEND THEIR TIME IN GETTING THE COUNCIL TO DISMISS THE DIRECTOR AND HIS DEPUTY.
>
> THERE IS NO LEADERSHIP IN THE SCHOOL. THE HEAD ALLOWS THE SWP[752] IN THE STAFF TO INTIMI-

---

748. 'Creation of Education Association at Hackney Downs', 21 July 1995, NRA ED 289/161p., Annex B.
749. Ibid, p. 3.
750. His company had supported the school financially since February 1994.
751. Letter to DfE, 18 July 1995, NRA ED 289/161 p. 3.
752. Socialist Workers Party.

> DATE US AND FORCE US TO PLEDGE LOYALTY TO HER.
> SHE COMPENSATES BY GIVING PROMOTION REGARD-
> LESS OF EXPERIENCE, ABILITY AND QUALIFICATION.
> THERE IS NO LEARNING. PLEASE SEND IN AN E.A. IN
> ORDER TO SAVE THE LESS THAN 200 PUPILS IN THE
> SCHOOL. INTERVIEW EACH MEMBER OF STAFF AWAY
> FROM THE HEAD AND THE SECRETARY OF STATE WILL
> KNOW THE TRUTH.
>
> ONE DOZEN CONCERNED TEACHERS WHO HAVE BEEN
> THREATENED BY THE SWP AND HEAD.[753]

In their report to the Secretary of State, submitted on 26 October, the Educational Association listed a catalogue of financial and managerial shortcomings they claimed had resulted in an unplanned deficit of some £80,000 for 1994–95, which it blamed on the London Borough of Hackney, the Acting Headteacher, the Governors and the ILEA.[754] The Association reported that the school buildings had

> an air of neglect and virtual abandonment ... there had obviously been a period for perhaps as much as ten years of almost total neglect of the buildings of the School. It is clear that the Hackney Authority have carried out very few repairs apart from a few comparatively minor jobs. However, it is evident that the start of the neglect goes back to ILEA days ... .[755]

Three inspectors commissioned by the Education Association reported on the quality of teaching at the school. One found Hackney Downs to be 'sound in most respects'; another concluded the English teaching to be 'good to very good'; a third judged maths teaching was 'at best satisfactory' but much of it, and of science teaching, 'unacceptable' and 'unsatisfactory'.[756] One inspector summarised his individual findings:

> There are no problems that I consider to be intractable. It [Hackney Downs] is much less a 'hopeless case' than in [sic] other former ILEA schools that I have experienced. Fundamentally the pupils want to learn and the teachers want to teach them ... My overall view, therefore,

---

753. Sent to Ms Marie Costigan, School Effectiveness Division, Department for Education and Employment, 25 July 1995. NRA ED 289/161.
754. *The Future of Hackney Downs School.*
755. Ibid., 9. The Association based these conclusions on an independent report commissioned from an engineering and design consultancy.
756. This evidence was not presented to the Court of Appeal in December 1995.

is that the school is rescuable, at a cost which is not prohibitive and which, taking a suitably long term view, would constitute value for money.[757]

The members of the Education Association disregarded or dismissed his findings. On 26 October 1995, they dispatched their report, recommending closure, to the Secretary of State, who then allowed a mere ten days for 'consultation'.

Michael Barber's impartiality is called into question by the inflammatory language and unsupported opinion of his article in the *Times Educational Supplement* a fortnight after the report was delivered:

> Hackney Downs is under-performing with a pupil-teacher ratio of 8:1 and a per-pupil expenditure of £6,489 per pupil[758] ... How can what is effectively daylight robbery from other Hackney schools be justified ad infinitum? ... The school is failing for many reasons: poor relations with the education authority, block-headed union militancy, lack of capital investment, and lack of quality among teachers.

Barber continued with an attack on supporters of the school:

> Rent-a-mob activists can be relied on to exploit the understandable and inevitable anxieties of parents and pupils ... the vociferous campaigns of semi-professional fanatics present a major challenge.[759]

The negative press, focusing on the school's problems, became a self-fulfilling prophecy.[760] By September 1995 the school roll had fallen as low as 200. On 31 October, the Education Association recommended closure of the school 'with effect from 31st December 1995,' with all pupils offered places at Homerton House.[761]

---

757. Derek Turner, 'Report on quality of teaching and pupils' response at Hackney Downs School.' UCL IoE Archive HD.
758. As Sally Tomlinson pointed out, HDS per pupil expenditure in 1993 was in fact £2900, rising to £3200 in 1994 after the LEA banned the first-form intake. *Times Educational Supplement*, December 11 1995.
759. *Times Educational Supplement*, November 17 1995. Barber continued to defend the closure, for instance in 'Why we closed Hackney Downs' in *The Times*, 3 November 1995.
760. In addition to invariably negative newspaper publicity, the school and Hackney's Director of Education, Gus John, were the subject of a controversial Channel 4 tv documentary, 'Closing Downs', broadcast on 3 August 1995. For an interesting psychoanalytical examination of this media exposure and its effect upon the school, along with the Conservative government's perceived marketisation of education (the 'league-table culture'), see Neurath.
761. Hackney Downs School: Report of the North East London Education Association. UCL IoE Archive HD.

One member of the Education Association, Bryan Bass (–2010), former Headmaster of City of London School, wrote a personal account of his time at Hackney Downs:

> [After the 1963 fire the buildings] were replaced by a cheap, drab structure, on which little or no maintenance has been carried out. Bits are falling off it, water comes in everywhere, and until we had them fixed the windows were in danger of falling out. . . The estimated cost of making the buildings good is in excess of £2 million. The effect of such an environment on the boys' morale may well be imagined, particularly as this comes on top of the background of social deprivation in which many of them live . . .
>
> Our decision, which I now see as having been inevitable, has of course dismayed the boys and staff of Hackney Downs School. There have been angry demonstrations (the Socialist Workers Party has been at the gates most of the time), and I have had to address and attempt to control several very turbulent meetings . . . What makes it particularly difficult for me is that I share the anger. The boys are losing their school, which for some is the only stable part of their lives, and the staff are losing their livelihood . . . What has happened to them is very largely the result of forces beyond their control, political manoeuvres, gross neglect, social injustice and years of mismanagement.[762]

On 1 November, the 206 boys remaining at the school attended an assembly to say farewell to a long-serving teacher.[763] They were informed that, in two months' time, they would be saying goodbye to the school itself.[764] Hackney Downs was to become the first school in the country to be shut down because it was 'failing'. On 12 December, parents of two pupils in year 11, the GCSE exam year, applied to the High Court for judicial review of the Education Association's report and recommendation. The court was restricted to reviewing solely the mechanisms by which the Secretary of State had made her decision – but neither the EA Report itself nor the evidence upon which it was based.[765] Rejecting the appellants' case, Justice Popplewell concluded:

---

762. 'They Call it Retirement', City of London School website, 1995.
763. Lesley Douglas, who taught English and History at the school for seventeen years.
764. *The Guardian*, 1 November 1995.
765. Tomlinson, Failing Schools, p. 85.

> Every professional who has had dealings with this particular school is satisfied that it is failing to give its pupils an acceptable education . . . OFSTED, the officer of the local education authority, the Association and the Secretary of State. In my judgment it is not possible now to challenge this decision of the Secretary of State which seems to me to accord with that professional view.[766]

On 15 December, the Court of Appeal rejected the case.[767] Transfer of pupils to Homerton House School now commenced. On 15 December, the remnant of pupils gathered for a final assembly. On 31 December 1995, 119 years after its foundation, Hackney Downs School was closed.

In the view of journalists Dave Hill and John Carvel:

> It was the money that talked. There were 300 empty places at Homerton House, Hackney's other boys' secondary school only a mile away. The cost of refurbishing Hackney Downs was £3 million. It occupied valuable housing land on a quiet street overlooking one of the borough's most desirable stretches of open space.[768]

The Conservative government's free market in school places was costing Hackney's Education Authority £9M a year, because it was losing almost one-third of its secondary pupils to nearby, richer boroughs, starving Hackney schools of much-needed funding.[769] John Major's government had declared war on 'failing' schools and on the mainly left-wing authorities that ran them:

> Few can doubt that Hackney Downs was used by the . . . Government as an example of its toughness. Once the E[ducational] A[ssociation] had recommended immediate closure and the Government had achieved its limited objective, the concept of the EA was quietly buried, never to be used again.'[770]

The decline and fall could be described as a vicious spiral, 'only . . . understood within a macro-context of historical, social, economic

---

766. Neville Harris, 'Too bad? The closure of Hackney Downs School under Section 225 of the Education Act 1993', in *Education and the Law*, Vol. 8, No. 2 1996, p. 119. At the hearing, Sally Tomlinson 'noticed Justice Popplewell had a Charterhouse tie on, as did one of the DES officials. At that point I thought "no chance"!' (Personal communication).
767. Neville Harris, 'Too bad?', p. 120.
768. *The Guardian*, 4 November 1995, p. 23.
769. Beckett, 'Scenes from the classroom war,' p. 16.
770. John Dunford, in the *Times Education Supplement Magazine*, 3 September 1999.

and political factors, and the interplay of vested interests. . .'.[771] At the same time

> it was clear by 1995 Hackney Downs was a special school in all but name, having taken in large numbers of students with severe learning and behavioural difficulties . . . [yet] it did not receive the extra resources that special schools are given.[772]

In her interesting paper attempting to understand the closure of the school in Kleinian psychoanalytical terms, Susanna Neurath describes a corkscrew of decline:

> Government cuts left the LEA unable to provide Hackney Downs with much needed support for English language needs, emotional and behavioural problems and learning difficulties within the pupil body. Lack of funds also meant that long overdue maintenance and repairs, which the ILEA too had failed to address, were never carried out. Years of neglect reduced the buildings to such an appalling state that closing the school and selling the site became the only financially viable option for the LEA. Furthermore other schools in the borough that were competing against each other for resources supported the closure in order to safeguard their own uncertain futures . . . All permanent appointments, including the headship, were frozen . . . de-stabilizing the staff group and contributing to the inexorable decline in the roll, and with it the school's formerly good reputation, made for great mistrust of the LEA within the school . . . Low morale was further fanned by the punitive, and at times deeply personal, press coverage[773] aimed at denigrating both staff and children, holding both groups responsible for the school's failure.[774]

There were several failing schools in Hackney at this time; all except Hackney Downs were rescued. Hackney Free and Parochial, a coeducational comprehensive – also dubbed 'Britain's worst school' by the tabloids[775] – was given the resources and support denied to Hackney

---

771. Tomlinson, p. 91.
772. Tomlinson, p. 94.
773. *The Daily Mail* labelled Hackney Downs 'The Worst School in Britain'.
774. Neurath, p. 8. During its final five years, the school underwent more than twelve inspections, by the LEA, HMI and Ofsted.
775. *Times Education Supplement Magazine*, 14 June 1996.

Downs and survived.[776] During the 1980s, some left-wing activists regarded Hackney Downs as elitist and wanted to prevent it evolving into a high-brow comprehensive preoccupied with university entrance.

Chronology of the final years

1984-85 School roll falls; fewer higher ability boys.
ILEA inspection warns of low academic standards.
Teachers' industrial action about pay disrupts classes.
1987 Removal of asbestos leads to temporary partial closure of school.
1989 Some Black staff and parents form 'action groups'.
Hackney prepares for the abolition of the ILEA.
Gus John is appointed Hackney's first Director of Education.
Michael Barber becomes Chair of Hackney Education Committee.
John Kemp retires as head.
1990 Hackney Downs is transferred from the ILEA to London Borough of Hackney.
Hackney Downs one of four Hackney secondary schools giving 'cause for concern'.
1991 New Head faces intensified disputes over role of Black staff and parents' group.
1992 LEA inspectors put school on 'at risk' register.
Head seconded to 'other duties'.
1993 New Acting Head appointed, assisted by Consultant Head, Daphne Gould.
Review of Secondary Schooling in Hackney proposes Hackney Downs becomes co-educational.
LEA recommends no Year 7 recruitment in 1994, in order to refurbish the school and prepare for admission of girls.
Acting Head leaves.
1994
Jan New Acting Head appointed, but goes on sick leave after two weeks
Feb Third Acting Head, Betty Hales, appointed.
Resignation/suspension of Head of Maths and public campaign against the school.
March Department of Education rejects the co-education proposal.
LEA refuses to allow Year 7 intake in September.
May OFSTED inspection.
July OFSTED says the school requires 'special measures', but praises progress.

776. O'Connor, p. 29.

Aug-Oct	School and LEA prepare action plans in response to OFSTED report. School roll falls to 300 because of missing Year 7. LEA decides to consult on closing school.
Oct-Nov	Governors oppose closure. Stormy consultation process: parents and pupils oppose closure.

1995

March	Education Committee ratifies closure: boys to be transferred to Homerton House School.
May	Labour councillors raise doubts about closure.
June	Education Committee rejects Director's report to Department of Education recommending closure. School prepares to recruit for autumn term.
4 July	Secretary of State no longer considering closure.
13 July	Secretary of State to set up Education Association.
27 July	Department of Education announces North East London Education Association.
28 July	Michael Barber writes in *The Independent* that the school is likely to be closed. Clove Club and former pupils support the school.
Sept	School opens with 200 boys and Education Association in control. Three independent inspectors appointed.
October	Education Association publishes report recommending closure.
14 Nov	Closure confirmed by Secretary of State. Staff issued with redundancy notices on minimum terms.
15 Nov	School told to commence transfer of boys to Homerton House School. Year 11 boys' GCSE preparation disrupted.
8 Dec	Leave granted for judicial review.
11 Dec	Mr Justice Popplewell hears case and rejects it. Leave to appeal.
15 Dec	Final school assembly. Staff told to leave premises that evening.
21 Dec	Appeal rejected. School closes.
1996	GCSE examination results no better at Homerton House than at Hackney Downs in 1995.

A blame game now started. The authors of *The School that Dared to Fight* spread culpability widely:

> A Conservative government and two Labour education authorities played their roles, some teachers, governors, parents and pupils behaved badly, and politicians of all shades frequently took advantage of the school's dif-

ficulties. Some sections of the media, at the end, were immensely supportive, while others tried to crucify the school, its staff and, most disgracefully, its pupils.[777]

For his part, in a book published the following year, Michael Barber concluded:

> Hackney Downs . . . is an example of the state a school can end up in if it is mismanaged over years and fought over by petty politicians and lobby groups who have forgotten that schools exist for their pupils. Hackney Downs also provides the clearest possible evidence that neither increased funding nor reducing class sizes are, on their own, the solution to this country's educational problems. Unless the management is good and the teaching of high quality even very large sums of money will change nothing.[778]

Both views were coloured by their respective authors' involvement in the final years of the school. Two of the team who wrote *The School that Dared to Fight* were on the Senior Management Team during the school's final five years, while Michael Barber served as Chair of Hackney's Education Committee and as a member of the Education Association. Having considered both books, the experienced educationalist Gerald Grace concluded:

> I am convinced by the judgement that Hackney Downs was a *failed* school, rather than a failing school . . . It was a failed school because market forces in education progressively recontextualised it from a successful comprehensive school, to a less attractive secondary modern school and finally to a struggling 'special needs' school with far more than its fair share of difficult and challenging pupils. It was a failed school because the tensions and struggle of institutionalised racism within the wider community were played out in the arena of the school, without sufficient external support for its hard-pressed staff. It was a failed school because Hackney Council was vacillating and unhelpful in its policy towards the school . . .[779]

---

777. O'Connor, p. xiii.
778. Michael Barber: *The Learning Game: Arguments for an educational revolution.* London: Indigo 1997, p. 116.
779. *British Journal of Educational Studies*, 2000, Vol. 48 No. 3, pp. 325–27.

The educationalist Richard Race points out that, while Barber criticises the teachers, pupils and parents and the prevalence of a drug culture in Hackney, he did not pursue Paul Harrison's linkage of poor education with socio-economic problems. While attacking the culture of the Hackney Downs staffroom and the London Borough of Hackney, Barber failed to examine the sociology of Hackney as a possible cause and solution of the problem; when the school closed, its pupils were simply transferred to a neighbouring Hackney school, with an identical socio-cultural profile and similar problems.[780] It is difficult to avoid the conclusion that Hackney Downs was arbitrarily selected by the government as a sacrificial victim, *pour encourager les autres*.

On 11 September 1998, the Clove Club, Hackney Downs' former pupils' association, arranged with Hackney Council for a final visit to the site of the school before its demolition. The buildings had stood empty for three years; on top of the dilapidation suffered during school's final decade, further serious deterioration had occurred:

> The hall was full of the London Borough of Hackney's Christmas street decorations . . . Some who had not quite appreciated the extent to which the Grocers' building had disappeared . . . asked in bemused voices 'But where's the school?' 'What have they done with the school?' The school had been picked over by staff from other schools and much that was usable had been taken away . . . which gave the school an even more abandoned feeling than it might otherwise have had. There was evidence of structural decay in some areas, floors heaving upwards, roofs leaking and windows broken . . . The technicians' room . . . was full of discarded specimens, many dating back to Mr. Gee's days and some now lacking their formaldehyde. The chemistry lab . . . looked like a second-hand wardrobe dealer's, with cupboards higgledy-piggledy . . . The new buildings were the greatest shock. They seemed more desolate than the remains of Grocers' [the Victorian buildings] and, being flimsier, seemed to be showing the wear even more than the older buildings.[781]

In recommending closure, the Educational Association had assumed the school site could be sold off for industrial, commercial or housing development, with a 'substantial part' of the proceeds invested in

---

780. Race, p. 185.
781. TCL, May 1999, p. 2.

The derelict swimming pool in 1998.

Homerton House School. However the terms of the 1906 transfer of the school from the Grocers' Company to the L.C.C. restricted use of the site to educational purposes. By 1999 Hackney Council became concerned that the area, which adjoined Hackney Downs open space, had become dangerous due to antisocial behaviour. However, the government refused to reopen the school as a co-educational secondary school, Hackney did not have the funds to reinstate, rebuild and run the school, and security for the abandoned site had become a heavy drain on the Council's Education budget. A hapless letter sent to Hackney headteachers requested any 'imaginative proposals'.[782]

In 2001 Russell Henderson, a former pupil, launched the Hackney Parents' Secondary Schools Campaign, pressing for the establishment of a new, secular coeducational comprehensive school on the site of Hackney Downs School. Several 'Old Grocers' agreed to serve as patrons, including Harold Pinter, Dr Michael Goldstein, Dr Douglas Gough, Professor Joshua Silver and Dr Barry Supple, along with Professor Sally Tomlinson. In 2002, the businessman Clive (later Sir Clive) Bourne (1942–2007), who grew up in Hackney, purchased what remained of Hackney Downs School,[783] and commissioned Sir Richard Rogers to design an Academy school on the site.[784] By May 2003, the last re-

782. Ian Turner, 5 Feb 1999; HDS Archive.
783. See Bourne's obituary in *The Jewish Chronicle*, 19 April 2007, p. 45 and *The Guardian*, 6 April 2007.
784. '[Andrew] Adonis and [David] Blunkett saw academies as a way of kick-starting the

maining parts of the original school, including the swimming pool and laboratory block, had been demolished, in preparation for the building work.[785] In 2004, the co-educational, non-selective and non-denominational Mossbourne Community Academy School (or MCA),named after Sir Clive's father, Moss Bourne) opened to its first intake of pupils, with plans eventually to cater for 900,[786] its first headmaster Sir Michael Willshaw.[787] Its achievements were soon declared outstanding:[788]

> On the ashes of Hackney Downs has risen a city academy that appears to be the kind of beacon of excellence in an area of deprivation that [Lord Michael] Levy's and my father's school once was. Called the Mossbourne Community Academy ... it is described by the standards watchdog, Ofsted, as 'outstanding', 'exceptional' and 'dynamic'. The school expects some 80 percent of its pupils, way above the national average, to achieve the five A* to C grades at GCSE (including English and maths) which represents a basic standard of academic achievement. Perhaps more importantly, there is a hunger among the kids to go on to university. The school, under its knighted head, Sir Michael Wilshaw, appears once again to be showing what can be achieved by the ambitious children of immigrants, but this time black and Asian ones, rather than the Jews of the mid-twentieth century.[789]

In a self-serving first chapter to his campaigning book, *Education, Education, Education*, the unelected New Labour Education Minister, Andrew Adonis, claimed Hackney Downs had 'long been a by-word for disaster in inner-city comprehensive education', inaccurately stating that 'As a comprehensive in the 1970s and 1980s, it became a sink school',[790] which enabled him to point up the purported contrast with his pet project, Mossbourne:

regeneration of struggling schools, usually in economically depressed areas, which had become so overwhelmed by so many problems, that the best thing seemed to be to hoover out their innards and transplant them with what Adonis called private-enterprise "DNA". The old Hackney Downs School ... was bulldozed and Mossbourne built in its place, with its jazzy new building and superhead, Michael Wilshaw ...' Jenny Turner, 'Barely Under Control', *London Review of Books* Vol. 37 No. 9, 7 May 2015.
785. Report by Willie Watkins, 15 May 2003; HDS Archive.
786. Authorised under the Learning & Skills Act of 2000, Academy schools are publicly funded through central government, but also have private sponsorship.
787. Wilshaw (1946–) had previously served as Head teacher of St Bonaventure's Catholic School, Forest Gate, London. In 2011 he was appointed Head of Ofsted.
788. Detailed in, for example, the *Daily Telegraph*, 23 February 2011.
789. Robert Peston: *Who Runs Britain?* pp. 258–9.
790. Adonis, p. 1.

It was tempting fate to set [an academy] up on the actual site of Hackney Downs. But the site was immediately available and the council was prepared to give it to the academy and to support the project... I even had a suggestion for the founding headteacher: the brilliant no-nonsense head [Sir Michael Wilshaw] of a high-achieving Catholic state secondary school in nearby Newham...[791]

In striking contrast to Hackney Downs in its final years, Adonis had access to all the resources and influencers he required. Sir Michael Levy – an 'Old Grocer' and Prime Minister Tony Blair's fundraiser – introduced Clive Bourne, an 'East End boy made good', who contributed £2M charitable sponsorship. The remaining £22M was provided by the state.[792]

> Richard Rogers designed a flagship school building. I chased progress at my weekly session with the Education Department. And I worked hand in glove with Sir Mike Tomlinson – former Chief Inspector of Schools, who became chair of the independent Hackney Learning Trust. .. to navigate the difficult local politics... Four years later, in September 2004, Mossbourne Community Academy was opened by Tony Blair.[793]

Adonis described the 'Wilshaw mantra':

> To make a success of an inner-city school... you needed to be more not less strict, expect more not less of the students, and compromise less not more with the world beyond the school gate... From day one, discipline, respect, hard work and politeness were at the core of Mossbourne Academy. The pupils stood up when a teacher entered the class, and at the start of lessons recited the mantra: 'I aspire to maintain an enquiring mind, a calm disposition and an attentive ear so that in this class and in all classes I can fulfil my true potential.'[794]

Is it fanciful to hear in this an echo of a Roman Catholic creed?

791. Adonis, p. 2.
792. Sally Tomlinson pointed out, 'Those of us who were trying to help the school would have been delighted to have been given a new school building and the £35 million that the much lauded Mossbourne Academy... finally cost.' *Renewal* Vol. 20 No. 4, 2012.
793. Adonis, pp. 3–4.
794. Adonis, p. 4. See also: 'One, Two, Three, Eyes on Me! George Duoblys on the new school discipline,' *London Review of Books*, Vol. 39, no.19, October 2017.

The sociologist Christy Kulz has published a critique of Mossbourne and the neoliberal education reform associated with the academy project. She argues that 'raced and classed pathological discourses [have been] mobilised both by Wilshaw and policy rhetoric...' and that 'neoliberal academy reforms are not about autonomy, but the imperative to comply with centralised policy demands at the expense of democratic participation and accountability.'[795] In her book, *Factories for Learning*,[796] Kulz suggests that Mossbourne – anonymized as 'Dreamfields Academy' – is re-enacting a type of nineteenth-century, colonial government, civilizing 'urban natives' with the lure of a dream future based on present hard work and discipline. The school buildings are literally isolated from the surrounding area behind high fences and locked gates, and the school is characterized as a 'well-oiled machine to combat urban chaos', drawing on a potent mixture of neoliberal and neoconservative dogma and practice to produce what Foucault might describe as a docile, productive workforce. She argues that Mossbourne's role under Wilshaw's headship was as a 'potentially transformative institution where children and their families [could] be monitored and regulated...'[797]

There is a paradox in Mossbourne's reported success. Kulz writes:

> Although [Mossbourne] ... was allegedly built to transform urban children, [it] has also become a haven for [Hackney's] middle classes, changing urban culture in unanticipated ways. Besides grafting cultural capital onto students, it actively seeks out those who already have the capital it requires to excel in the education market.[798]

Yet one cannot question the school's academic results. In 2009, Mossbourne's first GCSE year, more than 80 percent of students gained five or more good passes, making it one of a few dozen all-ability schools in the

---

795. Christy Kulz, 'Heroic heads, mobility mythologies and the power of ambiguity', *British Journal of Sociology of Education*, Vol. 38, No. 2, 2017, p. 85. Her PhD thesis, '"Structure Liberates?": Making compliant, consumable bodies in a London academy' (Goldsmiths, University of London), was submitted in October 2013.
796. *Factories for Learning: Making race, class and inequality in the neoliberal academy.* Manchester: Manchester University Press, 2017. 'This book draws on original research based at Dreamfields Academy, a celebrated flagship secondary school in a large English city, to show how the accelerated marketization and centralization of education is reproducing raced, classed and gendered inequalities. The book also examines the complex stories underlying Dreamfields' glossy veneer of success and shows how students, teachers and parents navigate the everyday demands of Dreamfields' results-driven conveyor belt. Hopes and dreams are effectively harnessed and mobilized to enact insidious forms of social control, as education develops new sites and discourses of surveillance' (Publisher's blurb).
797. *Factories for Learning*, p. 23.
798. *Factories for Learning*, p. 166.

Mossbourne Community Academy.

country to achieve such levels. In 2011, Mossbourne's first A-level group gained nine Cambridge University places and a total of seventy Russell Group university entrances.[799] The Mossbourne Federation of schools took up rowing again. In 2022 the under-15 boys took first place in the International Schools Head of the River competition, ahead of Westminster and Winchester public schools They were a full minute faster over the 4.5 mile course than the Eton College under-15s, who were competing in a different category.[800]

In September 2014 Mossbourne Federation was founded and a second school opened, Mossbourne Victoria Park Academy. In 2015 the Federation opened two primary schools, one near the Queen Elizabeth Olympic Park, named Mossbourne Riverside Academy, and also acquired the former Brooke Community School, renamed Mossbourne Parkside Academy. In 2024, concerns were raised about the Academy's treatment of children at both its secondary schools.[801]

---

799. Adonis, p. 7.
800. *The Times*, 26 March 2022.
801. *The Observer*, Saturday 23 November 2024

Afterword

Some Writers at Grocers'

Despite the lack of interest in English expressed by its long-term headmasters Gull and Jenkyn Thomas, Hackney Downs numbered some remarkable writers among its former pupils. In particular, a batch of Jewish writers explored their heritage and experience of London life, especially during World War II and the decades following.

The eminent literary scholar R. W. Chambers (1874–1942),[802] was educated at the school during the Gull era. In 1894 he gained a first class degree in English from University College, London, where he encountered the Classicist and poet A. E. Housman. In 1922 Chambers was appointed Quain Professor of English language and literature, holding the chair until 1941. His biography *Thomas More* (1935) – still in print – was awarded the James Tait Black memorial prize and made his name outside academic circles.

Ivor Bannet passed matric with honours at Hackney Downs in 1927 and edited the school magazine, *The Review*. His precocious poetry collection, *Verses of Youth* – the 'first efforts of a sixteen-year-old' – appeared in 1929;[803] a small collection apparently stimulated by the author's devotion to 'Lily', dedicatee of the book and object of its briefest poem:

> Just you
>   Do I love
> With my heart
> Just you

In 1931 Bannet won a scholarship at University College, Oxford;[804] after graduating he pursued a career in Customs and Excise. Bannet published

---

802. See ODNB.
803. Bannet included this note: 'The author is indebted for his appreciation of poetry to the English Examiners of the University of London, who set for detailed study at the matriculation examination of 1927 part of Palgrave's "Golden Treasury" – surely the most beautiful anthology in existence'.
804. The school celebrated with a half day's holiday. LMA EO/PS/4/34 25 October 1922, f. 108.

two novels based on Greek mythology: *The Amazons* (1948), [805] a tale written in the persona of the ageing Amazon commander Nessa;[806] and *The Arrows of the Sun* (1949),[807] which retells the myth of Perseus and Andromeda. Bannet died young in 1950, sufficiently regarded for a mention in the *American Jewish Year Book* for 1951.

Lazarus Aaronson,[808] who won a scholarship to Hackney Downs, belonged to a group known as the 'Whitechapel Boys'[809] – children of Jewish immigrants with literary and artistic ambitions. He was also involved in the Young Socialist League.[810] Aaronson converted to Christianity in the 1920s; his first poetry collection, *Christ in the Synagogue*,[811] dealt largely with his conversion and spiritual identity as a Jew and Englishman, recurring themes in his many mystical poems. Even his publisher acknowledged Aaronson's first book 'reached only a very small public . . .' *The New Age* claimed it as the 'most remarkable book of poetry in English for many years, bringing back belief to the sceptical nerveless life of our generation.' The poet Jon Silkin claimed Aaronson's poem 'The Fall' was '. . . a result of the conflict which is: Shall I or shall I not be a Jew?' A second collection, titled simply *Poems*, was published three years later,[812] and a third, *The Homeward Journey and Other Poems*, in 1946,[813] with subjects including World War II and the rise of fascism. Aaronson's short preface ended: '. . . the poet has, in the maze, the wilderness of our perplexed times, discovered that the

805. It appeared in an expensive folio limited edition, designed, produced and published by Christopher Sandford at the Golden Cockerel Press.
806. Illustrated with maps by Mina Greenhill and engravings by the artist Clifford Webb (1894–1972).
807. Released by Cresset Press, a literary publisher founded in 1927 by Dennis Cohen (1891–1970), who was possibly an MI6 officer, and helped organize Kindertransport during World War II.
808. Lazarus Leonard Aaronson (1894–1966) was born in Spitalfields to poor Orthodox Jewish parents, immigrants from Vilna.
809. Other members included John Rodker, Isaac Rosenberg, the poet and journalist Joseph Leftwich, Stephen Winsten, Clara Birnberg, the painter David Bomberg, and Abraham and Joseph Fineberg.
810. Diagnosed with tuberculosis and diabetes, Aaronson did not serve in World War I. He studied at the London School of Economics, but never completed his degree. Around 1934 he started lecturing in economics at the City of London College, where he taught for more than twenty-five years. Aaronson was married to Lily Shavelson (1903–1989), stage-name Lydia Sherwood, but divorced her for adultery with the theatre producer Theodore Komisarjevsky in a much publicized case. Often known as Laz, his circle also included the novelist Stephen Hudson, sculptor Jacob Epstein, media mogul Sidney Bernstein, artists Mark Gertler and Matthew Smith, and poets Harold Monro, Louis MacNeice and Samuel Beckett.
811. Published by Victor Gollancz in 1930 and dedicated to his wife.
812. Published by Victor Gollancz.
813. By Christophers, a small London publisher at 22 Berners Street, London W1.

only way out is "homeward," and "homeward" is "Back to God'..."'

In 1946, David H. Gillian, a pupil at the school in the 1920s, published a novel titled *Birthright of Multitudes*,[814] 'the story of a young man, the egotistical and ambitious son of a Clapton grocer, who was determined to escape from his narrow environment'.

Jacob Isaacs (1896–1973),[815] brought up in the Jewish East End and educated at Grocers' before gaining a first-class honours degree in 1921 in English at Oxford,[816] was in 1942 appointed the first Montefiore Professor of English at the fledgling Hebrew University of Jerusalem, returning to the UK in 1945 to become Professor of English at Queen Mary College, London. He wrote or edited more than thirty books and articles, on subjects ranging from Shakespeare and his contemporaries to Coleridge and twentieth-century poetry. His pioneering BBC Third Programme lectures in 1949[817] appealed to a wide audience with their wit, humour and irony. Six more Third Programme lectures became the basis of his book, *An Assessment of Twentieth-Century Literature* (1951). Isaacs' religious upbringing and knowledge were reflected in another series of Third Programme talks in 1966, on the influence of the Hebrew Bible on English literature. His obituary described a 'jovial, genial giant with his quietly patient corrective voice...'

Alexander Baron (1917–1999),[818] pen name of 'Alec' Bernstein, has been claimed as 'the greatest British novelist of the last war and among the finest, most underrated, of the post-war period'[819] and was educated at Hackney Downs between 1929 and 1935. Baron served in the Pioneer Corps during World War II, and experienced fierce fighting as an infantryman in Italy, Normandy, Northern France and Belgium, which left him scarred physically and emotionally. His first novel, *From the City, from the Plough* (1948), was a personal take on his war, and sold more than one million copies. It is a powerful account of the infantryman's experience before and after D-Day. War historian Anthony Beevor reckoned it to be

> undoubtedly one of the very greatest British novels of

---

814. Published by Andrew Melrose. The dustjacket has an artist's impression of the Narrow Way, Mare Street; Gillian is described as 'Secretary to a large Public Company'.
815. Born in London on 6 December 1896, son of the Revd. Moses David Isaacs and, Jessie, daughter of the Revd. Moses Bregman.
816. His examiners included R. W. Chambers.
817. Published as *The Background of Modern Poetry*. London: G. Bell, 1951. It was dedicated to Isaac Rosenberg and Alan Porter.
818. See *So We Live: The novels of Alexander Baron*, edited by Susie Thomas, Andrew Whitehead and Ken Worpole. Nottingham: Five Leaves Publications, 2019.
819. John L. Williams. He was born Joseph Alexander Bernstein, 4 December 1917. His father Barnet Bernstein, a Polish-Jewish immigrant, settled in East London in 1908, working as a master furrier.

the Second World War [which] provides the most honest and authentic account of front line life for an infantryman in North West Europe.

The author and critic V. S. Pritchett opined:

> This is the only war book that has conveyed any sense of reality to me. Gentle, modest, unaffected, it portrays the men of an infantry battalion very much as they must have seemed to each other, during their training, and later on in the Normandy battle. This is not a novel, nor yet an exhaustive documentary record, but lies somewhere between the two . . .[820]

From the City was followed by a second novel drawing on Bernstein's wartime experiences, *There's No Home*[821] (1950), focussing on a doomed love affair between an English soldier and an Italian woman in Catania, Sicily. *Rosie Hogarth* (1951) was Baron's first London novel, expressing his love of the city. He wrote:

> [The] man or woman who tries to settle in London without gaining admission to one of [its] communities, . . . is like a lonely traveller wandering, as night gathers, across the vast deserted moors . . .

In *With Hope, Farewell* (1952), about an injured Jewish RAF officer's return to post-war London, Baron describes Jewish life and antisemitism in post-war East London. *The Human Kind* (1953),[822] the third in his war trilogy, consists of a collection of short stories: 'an unqualified masterpiece; anyone wanting to understand the ordinary experience of soldiers in conflict should start here' (John L. Williams). All three books sold well, fitting the democratic new wave of British paperback publishing. They were followed by *The Golden Princess* (1954), Baron's only attempt to write a blockbuster; *Queen of the East* (1956), an historical novel about Zenobia, Queen of the Palmyrene Empire; and *Seeing Life* (Collins, 1958) set in contemporary London.

Baron next wrote two novels set in the East End underworld of a Jewish gambler. *The Lowlife* (1963), a novel about Jewish experience and for which he is best known today, is a portrait of a middle-aged man living alone in post-war Stamford Hill, his life divided between reading and gambling, and between the old East End and the new world of sub-

---

820. *The Bookman*.
821. American title: *The Wine of Etna*.
822. Later filmed as *The Victors* (1963), co-written and directed by the blacklisted Hollywood screenwriter Carl Foreman, with the characters changed to Americans to attract a US audience.

urbia. It includes a youthful affair in Paris, an illegitimate child, and the disappearance of the child and its mother on a train to Auschwitz. Its sequel, *Strip Jack Naked* (1966), follows the antihero Harryboy Boas from the East End to Paris and Venice. *King Dido* (1969) is a historical epic about Jewish gangs in Edwardian East London, and the rise and fall of a cockney tough. *The In-Between Time* (1971) is a semi-autobiographical account of a young man's political coming of age in 1930s Hackney and attempt to fight for the Republicans in the Spanish Civil War. Baron's *Gentle Folk* (1976) describes a Fabian country-house weekend in 1911, interspersed with brutal, premonitory visions of loss and horror.[823] Baron's final published novel, *Franco is Dying* (1977), tells the story of an ageing ex-communist revisiting Spanish Civil War battlefields around the time of Franco's demise.[824] *The War Baby*, published posthumously in 2019, is also set during the Spanish Civil War, and has been described as 'Baron's darkest work, a requiem for the years of grand ideals and untold deaths', and praised as 'one of the best accounts by any British writer of disillusionment with the left'.[825]

In addition to his 14 novels, Baron wrote many tv screenplays and radio scripts, including an Australian Western *Robbery Under Arms*[826] (1957) and *The Siege of Sidney Street* (1960). By the 1960s he had become a regular writer for BBC tv's 'Play for Today' series, also writing episodes for the series *A Family at War*, *The Further Adventures of the Musketeers* (1967), *Poldark* (1977) and *A Horseman Riding By*. From the 1960s to the end of the 1980s Baron adapted 17 classic novels for television, including *Daniel Deronda*, *Ivanhoe*, *Sense and Sensibility* (1981), *Jane Eyre* (1983), *Goodbye, Mr Chips* (1984), *Oliver Twist* (1985) and *Vanity Fair* (1987), as well as works by Dumas, Conrad, Tolstoy, Kipling and Walter Scott. He also scripted the pilot episode for Granada's successful *The Adventures of Sherlock Holmes* series (1984–85).

Roland Camberton (Henry Cohen, 1921–1965)[827] was born in Manchester but brought up in London, where he attended Hackney Downs. In December 1938, Cohen was awarded an L.C.C. Travelling Scholarship for study abroad: an inauspicious time for continental journeying by a young Jew. *Scamp*, his first novel, was published by John Lehmann in 1950 and is set in Soho, Bloomsbury and Fitzrovia in rented rooms, pubs and all-night cafés. The critic Julian Maclaren-Ross reviewed it harshly:

823. Adapted by Baron as a BBC tv drama in 1980.
824. Published posthumously in 2019 by Five Leaves Press.
825. David Herman in *The Times Literary Supplement*.
826. With W. P. Lipscomb.
827. Cohen's pen-name Camberton: apparently derived from **Camber**well + Brix**ton**. Cohen's father, Chaim Cohen, taught Gemara (rabbinical analysis and commentary on the Mishnah) at Montague Road Beis Midrash, Dalston (Cyril Domb: Reminiscences, p. 21).

Alexander Baron.

> ... Mr Camberton ... appears to be devoid of any narrative gift, [and] makes this an excuse for dragging in disconnectedly, and to little apparent purpose, a series of thinly disguised local or literary celebrities.[828]

Other reviews were more encouraging, and Scamp was awarded the 1951 Somerset Maugham award, while J. B. Priestley declared: 'Roland Camberton can write, and in Scamp he has produced one of the best novels I have read since the war.' Camberton's second novel, *Rain on the Pavements* (1951), is set in 1930s Hackney, with Blackshirts stalking Ridley Road Market and sketches of the Orthodox Jewish community. It consists of ten linked short stories, following David Hirsch

---

828. *Times Literary Supplement*, 10 November 1950. One derogatory portrait was of Maclaren-Ross, which possibly explains the excoriating review.

from early boyhood to his emergence as a young poet with a scholarship to study in France, and is clearly semi-autobiographical.

Stanley Dale Harris (1928–1996), who also attended Hackney Downs, claimed his first real exposure to culture occurred during the school's evacuation to King's Lynn, where he lived in an eighteenth-century house and encountered a world of 'unimaginable luxury and refinement'. After national service in the Royal Navy, Harris emigrated to the USA.[829] His only known novel (or novella) *Home Fires Burning*, published under the name Dale Harris, is a stark portrait of London during the Blitz, published in 1968.[830] It's a nasty little shocker, written in direct and unadorned prose, concerning wife-swapping, black-marketeering and a brutal rape. The *New York Times* opined:

> All the ingredients for a bad art film are present in this novel. The setting: a spooky bombed-out house during the London blitzes. The hero: a badly disfigured ex-serviceman named Oxley, who peddles black market goodies and operates a mini-agency devoted to wife-swapping (nightly capacity: three couples).[831]

Harold Pinter was also pupil at the school. His life and work are fully explored in Michael Billington's biographical study, Harold Pinter.[832] Pinter's lifelong friend Mick Goldstein wrote astutely:

> ...Hackney was a decisive factor, in the kind of rarefied breakdown and rebuilding of a language [in Pinter's work]... Hackney Downs School was a decisive factor in the nature and quality of its teaching staff and the natural acceptance by non-Jews of its large and undoubtedly talented Jewish content. This is not to say that Pinter would not have become a force in literature even without these factors. I'm sure he would. But *The Homecoming* and *The Dwarfs* could hardly have been written. I just can't imagine his writing about the Number 136 (if there is such a bus)

---

829. He enrolled at Columbia University and later Harvard, graduating in 1958, and was awarded a doctorate in 1965. In the early 1970s, Harris settled at Cooper Union, where he taught Art History and Humanities, and became a 'pre-eminent dance critic' at the *Wall Street Journal*.
830. By Macmillan in the US and Longmans in London in 1969.
831. In its theme and tone, the novel bears comparison with *Every Night and All* by William Miller, published by Anthony Blond in 1961, in which a bored, aimless Catholic teenager fortuitously encounters sado-masochism in upper-class London. Miller, like Harris, published only one novel. There is an extensive Dale Harris archive at New York Public Library.
832. 2nd edition, London: Faber and Faber, 1996.

from Wimbledon to Purley. It just doesn't sound right.[833]

Apart from short stories, Pinter's only fiction, *The Dwarfs*, written between 1952 and 1956, was first published in 1990.[834] The *Kirkus Review* judged it harshly:

> there's lots to pore over here for Pinter critics and other academics – but most readers will find this an affectless exercise, too mannered and too dated . . . to generate more than passing interest.

Billington is more positive:

> Set largely in Hackney, it is about competitive male friendship . . . Written largely in fast-paced dialogue full of cockney patter, the novel shows a born dramatist at work.

Steven Berkoff (Leslie Steven Berks, 1937–) spent his first two years of secondary education at Raine's Foundation Grammar School, where he was encouraged by his English teacher, Mr Shivas.[835] When his family moved to Manor House, North London, Berkoff transferred to Hackney Downs, which he claims to have hated: 'It was a ghastly school and I was put into a C grade for no reason that I could see, . . .' He left the school in 1952 aged fifteen, without qualifications, 'with all the speed the headmaster and I could summon'. Despite his protestations, he must have made some impression on Joseph Brearley, who in 1965 went to see him act in Albee's *Zoo Story* at Stratford East.[836] A prolific stage, film and television actor, Berkoff has also written many plays, including successful stage adaptations of Franz Kafka, Sophocles, Aeschylus, Strindberg, Shakespeare and Poe, as well as original plays with East End and Jewish themes.[837]

Henry Grinberg (1930–) was at Hackney Downs during the same period as Harold Pinter, playing Tybalt to Pinter's Romeo in Brearley's production. *In Variations on the Beast*,[838] a 'stunningly original novel',[839] Grinberg, a New York English professor and psychoanalyst,

---

833. Mick Goldstein: 'Letter written to Michael Billington in 1984', in Ian Smith: *Pinter in the Theatre*. London: Nick Hern, 2005, p. 121.
834. Pinter later made a radio adaptation, which, with the author's permission, was turned into a stage play (Faber: London, 2003) by Kerry Lee Crabbe (1946–2024).
835. Father of Mark Shivas (1938–2008), tv producer and later Head of Film at the BBC.
836. See Steven Berkoff: *Free Association: An Autobiography*. London: Faber and Faber, 1996.
837. See Robert Cross: *Steven Berkoff and the Theatre of Self-performance*. Manchester: Manchester University Press, 2004.
838. New York: The Dragon Press, 2006.
839. Edward Cone, Library Journal, January 2007.

explores Hermann Kapp-Dortmunder, a powerful musical maestro with no qualms about working under the Nazis. Perplexed that a whole nation – Germany – could be consumed by an overwhelming idea, Grinberg wrote about a man who helped bring this about. A reviewer wrote:

> *Variations on the Beast* . . . begins to answer the question 'How was it possible for a cultivated, cultured people to sink to the depth of supporting Nazism and participating in their heinous crimes?'[840]

After World War II, having served as a radio officer in the merchant navy, Morris Beckman, another former Hackney Downs pupil, helped found the 43 Group, to fight fascism in Britain. His only novel, *Open Skies and Lost Cargoes*, was published in 1944.[841] In the 1980s Beckmann documented his experiences in *The 43 Group* (1992), and followed this up with *The Hackney Crucible*, about growing up in Hackney before World War II; *Atlantic Roulette*, about the Battle of the Atlantic; *The Jewish Brigade: An Army With Two Masters* and *Flying the Red Duster* (Spellmount, 2011).

---

840. Charlotte Kahn in *The Psychoanalytic Review*, 2008, Vol. 95 (6), pp. 1045–1048.
841. Thacker & Co, Bombay.

Afterthoughts

> *That was the end of a marvellous place, not with a bang but a whimper. But it was marvellous once – and often – wasn't it?*
> John Kemp

Most official school histories are open-ended, looking forward hopefully to future growth and glory. In this respect, as in many others, the story of Hackney Downs differs, since – like all the best tales – it has a beginning, a middle and most definitely an end.

Since the school has now been dead for almost thirty years, it is possible to tell the story honestly and freely, hopefully without offending or taking sides. The decline of the school in its last period raised strong feelings – former pupils were angry, dismayed and in some instances felt betrayed by what they saw as the wanton destruction of their alma mater. Some teachers who served at the school in that period felt misunderstood, unheard and browbeaten; parents and pupils felt short-changed and abandoned.

Perhaps dividing the story into chapters defined by headships appears too neat – I hope I have justified this organization. Each Headteacher made a distinctive, and different, impression on the story of the school – whether liberal or conservative, authoritarian or permissive, progressive or conventional.

Undoubtedly, the school punched above its weight for much of its history. It experienced an unusual – possibly unique – initial period under Courthope Bowen, with his particular concern for child development and strong focus on English literature. Under the martinet Charles Gull, the school was re-modelled in an attempt to create a public school ethos for Hackney's aspirant lower-middle classes. Jenkyn Thomas managed successfully the transition from Grocers' Company ownership to control by the London County Council, though his fiercely independent combativeness, conservative attitudes and penny-pinching in a period of national economic stagnation inhibited progress. T. O. Balk not only reformed and refashioned what had become a backward-looking institution, but also led the school through the tough wartime evacuation in King's Lynn, the difficult period of resettlement back in London and the far-reaching reforms of the Butler 1944 Education Act.

There followed what have been described as 'golden years' of academic achievement, many of them during the uncelebrated headship of Barkway Pye. Alec Williams' stint as headmaster was dominated by the school fire in 1963 – not only the immediate disruption of teaching arrangements and class location, but also the impact of rebuilding and enlarging the school and its transformation into a comprehensive. John Kemp's initial years as Headmaster saw the school feted as a model, progressive comprehensive, but during the late 1980s, for many of the reasons rehearsed above – political, demographic, socio-economic, financial, architectural and racial – things declined inexorably. With hindsight, it is difficult to see how the school could successfully have survived without major injections of capital and a clear-sighted recognition of the profile, problems, needs and aspirations of its pupils.

Looking across the arc of the school's history, it is difficult to avoid feeling that bricks-and-mortar had a disproportionate impact on events. There is a suspicion that the original Victorian structure was built on the cheap, with the Grocers' Company underestimating realistic construction costs. In the early years, serious problems arose with the central-heating system and construction of the amphitheatre roof-supports, and there was repeated criticism of the school's depressing décor, dark corridors and dingy lighting. One of the major tasks awaiting Balk in 1936 was rebuilding the school, which by this date was already deemed unfit for purpose. The war put paid to any immediate plans and enemy action resulted in serious damage and further deterioration of the fabric.

The long-term effects of the catastrophic fire in 1963 cannot be underestimated. Although, through the efforts of the senior management, the school overcame most of the immediate housing and teaching problems, the next ten years were overshadowed by the controversy over transforming the grammar school into a comprehensive and by the physical disruption of the almost continuous demolition and building works on the school's restricted site. Here again the school seems to have been short-changed: the new premises put up between 1963 and 1970 were poorly designed and specified, and included hazardous asbestos, which was later removed, precipitating further controversy. During the school's final years – a mere twenty years after completion of the new premises – the neglected buildings decayed to the point of being judged unsafe. Such physical challenges inevitably affected pupil behaviour and aspirations.

Demography, too, hugely influenced the school's overall story. Initially catering for an aspirant lower-middle class, by the beginning of the twentieth century Hackney Downs' catchment area was increasingly peopled by the working classes, including first- or second-generation Jewish immigrants from Eastern Europe. Just at the time Hackney Downs transmuted from a fee-paying independent to a council-governed grammar school, open to scholarship boys, aspiring Jewish families were able to seize the opportunity of free secondary education. The proportion of Jewish pupils peaked in the 1940s and early 1950s, but fell quite rapidly as Jewish families moved out of the area. The evolution from grammar school to comprehensive coincided with the influx of Afro-Caribbean families to the area, and, later, migrants from Vietnam, Turkey, Nigeria, Eritrea and elsewhere.

TD

Some former pupils

Raymond W. Chambers (1874–1942) Literary scholar. Quain Professor of English, University College, London.[842]

Sir Edward Bairstow (1874–1946) organist at York Minster 1913–1946, composer. HDS 1889–1991.[843]

Millais Culpin, (1874–1952) Professor of Medical-Industrial Psychology at London School of Hygiene and Tropical Medicine. HDS 1931–1939.[844]

Sir John Jarvis MP (1876–1950) Lord Lieutenant of Surrey. Worked for the relief of the unemployed in Jarrow in 1936; bought the Cunard liner Berengaria for demolition to provide jobs.[845]

Frederic Sutherland Ferguson (1878–1967), bibliographer.[846]

Lt.-Col. Frederick John Roberts (1882–1964) Sherwood Foresters. Published trench magazine, *The Wipers Times*.[847]

F. [Frederick] Britten Austin (1885–1941), prolific fantasy, science fiction and military author.

Cecil Vandepeer Clarke (1888–1961) engineer, military inventor and soldier.[848]

Lazarus Aaronson (1894–1966) poet.[849]

Sir Ben Lockspeiser KCB FRS (1891–1990) First President, CERN. HDS 1905–1910.[850]

---

842. For a lengthy obituary see: Review 156, Autumn term 1942, pp. 12–17. See also ODNB; C. J. Sisson: *R. W. Chambers*. London: H. K. Lewis, 1951.
843. See ODNB.
844. See ODNB.
845. See Wikipedia, Sir John Jarvis, 1st Baronet.
846. See ODNB.
847. See IWM 'Lives of the First World War'; Wikipedia: 'The Wipers Times'.
848. See Wikipedia, Cecil Vandepeer Clarke.
849. See ODNB.
850. See ODNB.

Cecil J. Allen (1886–1973) Railway historian. HDS 1895–1900.[851]

Nathan (Menachem) Isidore 'Nat' Mindel OBE (1891–1961) Commissioner for Immigration, Palestine.[852] Born Dunilavichy, Vitsyebskaya Voblasts', Belarus.

Firth Shephard (1891–1949). Writer, theatre producer and presenter of plays.[853]

Sir Robert Barlow (1891–1976) Chairman of the Metal Box Company.[854] Married celebrated actress Margaret Rawlings (1906–1996)

William Harold Hutt (1899–1988) economist, and Professor of Commerce and Dean of the Faculty of Commerce, University of Cape Town, 1931–1964.[855]

Maj-Gen. S. W. Joslin, CB, CBE, MA (Cantab) (1899–1982) Chief Inspector of Nuclear Installations, First Director of Dounreay Atomic Power Station. HDS 1910–1917.

Sir Maurice Evans (1901–1989) nephew of actress Dame Edith Evans. In the USA a Shakespearean and classical actor-manager. He also acted in films and TV.[856]

Revd. Dr. Ernest Alexander Payne (1902–1980) B.A., B.D. (London), M.A., B.Litt (Oxon), C.H. President, World Council of Churches 1968–1975,[857] General Secretary Baptist Union of Great Britain & Ireland.

Norman Ginsbury (1902–1991) Analytical chemist, playwright, TV and film scriptwriter.[858]

Eric Fletcher, Baron Fletcher of Islington, Kt, PC, FSA, FRHistS (1903–90), Labour politician. As Sir Eric Fletcher MP was Deputy Speaker of the House of Commons.[859]

William Noble Warbey (1903–80) Labour MP 1945–1950 for Luton,

851. See C. J. Allen: *Two Million Miles of Rail Travel*. London: Ian Allan, 1965; Wikipedia, Cecil J. Allen.
852. See Jonathan Freedland: *Jacob's Gift: A Journey into the Heart of Belonging*. London: Hamish Hamilton, 2005, esp. p. 48. Mindel was General Allenby's aide-de camp and entered Jerusalem by his side in 1917.
853. Wikipedia, Firth Shephard.
854. See Encyclopedia.com https://www.encyclopedia.com › books › metal-box-plc
855. See ODNB.
856. See Maurice Evans: *All This and Evans Too*. Columbia S.C.: University of South Carolina Press, 1987; Wikipedia, Maurice Evans (actor)
857. See ODNB; W. M. S. West: *To be a pilgrim: a memoir of Ernest A. Payne*. Cambridge: Lutterworth, 1983 – possibly the first full-length biography of an Old Grocer.
858. See Wikipedia, Norman Ginsbury.
859. See Wikipedia, Eric Fletcher, Baron Fletcher.

1953–1955 for Broxtowe and 1955–1966 for Ashfield.[860]

Sir (Frank) Cyril James (1903–1973) Principal and Vice-Chancellor, McGill University. HDS 1913–1920. Professor of Finance at Pennsylvania University; member of the Economic Committee advising President F. D. Roosevelt.[861]

Albert Cyril Offord FRS FRSE (1906–2000) Distinguished mathematician, pioneer of probabilistic analysis.[862]

Solomon Kaufman (1908–1998) Lawyer and art historian. He defended author of *Exodus*, Leon Uris, in libel action brought by concentration camp doctor Wladislaw Dering.[863]

Ralph Shackman (1910–1981) Urologist and kidney transplantation pioneer.[864]

John Yudkin (1910–1995), nutritionist. Author of *Pure, White and Deadly* (1972), warning of the dangers of sugar consumption.[865] HDS 1921–1926.

John Lewis (1912–1969) Labour MP 1945–1950 for Bolton and 1950–1951 for Bolton West. Pursued a feud against the osteopath, Stephen Ward.[866]

Abram Games, O.B.E. (1914–1996) Graphic designer. Jenkyn Thomas told Games 'To be an artist you need talent and you haven't got it;' after leaving school he painted the headmaster.[867] HDS 1925–1930.

Dennis Lyons CB, (1916–2011) Innovative scientist at Royal Aircraft Establishment; director 1965–1971 of the Road Research Laboratory.[868]

Sir Arthur Abraham Gold CBE (1917–2001) President European

860. See Wikipedia, William Warbey. Though Warbey was not Jewish, he was one of the few Labour MPs who opposed the Attlee government's policy on Palestine, and made several strong attacks on Foreign Secretary Ernest Bevin. Jonathan Freedland has suggested this was possibly as a result of the influence of Zionist Jewish school friends. *Jewish Chronicle*, 18 June 2015.
861. See Stanley Frost: *The Man in the Ivory Tower: F. Cyril James of McGill*. McGill: Queen's University Press, 1991); Wikipedia, Frank Cyril James.
862. See Wikipedia, Cyril Offord.
863. Obituary, *The Independent* 12 January 1999.
864. See Wikipedia, Ralph Shackman; https://ukkidney.org › obituary › ralph-shackman
865. See ODNB; Obituary *BMJ* Vol. 311 p. 505, 19 Aug 1995.
866. See Wikipedia, John Lewis (British politician); Spartacus Educational, John Lewis.
867. Letter to Willie Watkins, 5 July 1996; HDS Archive. See also ODNB; Wikipedia; Abram Games: *Over my Shoulder*. London: Studio Books, 1960; Naomi Games, Catherine Moriarty and June Rose: *Abram Games Graphic Designer: Maximum Meaning, Minimum Means*. London: Lund Humphries, 2003.
868. Obituary, *The Guardian* 17 April 2011.

Athletic Association 1976; UK Athletics Team Leader for Olympic Games, 1968–1976. HDS 1926–1935.[869]

(Joseph) Alexander Baron (Bernstein) (1917–1999). Novelist, playwright, TV scriptwriter. HDS 1928–1935.[870]

Sir Alfred Sherman (1919–2006) fought with the Communists in the Spanish Civil War, after World War II active in Hackney Labour politics, moved to the right and became adviser to Margaret Thatcher. Founder of the Centre for Policy Studies.[871]

Dr Cyril Domb (Dombrowsky) (1920–2012) Regius Professor of Theoretical Physics, King's College London. HDS 1932–1939.[872]

Roland Camberton (Henry Cohen) (1921–1965) Novelist. HDS 1932–1938.[873]

David Abraham Galton (Goitein) CBE FRCP (1922–2006). Haematologist who performed UK's first successful leukaemia and lymphoma chemotherapy.[874] HDS 1931–1939.

Arnold Allen CBE (1924–2005) First Chair of UK Atomic Energy Authority. HDS 1932–1942.[875]

Reggie Bullen, Air Vice-Marshal GC CB (1920–2008) Awarded George Cross for returning to a burning plane to rescue a crew member.[876]

Morris Beckman (1921–2015) Writer and anti-fascist activist.[877]

Alfred 'Freddie' Mabbs CBE (1921–2009) Keeper of Public Records 1978–1982.[878]

Lord Arnold Goodman CH QC (1913–1995) Solicitor to the famous. Chairman of Arts Council, British Lion Films, Newspaper Proprietors' Association etc. Director of the Royal Opera House, Governor of the Royal Shakespeare Theatre, Master of University College, Oxford. HDS 1924–1929.[879]

869. See Wikipedia, Arthur Gold (sports administrator).
870. See *Chapters of Accidents: A Writer's Memoir*, ed. Colin Holmes and Nick Baron. Lonfdon: Vallentine Mitchell, 2022.; ODNB
871. See ODNB; Alfred Sherman: *Paradoxes of Power*. London: Societas, 2005.
872. See ODNB.
873. Iain Sinclair *The Guardian*, 30 August 2008; Wikipedia, Roland Camberton.
874. Obituary by Caroline Richmond, *BMJ* 24 March 2007, Vol. 334, p. 642; Wikipedia, David Galton.
875. Obituary, *The Times*, 3 March 2005.
876. See Wikipedia, Reggie Bullen.
877. See Morris Beckman: *The Hackney Crucible*. London: Vallentine Mitchell, 1995; Wikipedia, Morris Beckman (writer).
878. Obituary in *The Times*, 26 February 2009.
879. See ODNB; Brian Brivati: *Lord Goodman. Londonb: Simon & Schuster,* 1999.

John William 'Jack' Rawlings (1923–2016) Amateur footballer who represented Great Britain at the 1948 Olympic Games.[880]

Leon Kossoff (1926–2019) Artist. HDS 1938–1943.[881]

Stanley Clinton-Davis, Baron Clinton-Davis PC (1928– 2023) Labour MP for Hackney Central 1970–1983; Minister of State for Trade 1997–1998.[882]

(Stanley) Dale Harris (1928–96) Arts lecturer and dance critic.[883]

Michael Woolfson (1927–2019) Physicist and planetary scientist.[884]

Salman (Sidney) Mendel Greenbaum (1929–1996) Grammarian, Quain Professor of English language and literature.[885]

Frank Cass (1930–2007) Publisher. HDS 1947–1949.[886]

Henry Woolf (1930–2021) Actor, stage director. Commissioned and directed Pinter's first play.[887] HDS 1941–1947.

Harold Pinter, CH, CBE *Legion d'Honneur* (1930–2008) Nobel Prize for literature, actor, playwright, film and TV scriptwriter. HDS 1944–1949.[888]

Professor Barry Supple (1930–) CBE, FBA, economic historian. Master of St. Catharine's College Cambridge 1984–1993; Director of the Leverhulme Trust 1993–2001.[889] HDS 1942–1949.

Derek S. Pugh (1930–2015) British psychologist, business theorist. Emeritus Professor of International Management at the Open University Business School. HDS 1944–1948.[890]

John Bloom (1931–2019) Entrepreneur at the heart of 1960s 'washing-machine wars'.[891]

Lord Maurice Peston CBE (1931–2016)[892] Academic economist, set up the Economics department at Queen Mary College.

880. See Wikipedia, Jack Rawlings.
881. See Paul Moorhouse: *Leon Ksssoff*. London: Tate Gallery, 1996; ODNB.
882. See Wikipedia, Stanley Clinton-Davis.
883. Obituary by David Vaughan, *The Guardian* 16 March 1996.
884. Wikipedia, Michael Woolfson.
885. See ODNB.
886. See ODNB; Gerry Black: *Frank's Way*. London: Vallentine Mitchell, 2008.
887. Obituary by Irving Wardle, *The Guardian* 24 Nov 2021; Henry Woolf: *Barcelona is in Trouble*. Saskatoon: Comet Press, 2016; Wikipedia, Henry Woolf.
888. See ODNB; Michael Billington: *The life and work of Harold Pinter*. London: Faber, 2007.
889. See his autobiography, *Doors Open*. Cambridge: Asher, 2009; Wikipedia, Barry Supple.
890. See ODNB.
891. Obituary *The Times*, 13 March 2019; See John Bloom: *It's No Sin To Make A Profit* London: W.H. Allen, 1971, pp. 14–1; ODNB.
892. Father of the journalist Robert Peston. See ODNB.

Harry Kane (Cohen) (1933–) Olympic and Maccabean hurdler. HDS 1946–1949.[893]

Rabbi David Goldstein MA PhD (1933–1987), Curator of Hebrew Manuscripts, British Library; editor and translator.

Stanley Orman Principal Scientific Officer of UK Atomic Energy Authorit; Director-General of the US Strategic Defense Initiative, 1986–1990. HDS 1946–1953.[894]

Sir Michael Caine, (Maurice Micklewhite Jr.) CBE (1933–) Actor, Oscar winner. HDS 1944–1945.[895]

Efraim Halevy (1934–) 9th Director of MOSSAD, Israeli Intelligence Agency. HDS 1945–1948.[896]

Basil Feldman, Baron Feldman of Frognal (1923–2019) Entrepreneur dealing in Sindy dolls, aircraft kits and yo-yos. Conservative politician.[897] HDS 1935–1937.

Gerald Bernbaum FRSA (1936–2017) Vice-Chancellor and Chief Executive, London South Bank University, 1993–2001.[898]

Henry Richardson (1936–2017) Film editor who worked with director Andrei Konchalovsky.[899]

Steven Berkoff (Leslie Berks) (1937–) Actor, director, playwright, author. HDS 1950–1953.[900]

Keith Pavitt (1937–2002) Professor of Science and Technology Policy, University of Sussex.[901]

David Dolphin, OC, FRS, FRSC (1940–) Biochemist, inventor of Visudyne, Order of Canada.[902]

Douglas Gough FRS (1941–) Professor Emeritus of Theoretical Astrophysics, University of Cambridge. HDS 1952–1959.[903]

Mike Berry (born Michael Bourne) (1942–) Pop singer and actor.[904]

Right Honourable Sir Stanley Burnton (1942–) Lord Justice of

---

893. Wikipedia, Harry Kane (hurdler).
894. See Stanley Orman: *Uncivil Servant*. Twig Books, 2013.
895. Wikipedia, Michael Caine.
896. Wikipedia, Efraim Halevy. His father was Headmaster of the Dalston Talmud Torah Yeshiva.
897. Obituary, *The Times* 23 Nov 2019; Wikipedia, Basil Feldman.
898. Wikipedia, Gerald Bernbaum.
899. See Henry Richardson iMDb.
900. Wikipedia, Steven Berkoff.
901. Obituary, *The Independent*, 31 January 2003; Wikipedia, Keith Pavitt.
902. Wikipedia, David Dolphin.
903. Wikipedia, Douglas Gough.
904. Wikipedia, Mike Berry (singer).

Appeal 2008–2012. HDS 1954–1961.[905]

Dr Geoffrey Alderman (1944–) Historian and author.[906]

Geoffrey Sheridan (1944–2000) Journalist; founder member of Campaign for Press and Broadcasting Freedom and Campaign Against Racism in the Media.[907] HDS 1955–1962.

Michael Levy, Baron Levy (1944–) Philanthropist, political aide to Prime Minister Blair. HDS 1955–1962.[908]

Geoffrey Hanks DSc(Med), FRCP, FRCPE, FFPM (1946–2013) first European Professor of palliative medicine. HDS 1957–1964.[909]

Colin Shindler (1946–) First UK professor of Israeli Studies, SOAS. HDS 1958–1964.[910]

Neil Caplan (HDS c. 1960–1968) Member of Lindsay Kemp Theatre Troupe.

Eric Bristow MBE (1957–2018) Darts world champion.[911]

Metin Hüseyin (1959–) Film and television director.[912]

Dalton Grant (1966–) Olympic high jumper. HDS 1977–1982.[913]

---

905. Wikipedia, Stanley Burnton.
906. Wikipedia, Geoffrey Alderman.
907. Obituary, *The Guardian*, 29 Sept 2000.
908. Michael Levy, *A Question of Honour*. London: Simon & Schuster, 2008; Wikipedia, Michael Levy.
909. Wikipedia, Geoffrey Hanks.
910. See colinshindler.com.
911. Wikipedia, Eric Bristow.
912. Wikipedia, Metin Hüseyin.
913. Wikipedia, Dalton Grant.

Index

11-plus 97, 116
Aaronson, Lazarus Leonard 199
Abbott, Diane 181
Aberdare Intermediate School 54
Adler, Henrietta 65, 86
Adonis, Andrew 194, 195
Afro-Caribbean pupils 170, 171
Alec Bernstein *see* Baron, Alexander
Allen, Theophilus 20
Amherst of Hackney, Baron 19
anti-racism 151
anti-Semitism 69, 71, 72, 73, 143
Antigone 129, 132
asbestos removal 160, 161
athletics, school 68, 106, 124, 127,
attendance, pupil 159, 169

Balk, Thomas Oscar 81–112
Bannet, Ivor 198, 199
Barber, Michael 182, 185, 191,
Baron, Alexander 69, 70, 71, 73, 75, 76, 200-202
Barron, T. B. 93, 98
Bass, Bryan 186
Bath Street School 18
battalion, school 69
Beckman, Morris 73, 206
Bentley, Les 96
Berkoff, Steven 205
Black pupils 148, 153,
Boer War 43, 44
Bourne, Clive 195
Bowen, Herbert Courthope 17–36
Bowler, Allan 72
Box, Henry 12, 13
Boyd, W. G. 122

Boyle, Sir Edward 140
Brearley, Joseph 90, 96, 98, 105, 114, 115, 118, 123, 128, 132, 144, 148
Brereton, Dr. Cloudesley 78
Briault, Dr. Eric 134
Broughton, Revd. Reginald 26
Browning, Oscar 34
Bryce, D. L. 47
Buildings, unsatisfactory 98, 158, 168, 180
buildings, new 133, 139
buildings, design and construction 20, 23
Burford, W. E. 31
Burgess, Dr. Tony 180

Caine, Sir Michael 96
Calland, Albert 123
Camberton, Roland 71, 73, 202–203
Cambridge University 22, 66, 117
Central Foundation School 18, 113
Cesarani, David 73
Chambers, R. W. 47, 198
Charity Commission 13, 14, 33, 41
Chataway, Christopher 139
chronology, final years' 189–190
Clove Club, The 42, 160, 192
Clove's Lines, The 74
clubs and societies, school 76,
Cohen, Henry, see Roland Camberton
Collins, Sir William 51, 52, 55
colour, pupils of 150
Combined Cadet Force 106, 124

commercial classes 61, 62
Commons Protection League 25
Comprehensive intake 142
Certificate of Secondary Education 144
Comprehensive school controversy 108, 134–139
Cooper, A. A. 68
Corner, Cyril 98, 128, 132,
Corrigan, Pat 180
Costigan, Marie 184
Creevey, Thomas 15
Crimean War 13
CSE *see* Certificate of Secondary Education
Cuban Missile Crisis 128
Curriculum, school 24, 115, 144, 168

Davenport, Charles 62
Davies, Jeffrey 180
Day, Stanley 77
de Morgan, John 25
debates, school 67, 100, 127
discipline, pupil 26, 39, 48, 74, 75, 155, 156, 157, 161, 168, 169, 173, 174, 175, 178, 179
Domb, Cyril 68
Douglas, John 164, 168, 171–176
Downs Park Road 20
drama, school 59, 77, 90, 104 123, 141, 145, 149
Dulwich College 22, 37, 38
Dunning, Roy 128, 139

East and West India Docks and Birmingham Junction Railway 16
Edmonton, Lower 42, 69, 84
Education Act, 1944 97, 107
Education Reform Act (ERA), 1988 162
Educational Association 182, 183, 186, 192,
Elementary Education Act 32
Endowed Schools Act 13, 14
English as a Second Language 150
English for Speakers of Other languages (ESOL) 170, 178

English, teaching of 23, 27, 28, 60, 77, 82, 115, 184
Evacuation, school's 88–96
Eyre & Spottiswood 26

female teachers 64
Fenland 88
Finances, school's 29, 32, 40, 41, 42, 47, 49, 63
Finsbury Middle Class Boys School 18, 22
Finsbury Training College 34, 35
fire, school 129–132
Fitch, Joshua Girling 27
Froebel, Friedrich 22, 35, 79
From the City, From the Plough 200
Fry, Douglas 124

Galileo Galilei 123
Garnett, Sir William 50, 55
Gee, Adrian 92, 128
Gilbert and Sullivan 43
Gillian, David H. 200
Gold, Sir Arthur 69
Gosley, Margaret 143
Grace, Gerald 191
Grantham, W. W. 58
Great Eastern Railway 16, 26,
Greaves, William 90
Grinberg, Henry 99, 102, 205
Grocers' Company 12, 13, 14, 19, 33, 41
Grundy, G. Brandon 44
Gull, Charles George 37–53

Hackney Black Parents and Teachers Group 163, 164, 177, 178
Hackney Choral Society 27
Hackney Downs 14, 25
Hackney Education Authority 180, 182, 187
Hackney Empire Palace 74
Hackney Free and Parochial School 188
Hackney Proprietary Grammar School 15

Hackney Technical Institute 57, 67
Hackney, London Borough of 147, 166, 167, 176, 181, 184,
Hales, Elizabeth 169, 174, 178, 179,
Hardcastle, Dr. John 53
Hargreaves, Dr. David 153
Harris, Stanley Dale 89, 102, 204
Harrison, Paul 156, 157
Heath, Arthur George 47
Henderson, Russell 193
Henry, Philip 98
Hepburn, Peter 176, 178,
Holocaust 99, 103, 128
Homa, Dr. Bernard 86, 109, 122, 136, 138
Homerton House School 177, 181, 185, 187, 193
house system, school 42, 58
Humanities, teaching of 153
Hydeside House 42, 60

ILEA *see* Inner London Education Authority
Inner London Education Authority 134, 136, 149, 151, 153, 157, 158, 160, 162, 164, 170, 184,
inspection, school 26, 27, 28, 31, 44, 47, 60, 62, 65, 66, 77, 81, 110, 116, 152, 153, 154, 158, 159, 164, 171, 172, 173, 174, 181, 184
Isaacs, Jacob 200

James, Dr. Cyril 62
Jarvis, Sir John 47
Jewish pupils 30, 44, 67, 74, 82, 84, 86, 91, 99, 103, 112, 117, 122, 128, 142, 150
John, Gus 163, 170, 173, 177,
Johnson, Dr. Samuel 15
Jones, H. A. 74
Jones, W. H. S. 79
Joseph, Rev. Joseph 112

Kemp, John 118, 120, 128, 136, 140, 146, 147–164
King Edward VII School 88, 92, 94, 95, 113

King's Lynn 88, 89,
King's Lynn Technical School 92
Kingsley, Charles 24
Kossoff, Leon 89
Kulz, Christy 196

L.C.C. *see* London County Council
laboratories, school science 57, 114
Lammas land 25
Latin, teaching of 38, 60
Laxton, Sir William 13
Lea, River 69, 85
left-leaning staff 103
Levy, Sir Michael 195
Lockspeiser, Ben 59
London County Council (L.C.C.) 46, 50, 51, 54, 57, 78, 97, 109, 110,
London, University of 66
Low, Barbara 64

Macbeth 105
Madras House School 15
Magee, Frances 145
Mallen, David 162
Marley, E. J. 69
Medcalf, James 72, 102
Meiklejohn, J. M. D. 28, 29
Mercers' Company 12
Merron, David 103
Metropolitan Board of Works 25
Middle Class Schools 14, 32
Mitchell, Leslie 106, 124
Mosley, Oswald 73, 100, 103
Mossbourne Community Academy School 194, 195, 196
Munich 87
Murray, G. S. D. 33, 40,
music, school 43, 44, 77, 83, 90, 104, 120, 12, 141
Muslim pupils 163

Neurath, Susanna 188
Newcome's Academy 15
Newton, Ernest 43
Norfolk 88, 89, 96

Oberrealschule Soest, Germany 87

219

occupation, pupils' father's 25, 40, 49, 57, 60, 62, 66,
Ofsted 178, 179, 187
Ogilvie, David 90, 117
Oundle School 13, 52
Outwell 88
Oxford, University of 66

Palmerston, Lord 13
Pam, Jerry 96
Payne, Kenneth 121
Pepperers, Guild of 12
Pepys, Samuel 14
Peston, Lord Maurice 100, 138
physical education 84
Pinter, Harold 94, 99, 102, 103, 104, 105, 204
Popplewell, Sir Oliver 186
Prout, Ebenezer 27
Prussia 18
Pye, Vernon Barkway 113–125

Queen's Royal College, Trinidad 21

Race, Richard 192
racism 143, 151
Railway Club 120
Rayns, Alfred 66
Reform Act 13
refugees 64
religion, school and 27, 30, 39, 55, 122, 126
Review, The 43, 63
Richards, Samuel 58, 81
Rifle Corps, Old Boys' 43
Roach, Colin 167
Roberts, F. J. 64
Rogers, Revd. William 17, 18, 21, 30, 34
Rogers, Sir Richard 193
Rolph, C. H. 109
Romeo and Juliet 105
rowing 84
Rugby football 125
Russell, Ken 178

Sanderson, Frederick William 52

science laboratories 43
sex education 76, 154
Shephard, Gillian 179, 182,
sixth-form colleges 160
Skills for Living 154, 164
Societies, school 104, 119, 141
Sound Club, The 121
Spector, Cyril 71
sport, school 69, 91, 125, 14, 171
St. Botolph-without-Bishopsgate 17
St. John's Foundation School 16
St. Thomas, Charterhouse 17
Sullivan, Gilbert and 43
Supple, Barry 103
swimming pool, school 42, 106

Taunton Report 13, 19
Thomas, William Jenkyn 54–81
Thompson, Harry James 29
Three Holes 88
Tomlinson, Sally 180
Torn, David 155
Trinidad 21
trips, school 66, 76, 87, 104, 127, 141, 118
Tyssen-Amherst, William 19

uniform, school 58
Upwell 88
Uren, Ormond 129
Usherwood, Vivian 146

V1 93, 94
V2 94
Victoria Youth Club 132

Walcott, Derek 153
Walwyn, Humphrey 12
war damage 93
Watherstone, Dorothy M. F. 64
West Indian pupils 152
White City stadium   124
Widgery, Claire 154
Williams, Alexander Ernest 126–146
Wilshaw, Sir Michael 194, 196
Wilton Way School   132, 133
Wipers Times 64

Witney Grammar School 12
Woolf, Henry 99
World War I 43, 63, 65
World War II 88–96
Wormald, Dr. Richard 19